BLACK
CHILDREN

OTHER RECENT VOLUMES IN THE SAGE FOCUS EDITIONS

BLACK CHILDREN

Social, Educational, and Parental Environments

Edited by
Harriette Pipes McAdoo
and
John Lewis McAdoo

SAGE PUBLICATIONS
The International Professional Publishers
Newbury Park   London   New Delhi

For information address:

SAGE Publications, Inc.
2111 West Hillcrest Drive
Newbury Park, California 91320

SAGE Publications Ltd.
28 Banner Street
London EC1Y 8QE
England

SAGE Publications India Pvt. Ltd.
M-32 Market
Greater Kailash I
New Delhi 110 048 India

Printed in the United States of America

Library of Congress Cataloging in Publication Data

Main entry under title:

Black children.

   (Sage focus editions ; v. 72)
    1. Afro-American children—Addresses, essays, lectures.
I. McAdoo, Harriette Pipes. II. McAdoo, John Lewis.
E185.86.B524 1985   305.2′3′08996073   85-2307
ISBN 0-8039-2461-5
ISBN 0-8039-2462-3 (pbk.)

FIFTH PRINTING 1990

CONTENTS

This book is
dedicated to our own
Black children

Michael Garnett McAdoo

John Lewis McAdoo III

Julia BethAnn McAdoo

David Pipes McAdoo

PREFACE

This book was designed to explore in depth the unique experiences and situations that are common to Black children and their parents. The volume was developed within the framework that all children during their childhood—regardless of race, ethnicity, social class, or gender—must complete similar developmental tasks if they are to become competent adults. Therefore, the book does not attempt to duplicate the information that will be found in a comprehensive developmental textbook. Instead, it documents how these developmental tasks are uniquely experienced in the enivronments of children's growth and development.

This is an exploration of the diversities of childhood experiences that are confronted by children who are members of the largest American ethnic group of color. Members of this group are defined as those whose ancestors originally are from the many cultural groups of the African continent. This cultural group arrived in America in a variety of circumstances, but the majority were enslaved and continued, children and family members, to live lives that were dominated by the ethnic group composed of former Europeans. They merged their own cultures, assimilated from their enslavers, and created new and unique forms of family life that were functional for them within the situations in which they existed.

Afro-American children often have existed within environments that have been nonsupportive of their optimum development. The wider supportive network of the Afro-American family and the Black communities and their institutions have long attempted to provide a buffer for the Black child and to shield him or her from the reality of the negative images that continue to be perpetuated by the wider societal environment. Afro-American children develop a duality for their existence. To be fully functional, they must develop the skills to do well simultaneously in two different cultures, both Black and non-Black.

For this reason, this book has been developed around the themes of the significant *environments* within the lives of Black children. Each of the enivronments is viewed as presenting the potential for optimum

9

functioning and, simultaneously, presenting areas for negative and detrimental development. The selection of environments was based on our awareness of the developmental experiences of the majority of Black children. We do, however, attempt to avoid the all-too-common approach of presenting stereotypes of these children. In most literature the Black child is presented in a pejorative manner. In other literature the opposite tact has resulted in the Black child being presented in a totally positive manner. To use either approach is to perpetuate myths that shield the wider public, the developmental professionals, and, most important, the parents themselves from the complexities and diversities of the Black American experiences of young children.

There are two major assumptions made as this book is developed: One is related to the economic environment of many Black children and the other is related to the negative images that are carried about Black children by members of the wider society. The first assumption, which is so starkly presented in Marian Wright Edleman's chapter, is that despite the economic mobility of some Blacks, the vast majority of Black children live within environments that put their very existence in jeopardy. The second assumption, that non-Blacks view Black children through negative lenses, is shown clearly in several of the reviews of the child development literature in chapters throughout the book. The child either has been totally ignored or, when used within the empirical studies, has been treated in a negative manner that would be considered ridiculous, except the the consequences are so real and so painful for the Black child.

The environments that were selected to be developed in detail are as follows:

(1) the theoretical environment
(2) the socioeconomic environment
(3) the educational environment
(4) the parental environment: racial socialization
(5) the internal environments of children's racial attitudes and self-esteem

The importance of the theoretical frameworks and the empirical environments is stressed. The dominant views presented in the professional writing of these environments are those that are perpetuated within the child development literature by persons from the majority racial ethnic groups. Variation of Blacks from the norms formed by majority race children, who often are in adequate economic environments, too often are viewed as deviancy or pathology. The research methodology used and the interpretations made of the data often are clouded by the previously mentioned negative images held about Black children. The continuous reinforcement of negative images in the literature makes it difficult for researchers to provide objective examinations and interpretations of data achieved from Black children. To attempt to offset the prevailing images in the literature, we have attempted to present as many empirical studies as possible to provide real life data-based analyses of the lives of Black children.

Next, the socioeconomic environments are examined, for it is felt that these are the most crucial predictive determinants of the life experiences of young Black children. We feel that it would be superfluous to have extended theoretical or conceptual discussions about the Black child's developmental components unless all of the developmental aspects are placed within the dire economic realities of many Black children and families. Recent reports have only magnified the increasing poverty in the lives of Black children.

The third environment, in order of importance, is that of education. This is the battleground around which so much of the negative literature and experiences of Black children has been fought out. The educational environment has long been felt to be the one saving factor within the Black child's life, that would allow the child and his or her family to develop the skills to provide a more secure economic environment. It has been the source of inspiration, success, and mobility for hundreds of children. At the same time, however, it has been the place where thousands of children have been cowed into lower expectations and where they have experienced failure. Much has been written to document the failure of the Black child to succeed within this environment.

The socioemotional environment of Black children has had differential effects on their self-esteem and their ethnic group identities. The strains of belonging to an ethnic group that so consistently has faced economic disaster has been hypothesized to cause a lessening of feelings of self-worth. These empirical studies do not support this contention. Black children have been found to have the same distribution of self-esteem scores that is found in all other populations. Some feel good about themselves, while others do not. They have been able to maintain feelings of positive self-worth through their own tenacity and through the support of their wider family network.

The sociocultural environment is seen to have an interaction with the racial attitudes and the independently derived self-esteem of Black children. The pressures of the dominant society have tended to socialize all children to exhibit preferences for characteristics of the majority, non-Black population. These out-group preferences of earlier studies have been found to move gradually to the direction of racially neutral preferences and, finally, when the child has matured into middle childhood, to strong preferences for their own racial and cultural group. They are able to master the duality of their lives while maintaining positive evaluations of their own self-worth, independent of their racial preferences.

The parental environment is considered to be the most crucial of all. It is this environment that shields children from the often hostile external environment and prepares them to function within their own and the wider environments. This environment often enables children to function effectively within conflicting demands, lifestyles, and value systems. The maternal and paternal roles are highlighted. Too often, the paternal role is considered to be nonexistent or, at best, ineffectual within Black family environments. The adaptations that parents must make in order to raise their children are detailed in this section.

Many of the empirical chapters grew out of the nine-year efforts of Black researchers who have met, presented empirical papers, and soundly critiqued one another in closed sessions of the Empirical Conference on Black Psychology. This organization has held annual meetings and has provided a fertile environment for enthusiastic junior researchers and for exhausted, overextended senior researchers. Members of the planning committee for Empirical, in addition to the editors of this book, are Algea Harrison, Anderson J. Franklin, A. Wade Boykin, and, earlier, William Cross. Funding for these efforts has come from the Russell Sage Foundation, the Ford Foundation, and the Center for Studies of Minority Group Mental Health Programs of the National Institute of Mental Health.

The Empirical Conference on Black Psychology has become the key organization that encourages, in fact requires, that statements about Black children and their families must be substantiated by hard data. Rhetoric may have its place, but it is felt that Black children are too important to be used in polemic exercises of professional researchers, regardless of their race.

Attendance at the Empirical Conference is invitational, after a nationwide call has been issued and responded to by scores of researchers across the country. Papers are given blind reviews before an invitation is extended. It has become an increasing honor to be selected to attend and present work. It has been, and continues to be, a warm, unique experience. Several of the chapters in this volume are the result of this critiquing process that occurred during the past three years at Empirical. Their authors are considered to be among the best of those who are producing empirical work on Black children.

One earlier book has been produced from the the Empirical Conference process, *Reasearch Direction of Black Psychologists,* edited by A. Wade Boykin, James Anderson, and Frank Yates (New York: Russell Sage Foundation, 1979, distributed by Basic Books). That volume was nominated as an Outstanding New Text in Psycology by the American Psychological Association in 1980. The present work will follow the direction of the earlier volume by providing valuable information for those who are concerned about the optimal growth and development of Black children.

This volume was designed to be useful to undergraduate and graduate courses related to human growth and development, ethnic studies, family life education studies, and to professional students in social work, public health, and education. It also will be invaluable for practitioners working directly with Black children and their families. And it will be helpful to parents as they attempt to negotiate the evironments in which their children must develop.

Harriette Pipes McAdoo
John Lewis McAdoo

PART I

THEORETICAL FRAMEWORKS

1

OUR DESTINY

Authors of a Scientific Revolution

NA'IM AKBAR

Thomas Kuhn (1970), in his masterpiece *The Structure of Scientific Revolutions*, observed that "when recognized anomalies, whose characteristic feature is their stubborn refusal to be assimilated into existing paradigms, give rise to new theories which give identity to the anomalies, a paradigm shift or scientific revolution occurs." Translated, this means that when attributes of reality are not able to fit the existing models of reality, there is a natural process by which those models must change their structure. Those things not identified in the models must eventually begin to assert their identity and their defiance of their nonidentity or ignored identity vis-à-vis the existing models of reality. Kuhn defines this shift as being the dynamic process of a scientific revolution.

The destiny of the African-American social scientist is to be responsible for the paradigm shift or scientific revolution in the social sciences. It is important that we as social scientists begin to recognize that destiny before the inevitable movements of time deprive us of our well-deserved fate or legacy.

The question immediately arises: "What is the existing paradigm or model?" To the extent that "for a time paradigms provide model problems and solutions to a community of [scientific] practitioners"

(Kuhn, 1970), there obviously is a paradigm of human psychology. In the most simple terms, the currently accepted model is the middle-class, male Caucasian of European descent. There are many elements of linguistic and scientific jargon by which this model is identified, often in ways to obscure its true identity; but when properly analyzed and understood, there is no doubt of who is being characterized by the model of human functioning. In other words, throughout the existing conceptualizations of human psychology in the Western (and most of the rest of the industrialized) world, it turns out that the more that you look like, think like, speak like, and, in general, behave like the middle-class Caucasian male of European descent, the more you are defined in accord with the paradigm of an acceptable, functional, and effective (i.e., "mentally healthy") human being.

There are certain characteristics of this model that pervade the social science literature as implicit values of excellence. One such characteristic is the idea of individualism. The assumption is that the human being is paramount in his or her identity as an individual. There are many operational or conceptual models of this individuality throughout social, clinical, developmental, and general psychology. The much-researched concepts of internal versus external control epitomize the concept of the individual as ideally being one who stands separately as determiner of his or her own fate. There is growing controversy among Euro-American psychologists themselves that there has been an over-assertion of the role of independence as a desirable attribute to human beings. Some writers now are arguing that the kind of cold insensitivity and alienation among people in the Western world is a product of the emphasis on a kind of insular independence. Dependence has been identified as such an undesirable personality characteristic that it has become almost impossible to motivate people to cooperation or even to respect for leadership.

Concepts of internal fate control and independence as desirable personality traits are essentially camouflaged descriptions of the rugged individualistic immigrant from Europe who conquered and settled these shores of North America. It is conceived as healthy to defy environmental obstacles and subdue them at all costs. The idea of subjecting the environment to the control of the powerful is implicit in such conceptualizations of human personality and motivation. It is only incidental if those obstacles happen to be other people, such as Native Americans, Africans, or Aboriginal Hispanics. They all are dispensable if they stand in the way of European fate control. Of course, if your definitions assume a superordinate controller of fate, you are likely to suffer at least temporary subjugation by the egomaniacal force that has defined itself as self-determining. If you happen to be motivated by a sense of collective responsibility, belief in supreme providence, and a faith in a lawful, systematic, and orderly universe, then you are likely to be identified as having "low internal fate control" or being an "externalizer" which, of course, is correlated with the full range of negative traits from poor social and academic performance to the more serious forms of psychopathology.

Another characteristic of this model that expands the concept of individuality is the view that mentally healthy and effectively functioning people are "competitive." Human beings are axiomatically assumed to be in conflict and human accomplishment is realized through the triumph of one over the conflict. This is reflected in concepts such as achievement motivation and assertiveness. In fact, in recent years assertiveness has become such a desirable attribute that efforts have been designed for assertiveness training. If one is "too" passive, dependent, or cooperative, it is concluded that one needs skill in the assertive promulgation of self. This becomes a measure of one's mental health.

We all are familiar with the extensive work of McClelland and Atkinson (1953) on achievement motivation. In the classic McClelland (1961) document, *The Achieving Society*, the conclusion was that one could lay claims to civilized (industrialized) human development only if one's motivations were characterized by high need for achievement. Clearly, these dimensions repeatedly show non-Caucasian, non-European, nonmales, nonmiddle-class people to be predictably at the lower end of these dimensions of human strengths.

We have failed to realize that in the garb of "science" the Western world has used these conceptualizations to legitimize the assertion of their racial and national supremacy. What has been assumed to be an apolitical, objective system is, in fact, the essence of Euro-American, caucasian politics. When we as African-Americans innocently buy into these concepts, we become agents of our own inferiority-mongering and the establishment of the supremacy of Euro-American Caucasians.

Another characteristic of the existing model is its futuristic orientation. The extent to which one's behavior is directed toward some future goal is the degree to which one's behavior is viewed as appropriate. If one does not have proper "delay of gratification" for the accomplishment of some future goal, then something is adjudged as deficient about one's "individual ego." The degree to which you are able to delay processes to some future goal is the degree to which you are effective as a human being. Clearly, the degree to which you have developed the characteristics of this model improves your chances for success in the current societal structure. The argument is whether such a norm is a universal description of human nature or the description of a middle-class, Caucasian male of European descent. We have accepted as a model of reality his projection of himself as a universal image. Therefore, many of our descriptions and perceptions of ourselves and others is reflected by this alien mirror of self. Many of the judgements made by clinicians, educators, social service personnel, and others about the "ineffectiveness" of African-American behavior occur in contrast to the characteristics emanating from this model. That is, low internal control, achievement motivation, delay of gratification, and such are ways of describing the Afro-American as non-Caucasian, which ultimately is irremediable.

Another characteristic in this list of attributes of the existing paradigm (a list not intended to be exhaustive) is the affectlessness of the model man. This is discussed at length in a recent article that I have done (Akbar, 1980). In order to be effective as a human being, you are required to be affectless. Affect is considered irrelevant and disruptive to effective decision-making processes. Great energy goes into the prohibition of emotion in "sound rational" processes. What occurs is a kind of passive insensitivity to human emotion that permits an American slavery system, an Aushwitz, or a neutron bomb calmly described as capable of destroying all people, but leaving buildings and other physical structures standing. There is no need to reconcile the discrepancies of an economic system that affords excessive opulence to the few and privation to the many. To the degree that one shows affect or emotion is the degree to which one is viewed inappropriate, distracted, or just irrational and therefore deserves being discounted. Any people who tend to be affective and to guide reactions by subjective experience or responses are viewed as being cognitively defective. It's striking that the fantasy creation of Dr. Spock (on "Star Trek") is presented in striking contrast to the "feeling" earthlings in that Spock typifies the ideal of the Western scientist or scientific model of human beings (earthlings, even).

This is only a partial listing of these characteristics, but I am certain that just a cursory review of the literature would show these attributes to have great prominence as implicit models of human normalcy. The vast majority of the literature asserts in subtle ways in the name of "empirical data" the supremacy of the model that I have identified. It is important that we understand that such "data" become a way to define reality. It is also true that data are generated out of a paradigm that in turn substantiates the paradigm out of which it was generated. The questions that you ask are rooted in what ought to be asked (Clark et al., 1976, discussed this at length).

The next issue is to understand that a methodology emerges from the paradigm that ultimately augments the paradigm. What is that methodology for the paradigm that we are discussing? According to Kazdin (1980), quoting Nagel (1961), Weimer (1976), and others:

> The philosophy of science reveals among other things that there may be fundamental limitations from a logical standpoint in what experiments can provide in the way of knowing. . . . Even to speak of experimentation glosses over a host of assumptions about the legitimacy of empirical knowledge and how it is obtained. Philosophy of science can cogently challenge the assumptions about the basis of empirical knowledge by pointing to the tenuous nature of empirical knowledge and its logical limits.

In essence, we accept empiricism as incontrovertible truth, or at least a method to acquire such truth, while not dealing with the basis through which empiricism is evolved as a method. One such assumption that must be accepted is that the essence of reality is material. What is perceived by the senses is assumed to be more real than mental reality, and spirtiual reality is completely discounted. One defines oneself as a materialist when one accepts empiricism as the route to *total* truth. This is not to deny the dimensional validity of empiricism. The question is in regard to the Euro-American view that offers empirical fact as the truth. Europeans feel more comfortable and more in control of the material sphere, and it is for this reason that the material plane has been represented as the valid plane. Many African-American and even European historians and commentators have addressed this difference in approaches between the African and European frames of reality (Abraham, 1962; Diop, 1974; Mbiti, 1970; Nobles, 1980; Williams, 1974). Richard King (1978) and others have even suggested that there may be a physiological basis for this difference in approaches to reality. In fact, there is reason to believe that even the system of capitalism is rooted in a basic philosophy of materialism. Many people have argued that materialism is an outgrowth of capitalism; I suggest here that the inverse is true. Out of this comes the philosophical basis for even racism, which defines the essence of human beings as reducible to their physical (material) characteristics.

Another issue of Euro-American sciences is its methodology and particularly its reliance on statistical normalcy. The equation of central tendencies with naturalness or normality is an increasingly disturbing phenomenon. The pervasive and controlling concept of the average or mean in statistics produces some interesting conclusions about reality. Statements about normality can shift depending on increases and decreases in frequencies. It is interesting that such a tool, which essentially creates artificial or unnatural groupings depending on one's universe of observation, has become the major instrument of Euro-American social scientists. The effort to define himself as a majority influence in a world in which he has minority status becomes a primary objective of the Euro-American male. If you restrict your sphere of observation and observe varying frequencies, you are equipped to change your definition of normality. A mathematical instrument of precision has been used to authenticate an imprecise assertion of their authority and normality and as legitimate models of human excellence.

Natural laws are eliminated as irrelevant in the wake of statistical probability, central tendencies, and mathematically predictable variation. The norm then gets arbitrarily shifted as the field of frequency varies. In an earlier statement I have referred to this phenomenon as "democratic sanity" (Akbar, 1981). In the Diagnostic and Statistical Manual II (DSM II) there is a phenomenon known as sexual deviance or homosexuality. In the current edition (DSM III), this "disorder" no longer exists. The only related residual is transexualism, or a "disorder" whereby a person seeks surgical alteration of his or her gender. The point is that politics have effectively altered the normative grouping of deviations. By virtue of an alternation in frequency (or at least visibility), it became possible to reorder or reclassify normality. In other words, mathematics actually is being attributed systematically but arbitrarily to phenomena. To the extent that mathematics carries the aura of precision, by numbering phenomena, a guise of validity is projected.

The assumption of the empirical methodology also is one of objectivity, Jacob Carruthers (1972), in his paper entitled "Science and Oppression," argues against the allegedly greatest virtue of science, which is supposed to be its valuelessness. One fact, that often is denied, is that the use of an "objective" approach does not preclude values because objectivity is a value. When an observer chooses to suspend from his or her observations certain levels of reacting, this is a value judgment. This is a critical value because it often involves dismissing certain important sources of information that could critically alter what is perceived as real. If we deal with only literal meaning of objective reality as the face value of phenomena, we immediately see the limitation in the superficial information that comes from surface information. This is true of material objects themselves, the function of which is seldom revealed by surface observation, but more commonly through subjective analysis. Certainly, this limitation is even more striking in the case of human beings. Science argues, however, that "objectivity" is the "valueless value" that should be adopted for uncluttered observation.

Objectivity assumes that there is a controller who has the right to control objects. This controller has the right to subject things to his or her will, which begins to make him or her God-like. This may sound a bit extreme, but there is great revelation in the language that is required in scientific enterprise. First of all, the beginning science student is taught never to refer to him- or herself as "I," nor to his or her observations as "my." In order to avoid subjectivity, one must first objectify oneself (which is supposed to magically remove the observer from participation in the activity). One does so by referring to oneself as the E (xperimenter), and one works with S (ubjects). The E then subjects by objectifying what he or she works with. The E usually is or represents the paradigmatic image (i.e., Caucasian male of European descent). The subject becomes essentially everything and everybody else.

The other characteristic of the objective approach is the ordinal quantitative classification system. An ordinal classification system carries implicit requirement of a superordinate and subordinate or superior and inferior. Such a system justifies the presence of a controller (oppressor) and the controlled (oppressed). In other words, such a methodological approach replicates and legitimizes "scientifically" what has already been established politically. It is striking that an ordinal system actually is inconsistent with the principles of equality and democracy established in the American ideals.

Such a quantification system permits the objectification of human suffering and emotional difficulty. For example, personal turmoil and human misery become a score above 80 on the depression scale of the MMPI. People who either have alternative perspectives or are systematically blocked from adequate environmental opportunities are identified by a score of 85 in the dull normal range of intelligence on the WISC-R. Objectifying such imperatives for human action and reaction permits a neutralization of such conscience-provoking realizations. A score of 70 does not carry the impetus for help-giving that an emotionally depressed and unhappy human being carries. An IQ score of 85 does not carry the impetus for political and social reform that frustrated human beings seeking societal effectiveness carry. A value system based on the societal ideals would necessitate certain types of remedial actions for such human conditions, but objectification permits a comfortable hypocrisy.

As African-American social scientists particularly, we must be sensitive to such subtle manipulations of our thinking and activities. We must realize that many of our efforts that might be intended toward our liberation result in our greater enslavement. We must understand the nature of the limitations in using the opposition's weaponry in our own defense. Often the effort to destroy the barriers results in fortifying those barriers because we do not realize the intricacy of our borrowed tools. A case in point is the work of Kenneth Clark. He was a well-trained scientist who thoroughly understood the use of this methodology. He made the first major breakthrough in having the voice of the African-American scientist heard by having his scientific work documented in the 1954 Supreme Court decision. We, of course, realize some 25 years later that this probably was one of the greater disasters of the political decisions regarding our fate in North America. The price paid in the educational destruction of our children by that decision and its aftermath will, no doubt, take us 50 to 100 years to recover.

The kind of assumptions implicit in the Clark and Clark (1958) conclusions were so devastating that the outcomes of decisions based on such conclusions were predictably disastrous. We now know that even the data lacked validity, based on some recent findings and reanalyses (Semaj, 1979). Even short of the data, the paradigm that was utilized was already loaded with deadly assumptions. For example, one implication from the Clark findings was that it was psychologically unhealthy for "colored" children to go to school only with one another. The outcome is likely to be self-hatred, lowered motivation, and so on. Another conclusion implied from the data and made explicit in the Supreme Court decision is the idea that it is psychologically healthy for Black children to attend school with white children. Such an opportunity is likely to improve the African-American child's self-concept, intellectual achievement, and overall social and psychological adjustment. The entire statement of the 1954 Supreme Court decision speaks to damage done to "Negro" children by the system of school segregation:

> The segregation of white and colored children in public schools has a detrimental effect upon the colored children. The impact is greater when it has the sanction of law: for the policy of separating the races is usually interpreted as denoting the inferiority of the negro group. A sense of inferiority affects the motivation of a child to learn. Segregation with the sanction of law, therefore, has a tendency to retard educational and mental development of Negro children and to deprive them of some of the benefits they would receive in a racially integrated school system. We come then to the question presented—does segregation of children in public schools solely on the basis of race deprive children of the

minority group of equal educational opportunities. We believe that it does (excerpt from *Brown v. Board of Education of Topeka, Kansas,* 347 US 483).

At no point does the statement identify the reality that in maintaining a system of segregation, not only are African-Americans hurt by the thwarted opportunity and abuse, but Caucasian children are raised as delusional racists. No research was quoted to identify the pathological implications of the delusional system or of racism itself. If you assume that only African-Americans are being benefitted by such a system, then implicit in such a conclusion is a perpetuation of precisely that system that you allegedly are seeking to correct. It is not surprising that the drop-outs, push-outs, suspensions, achievement levels, and overall academic performance of African-American children probably is much worse than it was in 1954 in the overtly segregated school system. The kind of logic that was utilized in drawing these conclusions of dubious value to the oppressed people was rooted in the application of an implicitly destructive paradigm.

Empirical approaches to the study of human beings assume that such knowledge is primarily exoteric. The very devolved definintion of psychology as the "study of behavior" personifies this conclusion. The concepts of consciousness, mentation, and certainly unconsciousness have increasingly come to be looked upon as forbidden in "good scientific" psychology. From this perspective, material is sense, mind is nonsense, and spirit is nonexistent.

What then are the anomalies created by the existing paradigm that I am suggesting will give rise to the coming paradigm shift? Without a doubt, African-Americans and our genuine authentic characteristics personify these anomalies. In fact, women also are an anomaly within this paradigm, as is anyone who differs drastically from the essential (i.e., material) characteristics of the paradigmatic human being (i.e., Caucasian male of European descent with middle-class status). The greater the degree of your difference from this model, the more of an anomaly you are. African-Americans are anomalies because we become least capable of fulfilling the requirements of this paradigm.

According to Kuhn (1970), "scientific revolutions are inaugurated by a growing sense that an existing paradigm has ceased to function." For a long time the paradigm has remained functional because it simply negatively defined the anomalies who would not fit. A classification of "deviant" based on the model became a persistently simple way to dismiss the anomalies while maintaining control over their identity. Treatment of remediation were defined as techniques to bring the deviant more in accord with the model. The explosion of the Black psychology movement in the late 1960s was a reaction to growing discontent with the consistent failure to fit the model and the persisting demand that we should. When African-Americans consistently failed to fit the organization, leadership and decision-making strategies, and in every other sphere of personal and social life, people began to question the validity of the model. A few African-American psychologists began to question the model, although the vast majority of African-American psychologists persisted in trying to force the "deviants" into the alien model. This is why we are still inundated by volumes of deficit data emanating from Afro-American and Euro-American psychologists alike.

The Black psychology movement, women's psychology, Hispanic psychology, and Asian psychology all are statements about the limitations of the existing paradigm. The consistent claim is that the paradigm is malfunctioning and that new motions must begin to be articulated. An example of such an alternative concept has emerged from African psychology (an outgrowth of the Black psychology movement). The proponents of this conceptual framework (Clark et al., 1976; Nobles, 1980) suggest that a more valid ontological statement for African people is "I am because We are," as opposed to the Cartesian notion that has shaped Euro-American thought as "I think therefore I am."

The *cogito ergo sum* leads to a measure of intelligence as being one's familiarity with the objects and processes of an external environment. The volumes of data and controversy around the intelligence issue are based on this assumption of the *cogito* (I think, therefore I am). No one has yet dealt with implications for intelligence based on the assumptions of I am because we are. Such an assumption would lead to alternative measures of intelligence. Rather than assessing people's ability to effectively manipulate material objects of the outer world, one would be concerned with assessing people's adequacy in negotiating cooperative, amiable human relationships. With such criteria we might find the Western world to be a population of idiots, given their failures at effective family relationships, good human relations, transethnic relationships and cooperation, and the generally poor showing in effective interpersonal relationships. So long as the criterion remains one of adequacy in manipulating external objects, then people who often sacrifice objects on the basis of human values will continue to be seen as retardates while the human tyrants and technical tycoons will be models of human intellectual accomplishment. Again, I must caution that I do not condemn the value, and even the necessity, of technological accomplishment; instead, I am asserting that it is of even greater import that human beings should be adept at handling human relationships.

The paradigm shift comes with a recognition of the existing paradigm's inability to account for the failures in living. When that paradigm is unable to speak to the epidemic proportions of alchololism and other self-destructive processes growing out of people's failure to utilize their human resources and when emotional disorders begin to occur with greater frequency than physical disorders, we have a situation in which our technology has outflanked our mentality. We must begin to redefine reality in such a way that such problems can be corrected and a more universally applicable paradigm begins to emerge. Wade Nobles (1978) has defined power as the ability to define reality and to have others accept your definition as if it were their own. As long as we accept alien definitions of reality and internalize them, we remain powerless. If we can emerge with such new definitions and not be so thoroughly intimidated by the existing paradigm, we can begin to collect on our destiny.

There are movements even within the mainstream of psychology that are raising doubts about the effectiveness of the existing paradigms. Most prominent, perhaps, are the humanistic psychologists, who have thoroughly revolted against the increasingly mechanized, dehumanized, ethnocentric conceptualizations that have come to characterize psychology out of the behaviorist and Skinnerian models. Clinicians are admitting that their techniques do not work and are looking for other models to reduce human suffering. The family therapy movements, group therapy movements, and community psychology in general have been efforts to shift away from the insular, individualistic model described above. Paradoxically, these movements actually emulate traditional folk methods that have persisted in African and other non-Western societies. Unfortunately, we have failed to even research the folk traditions that often brought healing to ourselves in our culturally unique developmental experiences.

The African-American experience itself is an anomaly for Western psychology. Given the existing conceptualizations of human functioning, stress, tolerance, coping strategies, socialization influences, and so on, we are not supposed to be here. If physically still present, certainly we could not offer any examples of effective mental functioning from any frame of reference. Our very presence as effectively functioning scholars, fathers, mothers, citizens, even scientists actually defies their theories of human development. Western theories of psychology cannot account for just one DuBois at Harvard, or one King, or one Carver, or one Turner, much less the tens of thousands of successful, well-functioning human beings in all aspects of this alien cultural experience. The failures are predictable and the slave system and oppression of America are adequate explanations for the frustrated human failures. The paradigm does not account for the overwhelming evidence of human accomplishment that is more common among African-Americans than the failures their model would predict. The very theories that we as scholars use are erroneous by virtue of our presence here and ability to even utilize those theories. Too often we find ourselves advocating certain models for our people that do not even account for our success. The vast majority of us are not raised by a "Parenting Manual" but by good, intuitive maternal affection and guidance. We have tons of data about how the few do not make it and little information about how so many of us do. What are we doing here? How did we survive the oppression and assaults to our very physical being, not to mention our self-esteem? How did we survive the kind of material privation that, according to the existing paradigm, would assuredly destroy any vestige of humanity in the paradigmatic being? These are questions that our research has not bothered to address because the research has emerged from the alien paradigm. We must begin to address those exceptional cases of great accomplishment rather than being preoccupied with those exceptional cases of failure. The real anomalies are those who have achieved prominence despite oppression rather than those who have understandably succumbed to inhuman pressures.

Another area that presents horror to the proponents of the existing paradigm is spirituality. This aspect of human life has been so thoroughly eliminated from the purview of modern science that it probably will take a couple of generations to reintegrate it into our studies of human beings. There is considerable evidence that the European scientists' ongoing battle with the Christian church forced them to isolate themselves from spiritual enterprise. The only way left available to them to pursue their studies was to create a dualistic universe that gave the church sway over the spiritual sphere and gave science dominion over the material sphere. The result is that an essential page from the annals of human study was removed and the subsequent distortions represent efforts to understand the human makeup without its essence. Our experience and survival is the overwhelming evidence of the existence and potency of the transcendant human spirit and its resilience. The paradigm shift will necessarily accommodate this sphere as the absence of spirituality is probably the source of much of the anonymity created by the existing model.

It is difficult to project the form of the methodology that will begin to document the presence of such intangibles. Certainly the existing methods relying on objective measures could not adequately infer this superordinate dimension. It may require coerced presence of the skeptic in a "prayer meeting," or a "juke," and their subjective trepidation in experiencing vibratory intensity that they cannot cognitively assimilate. Certain types of people may never be able to grasp the "data" as some people are incapable of grasping the confusion of certain mathematical proofs. Clearly, the collection of data about spirituality will have to call on an instrumentation currently unavailable. Subjectivity does not preclude consensual validity. Some metaphysicians already have suggested that all knowledge is esoteric and all things may be known by knowing self.

The new paradigm that will emerge will be a balance between the extreme material and exoteric ontology represented in the Eurocentric model and the extreme spiritual and esoteric ontology represented in the Eastern models. The paradigm that will emerge will be a "natural" or general human paradigm (Akbar, 1980) rather than the ethnocentric paradigm that describes a particular human. This model will permit cross-validation between subjective and objective experience. The model will accept that the human being's experience of him- or herself is as "real" as the environment's influence on the human being.

A prototype of the emerging paradigm may be seen in the African traditional healer. Such healers were simultaneously herbalists (users of objective power) and griots (reciters of "self" or conjurors of subjective power). Such a model does not require a sacrifice of material mastery or technology, but it permits a balanced development of the inner and outer worlds. In such a world, one does not construct huge skyscrapers as a precipice for the deranged to throw themselves from. Instead, one's skill in scaling the heights of gravity is paralleled by insight into the depths of the human make-up.

The new paradigm will incorporate, as well, the teachings of affectivity. The capacity to feel emotionally attached to experiences and for emotions to modulate cognition will have legitimacy within the new paradigm. The kind of observational design implied by such a model takes on more of the form of pioneering efforts in Euro-American psychology. The early life of a paradigm has similar developmental processes. For example, participant-observer kinds of observational models would be essential for the new paradigm. The dichotomous assumptions of the old paradigm would not function in the new science. Consistent measure would not preclude the variability of the measurer. The person can remain a person without becoming the E(xperimenter) and still produce valid and reliable observations based on what he or she experiences by participating. Such an approach immediately eliminates the necessity for "human subjects' protection legislation." If the observer is what he or she observes, then he or she will also be compelled to preserve the integrity of what he or she observes. We must regain our capacity to immerse ourselves in our experiences and gain information from the outside and the inside.

Another device that could be used in moving toward the paradigm shift is natualistic observation. We simply need to describe what we see happening in our lives, communities, with our children—as Piaget did with his. Naturalistic observation should precede the experimental manipulations and creation of artifical realities that hold such prominence with the current paradigm. We must accept that there is much in human experience that is like astronomy, in which manipulation is not possible, but the science becomes precise and thorough observation and description. Particularly, as African-Americans we have not looked at ourselves "naturally" since the psychohistorical trauma of slavery took place. We have taken the naturalistic observations of Euro-Americans of themselves and their armchair theorizing and have arbitrarily attributed that reality and those assumptions to ourselves. Perhaps, step one would be to seek funding for a group of armchairs for a group of African-American psychologists to sit upon for several years and just theorize. Certainly, Euro-American psychology has a comparable genesis.

The new paradigm must restore the psyche to psychology. Strange as it may seem, there is considerable evidence that so-called "para-psychology" is going to be the warfare of the future. Evidence is already present that the Soviet Union has put considerable money and effort into the study of psychic phenomenon. More obscure evidence suggests a similar clandestine effort by the CIA, particularly in the area of mind control and psychic manipulation. This kind of study becomes a natural outgrowth of a shifting paradigm. However, it must be called para-psychology or dealt with in obscurity because it does not fit the current paradigm of psychology. However, I am convinced that there are insightful scholars who anticipate the shift, have pioneered the new spheres, and are probably cognizant of our destined role in the new order.

We as African-Americans are a natural bridge or kind of psycho-historical chiasma between the peaks of ancient civilizations, with their humanistic vision, and the peaks of modern civilization, with its technological opulence. If the range of human experience can be conceptualized on the model of the cerebral hemispheres, then we are the corpus collasum bridging the best of the aesthetic, esoteric, and affectional spheres with the best of the rational, cognitive, and exoteric effectiveness. Future generations will condemn us as traitors to our heritage if we do not collect on our destiny to bring about a scientific revolution by causing a paradigm shift.

REFERENCES

ABRAHAM, W. E. (1962) The Mind of Africa. Chicago: Univ. of Chicago Press.

AKBAR, N. (1981) "Mental disorder among African-Americans." Black Books Bulletin 7, 2: 18-25.

———(1980) "The evolution of human psychology." Presented to the SREB Student Conference, Atlanta.

CARRUTHERS, J. (1972) Science and Oppression. Chicago: Northeastern Illinois University, Center for Inner City Studies.

CLARK, K. B. and M. R. CLARK (1958) "Racial identification and preference in Negro children," in E. Maccoby et al. (eds.) Readings in Social Psychology. New York: Holt, Rinehart & Winston.

CLARK, X. C., D. McGee, W. NOBLES, and N. AKBAR (1976) Voodoo or IQ: An Introduction to African Psychology. Chicago: Institute of Positive Education Black Pages.

DIOP, C. A. (1974) The African Origins of Civilization. New York: Lawrence Hill.

KAZDIN, A. (1980) Research Design in Clinical Psychology. New York: Harper & Row.

KING, R. (1978) "Uraeus: from mental slavery to mastership." Ureaus 1, 3.

KUHN, T. S. (1970) "The structure of scientific revolutions," in International Encyclopedia of Unified Science, vol. 2. Chicago: Univ. of Chicago Press.

MBITI, J. (1970) African Religions and Philosophy. Garden City, NY: Anchor.

McCLELLAND, D.C. (1961) The Achieving Society. New York: Van Nostrand.

———and J. ATKINSON (1953) The Achievement Motive. New York: Appleton-Century-Crofts.

NAGEL, E. (1961) The Structure of Science. New York: Harcourt Brace Jovanovich.

NOBLES, W. W. (1980) "African philosophy: foundations for Black psychology," in R. Jones (ed.) Black Psychology. New York: Harper & Row.

———(1978) "African consciousness and liberation struggles: implications for the development and construction of scientific paradigms." (unpublished)

SEMAJ, L. (1979) "Reconceptualizing the development of radical preference in children: the role of cognition." Presented at the 12th Annual National Convention of the Association of Black Psychologists, Atlanta.

WEIMER, W. B. (1976) Psychology and the Conceptual Foundation of Science. Hillsdale, NJ: Erlbaum.

WILLIAMS, C. (1974) The Destruction of Black Civilization. Chicago: Third World Press.

2

BLACK CHILD SOCIALIZATION

A Conceptual Framework

A. WADE BOYKIN
FORREST D. TOMS

In this chapter our aim is to provide a viable conceptual framework for the study of Black child socialization processes. We believe such an effort is both timely and greatly needed. We say this for three important reasons. First, there is considerable complexity attendant to Black family life in America. A multiplicity of socialization agendas must be negotiated simultaneously. The demands that result from having to cope within the American social context are multifaceted and inherently contradictory. Consequently, a conceptual framework is needed to provide illumination and integration of the myriad of issues that must be taken simultaneously into consideration.

By common definition socialization refers to the preparation of children to take on the adult roles and responsibilities of society (Baldwin, 1980). As Zigler and Child (1973: 4) point out, it "deals essentially with the practical problem of how to rear children so that they will become adequate adult members of the society to which they belong." As Young (1970) states, this process is enacted principally through the teaching and learning of conventional beliefs, values, and patterns of behavior. Ideally, it is the principal process by which the codes and sanctions of a social order are imposed on individuals. The central, although surely not the exclusive, responsibility for socialization rests with the individual's family. Ideally, the socialization imperatives emanating from within one's family would not be inconsistent with those from other major socialization agents or institutions. That is, there ought to be compatibility between the initiatives and objectives attendant to family socialization and those of, for example, the system of schooling, the judicial system, the world of work, and the mass media. These additional socialization systems should thus play a reinforcing or augmenting role to that provided by one's family of origin.

These ideals of socialization may approximate the processes at work in the lives of individuals who can be characterized as monocultural, who participate in a relatively homogeneous society, or who belong to the dominant or defining group within the social order. Within the American social context, these ideals of socialization portray socialization processes attendant to Euro-Americans, and any attempts to capture those attendant to Afro-Americans have been patently inadequate.

For example, we must ask ourselves what does it mean for a Black person to become an "adequate" adult? What is the society of which he or she is a member? Similarly, when we speak of the imposition of the social order, is it not necessary to distinguish between the dictates of the larger society versus those of one's more immediate ecological circumstances? Moreover, to what extent might the more proximal socialization messages be incompatible with distal socialization messages? Further, the rewards for being "properly" socialized into the wider society may not be as readily expected or as highly valued (Banks et al., 1979). Such a set of circumstances (e.g., mixed socialization messages) is likely to lead to possibilities such as value or behavioral flexibility, rejection of and/or cynicism about mainstream conventions, a certain unevenness in the full inculcation of the extant "conventional" socialization imperatives, or the need to learn unique adaptive motifs. In any result, there is no obvious straightforward resolution of what it means to be an "adequate" adult, or what ought to be the outcome of the socialization process for Afro-Americans. The potential complexity attendant to Black child socialization is simply overwhelming. We believe that, to date, it has not been adequately and systematically understood. We believe that a viable conceptual framework is needed to bring adequate integration, coherency, and comprehension.

Second, a viable conceptual framework also is needed because existing schemes, in our estimation, are not fully appropriate to the task at hand. Within the mainstream of social science, the issues of socialization have been dominated by what we call the Freudian-Anglo-Behaviorist (FAB) conceptual complex. The dominant approach has been informed by an intellectual lineage that was instigated to create a theoretical rapprochement between behaviorism and Freudian psychology (Baldwin, 1980; Miller, 1983). This effort has been augmented by a tendency to promote Anglo-Saxon ideals (Sampson, 1977; Riegel, 1972). Consequently, behaviorism as a psychological translation of British empiricism, emphasizing the notions of tabula rasa, passive organism, rewards and punishments, drives and mechanistic cause-effect explanations, forms the processoral fabric and frames the methodology of the mainstream conceptual framework. The Freudian influence has contributed major socialization products and behavioral systems of interest such as aggression, imitation, dependency, toilet training, and attachment (Dollard et al., 1939; Miller and Dollard, 1941). Finally, such has been augmented by the Anglo-Saxon influence that contributed the value orientation that frames relevant personality characteristics and the proper categories and goals of socialization. Thus, we see emphasized such notions as strong achievement orientation, self-control, self-contained "rugged" individualism, and the elevation of the cognitive over the affective (Sampson, 1977; Sears et al., 1957, 1965; Bandura and Walters, 1963; Gerwitz, 1969). This conceptual framework has been highly influential since the 1930s, even up to the present time. It has been propagated through riding the crest of behaviorist dominance within mainstream American psychology. It has profited from this country's fascination with Freud and has helped to secure its place through the promotion of behavioral ideals and outcomes consistent with the dominant Anglo-Saxon value emphasis. The dominance of the Freudian-Anglo-Behaviorist conceptual scheme can be documented easily by perusing any of the recent major reviews in the field of socialization. It is clear that social scientists have routinely, even matter of factly, divided the domain of socialization into categories apparently inspired by the FAB complex (e.g., Zigler and Child, 1973; Gerwitz, 1969; Martin, 1975; Mussen, 1970).

We propose that no matter how well intentioned are our efforts, the extent to which we even implicitly work within this conceptual framework, the extent to which this conceptual complex frames our socialization agenda, we will not adequately capture the socialization fabric attendant to Black families. The quest for a Freudian-Behaviorist rapproachement surely was intellectually well intentioned and perhaps historically justifiable; yet it cannot serve adequately as a basis for organizing the behavioral systems attendant to Black families. It simply was not conceived with the distinct if not unique socialization agenda of Black families in mind. It was not offered to accommodate the particular complexities and diversities of Black families as its explanatory goal. Exporting it to the study of Afro-American family life could easily lead to what Nobles (1978) has called "transubstantive errors," or inappropriately characterizing the substance of one social reality in terms of a different one. Moreover, although it seems clear that extant Black parents often do hold mainstream child-rearing attitudes (Radin and Kamii, 1965; Bartz and Levine, 1978), it would be a mistake to conclude that Black family socialization can be fully understood simply in terms of its approximation to mainstream Euro-American ideals.

We believe there is a valuable lesson to be learned here. We are convinced that the articulation of conceptual frameworks should precede the offering of specific theories and empirical research. This is so because the conceptual framework utilized largely determines the research questions asked, the categories of experience scrutinized, the constructs examined, the range of observations possible, and the codification of behaviors (Allen, 1978; Boykin, 1979). Without appropriately construed conceptual frameworks, the research generated and the theory or model paid homage to may be inadequate or improperly focused. But beyond this, we also may run the risk of filling the knowledge void about Black family socialization in ways that belie our original intentions and even support the intentions of those with an unsympathetic scholarly agenda.

The third reason we believe that a viable conceptual framework is needed is to build upon the important work done in recent years by those scholars who have provided a revisionist perspective on Black family life. Indeed, over the past 15 years such work has led to important redirections in the approaches and images offered on the character, structure, and functioning of Black families (e.g., Billingsley, 1968; Hill, 1971; Ten Houten, 1970; Lewis, 1975; Peters, 1981). Revisionist scholars have helped to balance the pejorative perspective that has dominated for well over six decades (Myers, 1982). They have provided fresh insights into the resilience, adaptive strength, and integrity attendant to Black families. As Kilpatrick (1979: 347) has stated, "behaviors previously viewed as maladaptive or pathological because they differed from mainstream culture are now [within the revisionist position] interpreted as functional or having survival value within the Afro-American culture."

The work of revisionists has yielded several scholarly and paradigmatic benefits. Among the most salient are as follows: (1) It has led to greater appreciation for the adaptive and resourceful character of Black people (Hill, 1971); (2) it has led to greater appreciation for the complexity and diversity of what constitutes a structurally adequate family (Billingsley, 1968; Myers, 1982; Martin and Martin, 1978); (3) it has illuminated the limitations of taking an Anglocentric perspective and using an Anglometric yardstick by which to judge normalcy (Allen, 1978; Peters, 1981; Nobles, 1976); and (4) it has illuminated cultural features distinctive of Afro-American people (Nobles, 1976; Lewis, 1975; Young, 1970).

The revisionist perspective clearly has led to viable alternative characterizations of Black family life. It provides an orientation that seems well equipped to handle the complexities and distinctiveness of Black family functioning. To date, however, insufficient attention has been paid to Black family socialization processes from the revisionist perspective (Allen, 1978). Yet in our estimation, questions like "what are Black parents preparing their children to become as adults" or "what is an adequate adult role for an Afro-American" can be effectively addressed if we do so from a revisionist perspective.

In all then, we are persuaded that a lamentable void now exists in viable knowledge about Black family interactional processes, the dynamics of Black family life (Allen, 1979; Kilpatrick, 1979). We agree with Allen (1978) that the revisionist perspective has yet to generate viable conceptual frameworks to capture such processes. We advocate that until such frameworks are articulated the void will not be meaningfully eradicated. In the remaining pages of this chapter we will propose such a framework, building upon the revisionist perspective.

TOWARD A CONCEPTUAL FRAMEWORK

The task of offering a conceptual framework is fraught with difficulties. It cannot be principally guided by systematic empirical research, for a void exists in this regard within the revisionist perspective. Indeed, recent research done on Black family socialization processes seems informed by the FAB complex (e.g., Cummings, 1977; Durrett et al., 1975; Bartz and Levine, 1978; Baumrind, 1972). Yet the difficulty of the task cannot be a deterrent. For unless we can put some conceptual handles on capturing what Black children are being prepared to become, emanating from Afro-Americans' own social-cultural frame of reference, we will simply gain insight into how well these children approximate a Euro-American social-cultural frame of reference as the basis for successful socialization.

Insight into the difficulty of the task at hand can be readily gained. Consider, for example, that a cornerstone concern of revisionists has been Black culture. Yet there is considerable confusion over what is Black culture and how it is manifested in the lives of Afro-Americans. There even is confusion over what is culture. Some revisionist scholars seem to see Black culture as manifested in the various coping strategies and adaptive techniques used in the service of warding off racism and discrimination, and in the service of surviving under materially austere circumstances (Allen, 1978; Stack, 1974). Others speak of Black culture as a continuation of West African traditions within the American context (Nobles, 1974; Hale, 1980). Still others seem to mix these two notions freely without demarcation (Lewis, 1975; Staples, 1976). Yet, as Dennis (1976: 324) has stated, "a forced and dominated cultural base is different from an evolving cultural base that flows freely from the network of interlocking values that emanate from within the group itself."

Further complications exist. Those revisionists who offer various coping strategies and mechanisms do not make it clear whether such strategies represent reactions to the harshness and crises of life as best as possible or represent the active generation of certain family structures in order to better adapt to the confronted circumstances of life. Then, too, those who speak of an African-inspired intrinsic cultural base disagree on how such cultural phenomena are manifested. According to Nobles (1978), culture is manifested principally in the realm of belief systems and values. One can glean from the works of others (e.g., Lewis, 1975) that it is manifested essentially in terms of styles of behavior. Which position is correct? Or is it that both positions are legitimate? Even as various authors attempt to specify the scope and nature of Black culture, no one ignores that Afro-Americans participate to some degree in the cultural systems and institutions of mainsteam American society. Surely the diversity among Black families cannot be ignored.

Therefore, we believe that a viable framework must adequately address and distinguish between coping strategies and the intrinsic cultural base of Black family processes. A framework must reflect the extant bicultural character of Black family life. A framework must be comprehensive enough to accommodate diversity in Afro-American life. And, above all else, it must be responsive to the distinctive socialization agenda(s) attendant to Afro-American families. We need to guide our efforts at understanding Black family socialization by a comprehensive attempt to simultaneously capture the uniformity, diversity, complexity and the richness of Black family life.

The framework we will pose is based upon the position that Afro-Americans must simultaneously negotiate through three distinctively different realms of experience. These realms are the mainstream, minority, and Black cultural experience (Cole, 1970; Jones, 1979). The conceptual framework has been elucidated elsewhere to address the academic concerns of Afro-American children (Boykin, 1983, 1985). Given its close correspondence to the observations of several revisionist scholars attempting to account for the complexity of Black family life (e.g., Young, 1970; Lewis, 1975; Peters, 1981), we believe it is applicable to the domain of socialization proper as well.

THE TRIPLE QUANDARY

Surely Afro-Americans have their lives significantly shaped by mainstream American society. Of course, the susceptibility to such influence can vary among Afro-Americans. As Young (1970: 406) has stated, however, "participation in standard American culture is characteristic of [Blacks] of all social classes, rural and urban. [Blacks] participate in work systems, judicial systems, in consumption systems, in bureaucratic organizations both as clients and employees." Moreover, values transmitted via the mass media, especially television, are likely to be picked up by Afro-Americans. Then, too, the educational institutions of this society surely exert a homogenizing influence on its participants in terms of values, practices, and outlooks. Thus, it is not unexpected that working-class Black mothers display similar child-rearing values as their middle-class counterparts (Radin and Kamii, 1965); that there is greater convergence than divergence in the child-rearing attitudes expressed by Black parents and Euro-American parents (Bartz and Levine, 1978); and that success within the legitimate occupational channels is aspired to by Black children (Simmons, 1979). Likewise, we can be persuaded by Leibow's (1966) finding that Blacks substantially internalize mainstream American norms. Regardless of what criteria revisionist scholars use to offset the argument of inadequacy in Black family life, extant Black families do substantially judge their own success and failure against white middle-class standards. The hope of attaining the American dream has not eluded Afro-American families. But while the hope may be espoused, overwhelming evidence, too obvious to enumerate, shows that attainment of this dream has not been forthcoming. Reasons for this are legion. Yet presently it is relevant to emphasize that although Black families may pay homage to Euro-American values, their emulation of these values and their living out the ensuing behavioral practices are not so much in evidence. Hence, we find Black parents espousing Euro-American values but engaging in practices that run counter to those values (Radin and Kamii, 1965; Hess, 1970). Thus it is plausible that Black families have not done as adequate a job in preparing their children to embrace a Euro-American mainstream ethos as have their Euro-American counterparts. It is one thing to refute that Black parents do an inadequate job of raising their children. Revisionists have adequately rebutted this claim. But it remains tenable that Black parents do an inadequate job of raising their children to be middle-class Americans. We submit that principal among the reasons for inadequate mainstream socialization attendant to Black families is that two other domains of experience require socialization attention as well. The mainstream socialization agenda has to be negotiated in lieu of the minority and Black cultural agendas. These other agendas clearly conflict with the mainstream one; and, for that matter, with each other as well.

Over the last 20 years in particular, an impressive array of scholars have converged on the specification and delineation of Black cultural expression in lives of Afro-Americans (Gay, 1975; Akbar, 1976; Hale, 1982; Thompson, 1966; Jackson, 1976). The common thread running through these scholars' work is that the core character of Black cultural expression is emphatically linked to traditional West African cultural ethos. Given the debilitating intrusions of racism and oppression and the necessity to function for 300 years within the American social context, it would be unrealistic to presume that African culture remains intact and is expressed full-blown in the cultural modes of Afro-Americans. Yet, as Baldwin (1979) and others have argued, it would be erroneous to understand Black psychological functioning only as an approximation of Euro-American norms or as a reaction to racial oppression. Such would obscure and misrepresent the full meaning of the phenomena observed. To be sure, if West African culture had remained untransformed and unmitigated in the lives of Afro-Americans, we would expect to find the ethos displayed in terms of world views, which would eventuate in a set of values that in turn would get displayed in a repertoire of culturally informed behavioral styles (DuBois, 1972; Boykin, 1983). This does not seem to be the case for extant Black families. We do not witness the espousal of untransformed African belief systems, which inform a full complement of core values and which then dictate cultural styles. Yet evidence of behavioral practices consistent with West African traditions do abound and are witnessed within Black family life (Young, 1970; Hale, 1982; Nobles, 1978). Values and outlooks consistent with African tradition also exist, even if their proponents cannot articulate the origin of such stances and even if the entire coordinated cultural system has not been preserved intact.

In distilling the work of scholars who address the character of Black culture, Boykin (1983) has specified nine interrelated but distinct dimensions that find expression among Afro-Americans. These dimensions are as follows:

Spirituality—conducting one's life as though its essence were vitalistic rather than mechanistic and as though transcending forces significantly govern the lives of people

Harmony—placing a premium on versatility and placing an emphasis on wholeness rather than discreteness

Movement—approaching life rhythmically, particularly as expressed through the patterned interwoven mosaic of music, movement, and percussiveness

Verve—psychological affinity for variability and intensity of stimulation, particularly stimulation emanating from the movement mosaic complex

Affect—a premium placed on emotional sensibilities and expressiveness

Communalism—sensitivity to the interdependence of people and the notion that group concerns transcend individual strivings

Expressive Individualism—a premium attached to the cultivation of distinctiveness, spontaneity, and uniqueness of self-expression

Orality—a special emphasis on oral and aural modes of communication, especially the use of the spoken word to convey deep textural meanings not possible through the written word

Social Time Perspective—a commitment to time as a social phenomenon much more than a concoction objectively drawn through clocks, calendars, and other inanimate markers

Recognizing that these dimensions find expression in the lives of Afro-Americans is one thing: Understanding how such phenomena are manifested and conveyed within the Black family socialization context is another matter. We posit that Black culture typically is not overtly socialized in the sense of conventional teaching of rules and values informed by an overarching belief system. Instead, we are persuaded by Young (1974: 412), who, after extensive anthropological observations, stated that Black parents tend to socialize a

mode of behavior rather than [concentrate] on the conventions or rules which govern behavior. This is perhaps why Black Americans' behavior has often been analyzed as pragmatic rather than culturally conditioned. Culture is more easily recognized when it takes the form of specific rule-based and value-based behavior than when it consists of modes, sequences, and styles of behavior.

The key phrase here for understanding Black cultural socialization is "culturally conditioned." We posit that Black cultural motifs are typically what is passed on. As such Black culture is socialized more so through a tacit cultural conditioning process, a process through which children pick up "modes, sequences, and styles of behavior" through their day-to-day encounters with parents and other family members; encounters in which such modes, sequences, and styles of behavior are displayed to these young children in a consistent, persistent, and enduring fashion. This is so even if the cultural import of such displays is unarticulated, and even if they are not accompanied by directives or imperatives to learn them. As motifs or styles become the basis, the foundation for the child's behavioral negotiation with the world, they conceivably can extrapolate to tacit embracement of the values if not belief systems that correspond to a lost cultural legacy of their African ancestry. Of course we cannot rule out that Black cultural values or beliefs are overtly taught per se. But if and when this happens, it typically is done without awareness that they are embedded within a comprehensive cultural complex of West African origins, or it is done without the full complement of interdependent values being consistently and fully applied. This, then, is a tacit socialization process. Tacit because, for all intents and purposes, Black parents typically are unaware that they are transmitting *cultural* styles (or even cultural values). There also is a general unawareness that the culture being transmitted is informed by a traditional African ethos that in its purest form is an elaborated complex of interdependent, internally coherent beliefs, values and behavioral motifs. There also is general unawareness that these styles, which amount to habitual patterns of behavior, foster a set of extrapolated values and beliefs; values and beliefs that may go unarticulated and even when grasped are done so without understanding their ultimate source, and thus they are robbed of their full cultural meaning and significance. Thus, Black cultural styles are enacted by Black parents (and other family members and friends) and passed on to the children essentially because such are habitual forms of behavior, ingrained patterns of actions, motifs that are displayed with such consistency and that help to provide an ambience so compelling that the child can pick them up through an unarticulated conditioning process. Black cultural motifs, thus, can get conditioned even as parents might belie what they articulate to be their value and child-rearing objectives.

As the literature bears out, Black parents do show evidence of embracing mainstream ethos and participating and being influenced by mainstream institutions. Consequently, biculturality is a fact of life for Afro-Americans. Biculturality does not have to be problematic. It is probable that individuals can easily if not effortlessly integrate or negotiate two cultural agendas. Yet we argue that owing to the character of the cultures in question, for Afro-Americans the attendant negotiational demands are inherently problematic. Praeger (1982: 111) brilliantly illuminates this point when he states:

> [I]t is not the mere fact that Blacks hold a dual identity in this country which has constrained achievement; to one degree or another, every ethnic group and racial group has faced a similar challenge. The Black experience in America is distinguished by the fact that the qualities attributed to Blackness are in opposition to the qualities rewarded in society. The specific features of Blackness as cultural imagery are, almost by definition, those qualities which the dominant society has attempted to deny in itself, and it is the difference between Blackness and whiteness that defines, in many aspects, American cultural self-understanding. For Blacks, then, the efforts to reconcile into one personality images that are diametrically opposed poses an extraordinarily difficult challenge.

We contend that the "qualities attributed to Blackness" are to be understood chiefly in psychocultural terms. We thus take this quotation to signify that the cultural orientation of Afro-Americans, which is linked to traditional African ethos, is essentially antithetical to mainstream American "cultural self-understanding." Thus, such Black cultural qualities would not be easily integratable with the dominant societal cultural ethos. Boykin (1985) has more fully elaborated on the profound incompatibility between Black and mainstream cultural frames of reference. Suffice it for now that it is difficult to put spirituality, communalism, a rhythmic-movement orientation, expressive-individualism, an affective orientation, and the likes in the service of mainstream institutional strivings. Likewise, Euro-Americans find it easy from their dominant cultural-definitional viewpoint to view spirituality negatively as "voodoo" and "superstition," communalism as dependency, a movement rhythmic orientation as hyperactivity, expressive-individualism as being unsystematic or showing off, or to see an affective orientation as immature, irrational, and too emotional. Such characteristics are ones that Afro-Americans may habitually possess, implicitly value, and feel comfortable with, and yet overtly deny in themselves if not denounce, particularly if their orientation is toward succeeding in mainstream American society. To any degree that they are influenced by or seek to participate in mainstream institutions, these are characteristics that they, through holding up society's mirror to themselves, may deride and castigate when observed among their own people. Yet in spite of their intentions, their own cultural habits may continue to get in their way. In any case, they are unlikely to be aware that such habits are cultural.

Such a dilemma is surely what DuBois (1903: 17) must have had in mind even back in 1903 when in *Souls of Black Folks* he stated: "One ever feels his twoness—an American; a Negro; two souls, two thoughts, two unreconciled strivings; two warring ideals in one dark body, whose dogged strength alone keeps it from being torn asunder."

At the very least, this bicultural expression complicates socialization matters for Black parents in a profound way. Yet socialization concerns get complicated even further because Black people have minority status within the American social order. This status breeds an experience that brings its own unique set of forces, responsibilities, and necessities for negotiation.

It seems appropriate to posit that though a Black cultural orientation may be present, Blacks still must possess distinctly pragmatic and expedient ways of responding to racially and economically problematic life circumstances. Thus, adaptive reactions, coping styles, and adjustment techniques have surely become part and parcel of the social negotiational reality for Afro-Americans as well. Indeed, the particular ways Black families cope with the exigencies of racism and oppression have crucial and distinct implications for the socialization process. Such ways surely depend on the orientation to and the meaning Black families ascribe to the exigencies of oppression and racism. We believe that there are a myriad of ways in which Black families conceivably could orient themselves. There also is considerable complexity and multidimensionality attendant to the coping processes utilized. Given this wide array of possibilities, surely an organizational scheme is needed.

Toward this end, we posit that a given Afro-American's characteristic adaptive reaction(s) should be understood as an intersection of several dimensions of adaptive orientation. Relevant dimensions would be the following: (1) whether one takes an active versus a passive role in the confronting of the realities of racism and oppression, that is, does one acquiesce or does one put forth active effort to confront such circumstances; (2) whether there is system engagement or disengagement, that is, is one oriented toward participation in mainstream institutions, tying one's fate to mainstream avenues and prescriptions for appropriate and successful attainment, or does one seek to function as orthogonal to such participation as possible and operate separate from such avenues and prescriptions; and (3) does one orient toward system maintenance or toward system change? This can be further divided into two thrusts: Is one's orientation toward system blame or person blame? Essentially at issue here is whom to hold responsible for one's plight. Then, too, we could consider whether one seeks maintenance or change with regard to social structural concerns and/or with regard to cultural concerns. At issue in the former case is the allocation of status, wealth, and power; at issue in the latter case is change in the dominant or in the range of acceptable values, beliefs, and behavioral practices of the system.

This classification system affords us the opportunity to shed some systematic light on the range of possible adaptions. For example, if one's adaptive orientation is to work vigorously at doing well in the system as it stands and by the rules of the system, this would be an active adaptive orientation that is system maintenance and system engagement in nature. If one's orientation is to accept one's lot and to depend on the system for survival, this would be a passive maintenance and system engagement orientation. Then, too, if one is covertly subversive but openly patronizing, one's orientation would be characterized as passive yet system engagement and system change. If a person had an openly defiant, Black nationalist orientation, that person would have an active system change attitude; and if there was advocated the building of and participation in separate Black-oriented institutions, we would have one that also is system disengagement in nature. When one is aware of the built-in hypocrises of American society but takes an essentially cynical stance, one is embracing a posture that is passive system change, yet possibly system disengagement in character. In all, then, we hold that how a Black family views its minority status and orients itself accordingly is a major determinant of its socialization agenda.

To be sure, several issues must await further specification and delineation; for example, how adaptive orientations and coping styles are transmitted to successive generations; how adaptive orientations get translated into actual-to-be socialized behaviors; and what are the socialization-behavioral dynamics attendant to such adaptive considerations. One thing, however, seems clear: The socialization processes at work would be essentially distinct from those operative within the Black cultural realm. Given that Black culture is operative in a more tacit and implicit fashion, we should not expect it to be used as a buffer against racism and oppression. Culture could, however, serve as a buffer for minority groups who can draw upon a more intact, fully elaborated, hierarchically integrated, and explicit cultural frame of reference (DeVos, 1982). In this case, one's cultural experience repertoire can serve as one's minority experience repertoire. For Afro-Americans, however, the adaptive orientation is likely to be distinct from the Black cultural orientation. Moreover, as extant Afro-Americans do not participate fully in the mainstream of American life, as they (for a variety of reasons) do not as securely grasp the requisite values and behaviors, and given the very nature of the isolating effects of oppressed minority status and the reactive posture that is thereby garnered, the adaptive orientation is likely to be distinct from the mainstream psychological repertoire as well.

So in all, then, we can note three distinct arenas of experience, three distinct realms of social negotiation. It should be understood that these realms—the mainstream, minority, and Black cultural—require essentially three distinct psychological/behavioral repertoires. Yet any given Black person's life changes are linked to successful negotiation in all three realms. If we are on target in our conceptualization, successful negotiation leads even beyond what DuBois (1903) called a "double consciousness" to a "triple consciousness," a consciousness potentially fraught with contradictions, inconsistencies, and surely complexity. In all, then, Afro-Americans are faced with a triple quandary. There is dynamic interplay among three competing contexts for socialization: socialization in the mainstream of American society, socialization informed by oppressed minority status, and socialization linked to a proximal Black cultural context that is largely noncommensurate with the social dictates of mainstream American life.

Thus, a scenario has been provided that we believe more adequately captures and elaborates the complex socialization context for Afro-American families. A preponderance of Afro-American children are overtly socialized consistent with the dominant beliefs and values of American society. Afro-American parents, however, in dispatching their responsibilities as value transmitters and socialization agents, do not have the same access to this mainstream socialization process as their Euro-American counterparts. In turn, the resources available to expedite such socialization are not as available. The parents' grasp of the commitment to this process would not be as great as well. Consequently, the pervasiveness and degree of ingrainment of Euro-American ideals is lessened. The lessened success, facility, and commitment are linked directly to the fact that socialization time must be shared with two other critical concerns: minority and Black cultural. Of course, the facility and commitment to mainstream dictates also are lessened because the Black cultural experience is fundamentally at odds with Euro-American ethos. Relatedly, one's minority status typically does not breed full embracement of mainstream ideals. So the triple quandary can be stated succinctly: Afro-American children are incompletely socialized vis-à-vis the Euro-American ethos. They develop a distinct repertoire which, being rooted in their African lineage, is culturally at odds with mainstream strivings. They must, furthermore, learn to cope with their racial and economic victimization within the American social order.

In all, then, we posit that Black child socialization can be understood largely in terms of the conditioning of cultural predilections that are incongruent with the socialization goals of mainstream American society: the proactive effort to realize mainstream ideals while explicitly or implicitly being reluctant to fully shed Black cultural motifs and the preparation of the next generation to be aware of and cope with institutional and individual oppression.

Given the complexity of these socialization demands, it should be expected that various Black families attend to this triple quandary in varying ways. There is no monolithic Black experience. There is no singular socialization pathway. Indeed, there is a tapestry of variegated socialization possibilities. The particular socialization experiences in any one Black family would be represented by (1) the extent to which mainstream goals and values are promoted or embraced; (2) the particular domains in which these goals and values have been promoted or adopted; (3) the extent to which Black cultural socialization goals have been overtly articulated and promoted; (4) the orientation pattern and the display of responses utilized to cope with oppressed minority status; and (5) the extent of Black cultural conditioning of children. These kinds of concerns should frame our discussion of the socialization processes attendant to Black families.

IMPLICATIONS FOR RESEARCH

Several important research implications arise from this triple quandary conceptual framework. We will mention a few: First, it would follow that Black families can be characterized in terms of the relative weightings given to mainstream, minority, and Black cultural socialization. In this regard, we believe that Black families generally can be classified as mainstream, minority, or Black cultural in their modal socialization orientation. Research needs to be done that examines extant socialization practices as a function of such a classification. Moreover, although surely no family would operate exclusively within one experiential domain, the particular patterns of emphasis across the three domains largely frames a particular Black family's socialization agenda. Research needs to be conducted that examines behavioral and attitudinal outcomes as a function of a Black family's socialization agenda. Then, too, we should discern what psychological or social processes might account for a given parent's orientation toward the socialization task at hand. That is, what are the antecedents for why a given parent defines the socialization task as he or she does?

In light of the arguments in this chapter, a further issue worth pursuing would be, what are the implications of whether a given socialization message is overt and attitudinal or whether it is essentially tacit and behavioral? That is, what are the consequences of whether parents consciously embrace a particular value and overtly attempt to impose it on their offsprings; or whether parents typically and habitually display a given behavior pattern or motif so consistently that tacitly such a motif becomes conditioned in the children.

We feel strongly that empirical investigation of the expressions, functions, and family origins of Black culture is long overdue. Surely, of the three experiential realms, the Black cultural has been the most neglected and least understood. We especially believe that it typically forms the intrinsic base that all later socialization must build upon (or tear down). We find ourselves agreeing with Lewis (1975: 237) when she states:

> In early childhood socialization when patterns are probably most unconscious and at an age when the child is minimally influenced by dominant society expectations, there is a greater cultural influence; [however] later socialization . . . reflects more closely the structure of expectations and opportunities provided . . . by the dominant society.

If it is the case that for a preponderant number of Black families Black cultural motifs are readily and consistently displayed, then the character of this cultural socialization process surely is in need of documentation and specification. Indeed, we argue that the efficacy of this position surely deserves exploration. The conditioning of Black cultural styles early in life should become the focus of concentrated research and scholarship among students of Black family socialization.

Therefore, the triple quandary allows for the meaningful consideration of the biculturality of the Afro-American experience. It allows us to move away from Anglocentric and Anglometric perspectives on socialization. It affords a vantage point for considering, within the same conceptual framework, the uniformity as well as diversity, adaptiveness as well as Africanity, of Black family life.

We hope, further, that the framework has sufficient heuristic value to help determine the important questions asked and the nature of the observations made in future research on Black child socialization. We also hope that future research can specify, clarify, and, when needed, modify the considerations offered in this chapter.

REFERENCES

AKBAR, N. (1976) "Rhythmic patterns in African personality," in L. King et al. (eds.) Assumptions and Paradigms for Research on Black People. Los Angeles: Fanon Center Publications.

ALLEN, W. (1979) "Class, culture, and family organization: the effects of class and race on family structure in urban America." Journal of Comparative Family Studies 10: 301-313.

———(1978) "The search for applicable theories of Black family life." Journal of Marriage and the Family 40 (February): 117-129.

BALDWIN, A. (1980) Theories of Child Development. New York: John Wiley.

BALDWIN, J. (1979) "Theory and research concerning the notion of Black self-hatred: a review and reinterpretation." Journal of Black Psychology 5: 51-77.

BANDURA, A. and R. WALTERS (1963) Social Learning and Personality Development. New York: Holt, Rinehart & Winston.

BANKS, W., G. McQUATER, and J. HUBBARD (1979) "Toward a reconceptualization of the social-cognitive bases of achievement orientations in Blacks," in A. W. Boykin et al. (eds.) Research Directions of Black Psychologists. New York: Russell Sage.

BARTZ, K. and E. LEVINE (1978) "Childrearing by Black parents: a description and comparison to Anglo and Chicano parents." Journal of Marriage and the Family 40: 709-719.

BAUMRIND, D. (1972) "An exploratory study of socialization effects on Black children: some Black-White comparisons." Child Development 43: 261-267.

BILLINGSLEY, A. (1968) Black Families in White America. Englewood Cliffs, NJ: Prentice-Hall.

BOYKIN, A. W. (1985) "The triple quandary and the schooling of Afro-American children," in U. Neisser (ed.) The School Achievement of Minority Children. Hillsdale, NJ: Erlbaum.

———(1983) "The academic performance of Afro-American children," in J. Spence (ed.) Achievement and Achievement Motives. San Francisco: Freeman.

———(1979) "Black psychology and the research process: keeping the baby but throwing out the bath water," in A. W. Boykin et al. (eds.) Research Directions of Black Psychologists. New York: Russell Sage.

COLE, J. (1970) "Black culture: negro, black, and nigger." Black Scholar 1: 40-43.

CUMMINGS, S. (1977) "Family socialization and fatalism among Black adolescents." Journal of Negro Education 46: 62-75.

DENNIS, R. (1976) "Theories of the Black family: the weak family and strong family schools as competing ideologies." Journal of Afro-American Issues 4: 315-328.

DEVOS, G. (1982) "Adaptive strategies in U.S. minorities," in E. Jones & S. Korchin (eds.) Minority Mental Health. New York: Praeger.

DOLLARD, J., L. DOOB, N. MILLER, O. MOWRER, and R. SEARS (1939) Frustration and Aggression. New Haven: Yale Univ. Press.

DUBOIS, C. (1972) "The dominant value profile of American culture," in R. Shinn (ed.) Culture and School. San Francisco: Intext Educational Publishers.

DUBOIS, W.E.B. (1903) Souls of Black Folk. Chicago: McClurg.

DURRETT, M., S. O'BRYANT, and J. PENNEBAKER (1975) "Childrearing reports of White, Black, and Mexican-American families." Developmental Psychology 11: 871.

GAY, G. (1975) "Cultural differences important in education of Black children." Momentum (October): 30-33.

GERWITZ, J. (1969) "Mechanisms of social learning: some roles of stimulation and behavior in early human development," in D. Goslin (ed.) Handbook of Socialization Theory and Research. Chicago: Rand McNally.

HALE, J. (1982) Black Children: Their Roots, Culture, and Learning Styles. Provo, UT: Brigham Young Univ. Press.

———(1980) "Demythicizing the education of Black children," in R. Jones (ed.) Black Psychology. New York: Harper & Row.

HESS, R. (1970) "The transmission of cognitive strategies in poor families: the socialization of apathy and underachievement," in V. Allen (ed.) Psychological Factors in Poverty. Chicago: Markham.

HILL, R. (1971) The Strengths of Black Families. New York: Emerson Hall.

JACKSON, G. (1976) "The African genesis of the Black perspective in helping." Professional Psychology 7: 292-308.

JONES, J. (1979) "Conceptual and strategic issues in the relationship of Black psychology to American social science," In A. W. Boykin et al. (eds.) Research Directions of Black Psychologists. New York: Russell Sage.

KILPATRICK, A. (1979) "Future directions for the black family." Family Coordinator 38: 347-352.

LEIBOW, E. (1966) Tally's Corner. Boston: Little, Brown.

LEWIS, D. (1975) "The Black family: socialization of sex roles." Phylon 26: 471-480.

MARTIN, B. (1975) "Parent-child relations," in F. Horowitz (ed.) Review of Child Development Research. Chicago: Univ. of Chicago Press.

MARTIN, E. and J. MARTIN (1978) The Black Extended Family. Chicago: Univ. of Chicago Press.

MILLER, N. and J. DOLLARD (1941) Social Learning and Imitation. New Haven: Yale Univ. Press.

MILLER, P. (1983) Theories of Developmental Psychology. San Francisco: Freeman.

MUSSEN, P. [ed.] (1970) Carmichael's Manual of Child Psychology. New York: John Wiley.

MYERS, H. (1982) "Research on the Afro-American family: a critical review," in B. Bass et al. (eds.) The Afro-American Family: Assessment, Treatment, and Research Issues. New York: Grune & Stratton.

NOBLES, W. (1978) "Toward an empirical and theoretical framework for defining Black families."Journal of Marriage and the Family 40: 679-688.

———(1976) "A formulative and empirical study of Black families." A Final Report, DHEW, Office of Child Development, 90-C-255, December.

————(1974) "African root and American fruit: the Black family." Journal of Social and Behavioral Sciences 20: 52-63.

PETERS, M. (1981) "Parenting in Black families: a historical perspective," in H. McAdoo (ed.) Black Families. Beverly Hills, CA: Sage.

PRAGER, J. (1982) "American racial ideology as collective representation." Ethnic and Racial Studies 5: 99-119.

RADIN, N. and C. KAMII (1965) "The childrearing attitudes of disadvantaged Negro mothers and some educational implications." Journal of Negro Education 34: 138-146.

RIEGEL, K. (1972) "Influence of economic and political ideologies on the development of developmental psychology." Psychological Bulletin 78: 129-141.

SAMPSON, E. (1977) "Psychology and the American ideal." Journal of Personality and Social Psychology 35: 767-782.

SEARS, R., E. MACCOBY, and H. LEVIN (1957) Patterns of Childrearing. New York: Harper & Row.

SEARS, R., L. RAU, and R. ALPERT (1965) Identification and Child Rearing. Palo Alto, CA: Stanford Univ. Press.

SIMMONS, W. (1979) "The relationship between academic status and future expectations among low-income Blacks." Journal of Black Psychology 6: 7-16.

STACK, C. (1974) All Our Kin. New York: Harper & Row.

STAPLES, R. (1976) An Introduction to Black Sociology. New York: McGraw-Hill.

TEN HOUTEN, W. (1970) "The Black family: myth and reality." Psychiatry 33: 145-173.

THOMPSON, R. (1966) "Dance and culture: an aesthetic of the cool." African Forum 2: 85-102.

YOUNG, V. (1974) "A Black American socialization pattern." American Ethnologist 1: 405-413.

————(1970) "Family and childhood in a southern Negro community." American Anthropologist 72: 269-288.

ZIGLER, E. and I. CHILD (1973) Socialization and Personality Development. Reading, MA: Addison-Wesley.

3

DEVELOPMENTAL IMPERATIVES OF SOCIAL ECOLOGIES

Lessons Learned from Black Children

BERTHA GARRETT HOLLIDAY

First, you got to understand that it is not in the color but the thinking, how you might say, the attitude. And it's not in *your* attitude, but in the attitudes of all the people that growed you and of the people that you seen and heard about. My mother's father told me this thing and I remember it: He used to say, "White folks are *how* folks and black folks are *what* folks."

—J. L. Gwaltney,
"Porter Millington," *Drylongso*

Porter Millington is, intuitively, an ecologist. He believes the adult the child becomes is determined largely by his or her experiences and relationships with others. Millington recognizes that differences in experience are related to different and competing perceptions of social reality. He would not be surprised to be informed that, more often than not, child researchers describe Black children as culturally or cognitively deficit—that is, unable to talk right, think right, act right, or feel right, and that such views are based on scientific studies that primarily investigate the developmental process focusing on *how* Black children talk, think, act, or feel, instead of the *content* of these activities.

This dominant view of Black children is supported by widely cited, well-controlled studies based on a research paradigm distinguished by its focus on a limited number of discrete cognitive abilities or developmental processes, systematic comparisons of Black and white children on these abilities and processes, and frequent use of experimental tasks in laboratory settings on a single occasion.

Child researchers, however, increasingly are articulating various limitations of this dominant paradigm and its related findings. It has been noted that behaviors evoked by atypical (manipulated research) tasks in atypical (laboratory) settings cannot necessarily be interpreted as accurate and valid indicators of abilities that are demonstrated in routine activities (Cole and Bruner, 1971; Tulkin, 1975). Use of the single control variable of social class has been questioned as an adequate means for statistically equating experiential differences between Blacks and whites (Tulkin, 1975). Small but statistically significant Black-white differences have been cited as insufficient for making substantive and predictive inferences (Zigler, 1979).

Researchers also have been chastised regarding their frequent failure to determine whether observed racial differences indicate developmental "lag," or a qualitatively different developmental process (Dill, 1976; Dusek, 1974). It also has been noted that the dominant paradigm assumes that Black children, at critical developmental periods, lack those quantities and qualities of stimuli inputs (e.g., linguistic, visual, tactile, psychomotor experiences) essential for later normative development (Hunt, 1969; Passow, 1963; Riessman, 1962). Consequently, the paradigm both encourages gross misprediction of Black children's later adult characteristics and fails to explain the adequate social adjustment demonstrated by the overwhelming majority of Black adults (Glaser and Ross, 1970; Hilliard, 1974; Sullivan, 1973).

In general, the dominant paradigm is being questioned and scrutinized because of its failure to address or "factor in" the effects of historically rooted social factors. These factors structure the environments of children and exert pushes and pulls on developmental processes (Ingleby, 1974; Ogbu, 1981; Riegel, 1976; Siegel, 1979). As Bronfenbrenner (1979: 259) astutely observes, the typical deficit-oriented comparative study investigates race merely as a marker variable, "a sign on the door of an environmental context that leaves its nature unspecified" and consequently results in inferences that are "little more than speculation."

The study presented in this chapter concerns the social realities of Black children's development and represents an alternative to the dominant and deficit-oriented paradigm. More specifically, the study examines the breadth and flexibility of Black children's behavioral repertoires. Two of the study children's primary socializing agents (their mothers and teachers) assessed the frequency and effectiveness of various skills used by the children at home, in the neighborhood, and at school. These assessments were statistically analyzed to determine the extent children are meeting role requirements of a given setting and the extent of variation in their reported behavioral competence across settings.

TOWARD A NEW PARADIGM:
IN RECOGNITION OF SOCIAL FACTORS

AN EMPHASIS ON COMPETENCE

The concept of competence suggests alternatives to the dominant paradigm of Black child research. Robert White (1959) introduced this concept to the psychological community. He viewed competence as a biologically based exploratory drive and defined it as the capacity to effectively interact with the environment. The motivational component of competence was termed "effectance." And the affective element of effectance was termed "a feeling of efficacy."

Other competence theories are modifications of White's and reflect the theoretical perspectives of subdisciplines within psychology. In addition to White's motivational perspective, three other types of perspectives are prevalent: those emphasizing cognitive operations (e.g., Fullan and Loubser 1972; Goldfried and D'Zurilla, 1969; Spivak and Shure, 1974); those emphasizing social roles and reinforcements (e.g., Gladwin, 1957; Phillips, 1976; Smith, 1968); and those concerned with developmental indicators and their related patterns of stability and change (e.g., Foote and Cattrell, 1955; Murphy and Moriarity, 1976; Rutter, 1979; White and Watts, 1973). Theories of competence also can be classified in terms of those attributes chosen as indices of competence. Three types of indices are used: (1) personal behavior and attitudes; (2) interpersonal behavior; and (3) role behavior.

There is a small but growing body of empirical competence-oriented Black child research (e.g., Davidson and Greenberg, 1967; Glaser and Ross, 1970; Hendrix and Dokecki, 1973; Ladner, 1971; Mercer, 1971, 1972; Ogbu, 1974; Slaughter, 1977; Wilkinson and O'Connor, 1977). These studies are distinguished by the presence of two or more of the following characteristics: (1) a focus on psychological and behavioral strengths; (2) adoption of an ecological perspective as reflected by the absence of laboratory tasks, use of multiple indicators of environment, investigation of multiple attributes and behaviors across two or more settings, and emphasis on interactive (rather than cause-effect) relationships; and (3) abandonment of a racial comparative design.

The current study is an attempt to extend this new Black child research perspective by elaborating an ecological framework in support of the investigation of Black competence.

AN EMPHASIS ON ECOLOGY

Kurt Lewin, a field theorist and ecologist, defined the structure of person-environment interactions as a "lifespace." Lewin (1951, 1954) views development as that process associated with changes in person-environment interactions (i.e., the content and context of our activities) through which we become increasingly aware of the world, especially in terms of its dimensions of activity, space, time, and reality/irreality (i.e., changing classifications of what is fantasy, a possibility, or a fixed social reality).

IMPLICATIONS FOR BLACK CHILD RESEARCH

Theories of competence and ecology suggest that any distinctiveness of black children's development is rooted in the structure and process of their person-environment interactions. An urban Black child's lifespace is composed of seven hierarchically nested lifespheres: (1) the child; (2) the family or home; (3) the neighborhood, that is, peers and adult friends; (4) the Black community, that is, Black social, civic, and religious groups and other formal and informal interactions among Blacks; (5) the service community, that is, predominantly white-administered and/or owned services, businesses, and institutions located in the Black community; (6) the broader community, that is, non-Black residential, service, and business communities; and (7) social structure, that is, social, economic, and political structures, processes, and policies. Each of these spheres is distinguished from the others by differing socializing agents and agencies and by differing opportunities for role taking and accomplishment.

Black children's transitions among these lifespheres are fraught with various historically rooted barriers that progressively limit access to larger portions of the lifespace as one proceeds upward through the spheres, thereby restricting the range of the children's environmental experiences. These barriers are occasioned by beliefs and practices emanating from institutional and social structural levels, and manifested in inequitable distributions of status, income, power, wealth, and differential access to social goods, knowledge, privilege, and choice. In response to such barriers, Black children must attempt to develop skills appropriate for the social demands of both the Black and white communities. They also must develop skills appropriate for negotiating the transition between the two communities (Peters, 1978).

This ecological perspective suggests that the process and content of Black children's development differ from those of white children in five critical ways:

(1) The ecological structure of Black children's lives is more complex than that of white children. Black children's interactions with both Black and white communities result in their potential involvement in more settings.

(2) Relationships between white and Black communities are defined by patterns of domination and subordination and punctuated by differences in values, social relations, and institutional patterns. Therefore, Black children, who must interact with both communities, are confronted with more role requirements that are qualitatively more varied.

(3) Variations in role requirements within Black and white communities coupled with systematic social barriers cause Black children to develop skills appropriate for effecting transitions within both white and Black communities as well as between the two. Black children therefore must develop more extensive behavior repertoirs that must be demonstrated with greater flexibility in anticipation of more problematic situations.

(4) Relationships between Black and white communities result in Blacks' having less access to and reduced control of schedules and contingencies of reward. Consequently, Black children frequently are unable to predict if their efforts in problematic situations will be associated with success or failure. This lack of probability is double-edged in its developmental consequences. On one hand, it provides Black children opportunities for that kind of sweet success against the odds that undergirds exceptional competence. But it also provides them opportunities for that kind of unexpected, mystifying, paralyzing failure that overwhelms children and leads them to assume postures of stagnation, indifference, and hostility.

(5) Black children are older younger. Their experiences in bicultural settings encourage that kind of social-cognitive and behavioral precocity ("motherwit") that spurs earlier maturity and independence.

The following study, which focuses on differences in children's role requirements across settings and the flexibility of children's behavioral repertoires, represents an attempt in structuring Black child research in directions supportive of those competence and ecological perspectives that incorporate the social realities of Black children's lives.

THE STUDY'S METHODS

SAMPLING

In consideration of the study's ecological thrusts, sampling procedures were designed for selecting a group of children experiencing similar physical and social settings. United States Census Block Data (1970) were used to identify a two-mile by one-mile geographic area inhabited predominantly by low- and moderate-income Black families. I then identified all moderate-income government subsidized housing units in this area. Managers of these units provided addresses of those units in which 9- and 10-year-old children resided. A 14-item screening interview was administered to an adult occupant of each of these households to determine if the target child met the study's other social and environmental criteria (e.g., enrollment in a predominantly minority neighborhood public school for at least two years, absence of mental, emotional, or physical handicap). Interviews and tests were administered orally to the children and their mothers in their homes by trained Black female examiners. School data were collected from the children's school records and teachers.

SUBJECTS

The 44 children (22 males, 22 females) were 9 (N = 29) and 10 (N = 15) years of age and enrolled in the fourth (N = 32) and fifth (N = 12) grades of predominantly minority public schools located in their neighborhoods. Of the children's households, 73% (N = 32) were headed by mothers or mother surrogates. Adult males were present in 34% (N = 15) of the households. Full-time employment status was reported by 61% (N = 27) of the mothers and mother surrogates and by 70% (N = 10) of the adult male household members. Equal numbers of mothers were high school graduates and nongraduates. The sample's modal 1978 gross household income was in the range of $5,000 to $8,900. In return for their participation in the study, mothers received monetary compensation and children were awarded a "Certificate of Merit."

INSTRUMENT

THE PARENTAL QUESTIONNAIRE
ON CHILDREN'S BEHAVIORAL COMPETENCE (PQCBC)

Mothers were administered the PQCBC, an instrument newly developed for this study (Spearman-Brown reliability: r = .82). This instrument consists of 171 items, of which 144 served as the study's primary data sources. On these items, mothers reported their perceptions of their child's behavioral competencies as typically demonstrated in the home and neighborhood. Response choices (3-point scale) for each of these items are indicative of mastered, emergent, or latent behavior (relative to the frequency and/or effectiveness of the behavior). The items assess the following three skill areas:

Functional Life Skills (80 items)—the ability to effectively use and manipulate objects, technology, and social instruments encountered in day-to-day living. Such skills are indicated by behaviors related to mobility in space, communication, management and independence, caretaking and supervising, and consumerism.

Interpersonal Skills (28 items)—the ability to become a participant, to gain leadership, and to cooperate and collaborate. Such skills are indicated by the quality and frequency of the child's interactions with peers, siblings, and adults.

Problem-Solving Skills (36 items)—the ability to recognize, adapt to, circumvent, or change an encountered predicament. Such skills are indicated by behaviors related to the child's reaction to personal, interpersonal, technical, and social predicaments.

Because of the broad range of behaviors assessed, items were drawn from varied sources (Doll, 1947; Gesten, 1976; Lambert et al., 1974; Mercer and Lewis, 1979; Stott and Sykes, 1967). Other items were newly developed. All items were submitted to a panel of judges for skill area and sphere assignment. The PQCBC was pilot-tested and revised prior to study administration.

OTHER INSTRUMENTS

Children were administered the Coopersmith Self-Esteem Inventory, Form A, and the Bialer-Cromwell Children's Locus of Control Scale. Teachers of the study children completed a newly developed 48-item Teacher Rating of Behavioral Competence (Spearman-Brown reliability: $r = .84$). This instrument assesses those functional life, interpersonal, and problem-solving skills demonstrated in the school. Children's mathematics and reading achievement scores and grade point averages were secured from school records.

RESEARCH ISSUES

This study addresses issues related to those behavioral skills routinely demonstrated by Black children in the settings of home, neighborhood, and school, and the effectiveness of these skills as perceived by two of the children's primary socializing agents. The specific issues addressed by the study are as follows: Do these children reportedly exhibit different patterns of behavioral competence in different settings? How are children's perceived behavioral competencies in different settings related to their academic achievement? What is the relationship between perceived levels of the children's competencies and the psychosocial characteristics of children's home environments? How do children with high and low competence differ?

RESULTS AND DISCUSSION

As previously indicated, competence items were classified into three lifesphere areas (home, neighborhood, and school) and three skill areas (functional life, interpersonal, problem solving). Consequently, scores could be displayed in a 3×3 table (skills by spheres). The table's marginals consist of three composite scores across rows (i.e., skills) and three composite scores across columns (i.e., spheres). The sum of these composites is termed the children's "overall competence score."

All raw scores were converted to a 100-point scale. Low and high competence groups were defined by a median score split on overall competence. Twenty-one children (11 males and 10 females) were classified as high competence, and 23 children (11 males and 12 females) were classified as low competence. The mean score difference between low and high groups was highly significant ($t = -.6.99$, $p < .001$).

Do these children reportedly exhibit different patterns of competencies in different settings? The study's data suggest that differential patterns or ranking of skills is observed across settings. As indicated by Figure 3.1, both the high and low groups were perceived as demonstrating identical patterns within the spheres of neighborhood and school and an overall competence.

Group patterns differed in the home sphere. Those skills ranked 2 and 3 in the high group were respectively ranked 3 and 2 in the low group. But for each group, statistical tests revealed no significant differences between the levels of these two skills (for lows: $t = 1.48$, $p =$ n.s.; for highs: $t = -.94$, $p =$ n.s.). For both groups, the greatest press for functional life skills occurred in the home; the greatest press for interpersonal skills occurred in the school; the greatest press for

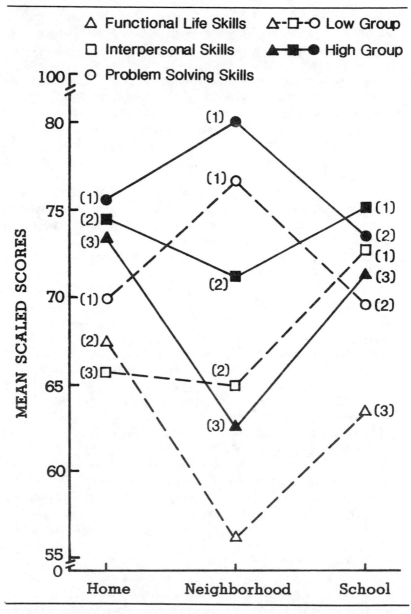

Figure 3.1 Skill Levels (and Ranks) in Three Lifespheres for Low and High Groups

problem-solving skills occurred in the neighborhood. Such "press" reflects the type of behavioral skill most demanded by the tasks and social role requirements of a given lifeshpere. Other such similarities of press were demonstrated by both groups. The children's uniform patterning on overall competence suggests that they experience the structure and demands of their world as ones in which they must act foremost as problem solvers.

How are children's perceived competencies in different settings related to their academic achievement? According to the proposed model of the lifespace of urban Black children, the public school is located in the sphere of the "service community." Thus, the school's values and role requirements, as reflections of those of the "broader community," are not necessarily continuous with those of the home and neighborhood, which are more fully defined by the Black community.

The study's data support this hypothesis. Through use of multiple regression analyses, nonsignificant relationships were found between children's academic achievement (as indicated by their grade point averages and standardized mathematics and reading achievement scores) and their competence at home ($F = .25$, $p = .86$), in the neighborhood ($F = 1.02$, $p = .40$), and their combined competence at home and neighborhood ($F = .46$, $p = .712$). Thus, mothers' perceptions of the children's skills bear no relationship to the children's academic achievement. But teachers' perceptions of the children's skills are highly predictive of children's academic achievement ($F = 13.39$, $p < .001$).

These children had relatively low mathematics achievement scores ($\overline{x} = 32.30$ percentile, S. D. = 19.32) and reading achievement scores ($\overline{x} = 34.10$ percentile, S. D. = 22.81), but their grade point averages were relatively high ($\overline{x} = 2.94$, S. D. = .36). Low and high groups did not significantly differ on mathematics achievement, but the high group had significantly higher reading achievement scores ($t = -1.76$, $p < .05$) and grade point averages ($t = -1.98$, $p < .03$).

These analyses suggest that discontinuities exist between the role requirements of the home and neighborhood and school. In the home and neighborhood, children's roles most frequently demand problem-solving skills. But at school, children's interpersonal skills, as well as academic excellence, are in greatest demand. In fact, low competence children demonstrate school interpersonal skills and school problem-solving skills at high levels that were not significantly different from those of the high competence children. These findings also suggest that low and high competence children approach the demands of the school with a plasticity or flexibility of response that Murphy and Moriarity (1976) suggest is characteristic of children actively coping with their environment. The data, however, further suggest that the competing demands for both academic and interpersonal excellence, coupled with discontinuities between home and neighborhood and school, are especially detrimental for low competence children, who simply do not have a competence repertoire that is broad and stable enough to meet both the school's demands. Consequently, these children settle for meeting the demand for interpersonal skills (i.e., behaving acceptably), which is most essential for their literal survival in school.

Ecological discontinuities, competing demands, and mixed messages in the form of relatively high grade point averages and relatively low achievement scores combine to structure these study children's problematic school experience.

What is the relationship between perceived levels of children's competencies and the psychosocial characteristics of their home environments? Developmental research studies frequently report that Black children's characteristics are strongly related to those of their homes. In this study, however, differences in children's environments were not systematically related to the level of the children's competencies ($F = 1.25$, $p = .310$). This unexpected finding might be related to the type and number of the study's environmental indicators. Typically, researchers choose to assess children's environments by using indicators of either maternal characteristics (e.g., her education or income) or mother-child interactions. In this study, environment was more broadly conceptualized and indicated by 7 variables: family size, crowding (i.e., number of persons per room), family type (i.e., presence or absence of an adult male), structured home environment, parental expectations, child's self-esteem, and child's locus of control. These served as the independent variables for a multiple regression analysis in which the dependent variable was the children's overall competence scores.

Of course, in this study the lack of relationship between competence and environment may be an artifact of procedures used for selecting a sample of children experiencing "similar ecological worlds". It should be noted, however, that high and low groups significantly differed on 2 of the 7 environmental indicators. Children with high competence were members of larger families ($t = -1.96$, $p < .03$) living in more crowded homes ($t = -3.35$, $p < .001$). In addition, one-way ANOVA indicated children's overall competence was unrelated to their gender ($F = .09$, $p < .76$). These findings suggest that Black children's behavioral competence cannot be predicted by the multivariate characteristics of their home environments, nor by their gender.

How do children with low and high competence differ? As previously noted, both low and high groups reportedly demonstrated similar patterns of competencies across lifespheres. This suggests that low and high groups are not perceived to use qualitatively different approaches to mastery of their social world. This led me to investigate the quantitative differences between the two groups' scores. I found that the two groups are perceived to differ in terms of the level of their skills and

TABLE 3.1   t-Values and Associated Probabilities for Differences
in Level of Lifesphere by Skill Area Competencies
Between Low and High Competence Groups

	Home		Neighborhood		School		All Spheres	
Skill Area	t-Value	P	t-Value	P	t-Value	P	t-Value	P
Functional life	−4.31	.001	−3.82	.001	−2.45	.019	−6.88	.001
Interpersonal	−2.94	.005	−2.80	.008	− .52	ns	−3.25	.002
Problem solving	−3.03	.004	−1.62	ns	−1.30	ns	−4.95	.001
All skill areas	−5.17	.001	−4.48	.001	−1.80	ns	−6.99	.001

NOTE: Probabilities are for two-tailed test of significance. Negative values of t indicate the mean of high group is greater than that of low group; positive values indicate
the mean of low group is greater than that of high group.

the extent to which skills are demonstrated at consistent levels across
spheres. High competence children are perceived to demonstrate skills
at higher levels, and doing so more consistently across settings.

Low and high groups were compared on each of their 7 lifesphere-by-
skill scores. Through use of between-groups t-tests, significant differences were observed on 6 of the scores. The low and high groups also
significantly differed on three total skill area scores and on total home
and total neighborhood scores (Table 3.1).

The range in t-values resulting from these group comparisons
suggested that the groups also might differ in terms of the consistency or
stability of their scores across both lifespheres and skill areas. For each
group, 9 paired t-tests were performed on pairs of skill area scores within
lifespheres (Table 3.2). Among the 18 skill pairs thus compared, 9
significant differences were found. Six of these were between skill scores
of the low competence group and 3 were between skill scores of the high
group.

Similar paired t-tests were conducted on pairs of lifesphere scores
within skill areas (Table 3.3). Ten significant differences were found. Six
of these were among low competence children, and 4 were among the
high group.

Both sets of analyses indicate that the competencies of the high group
are perceived as higher and more stable than those of the low group.
Consequently, low and high competence children differ in terms of the
level and stability of their behavioral skills.

High competence children demonstrated their highest level of
competence and their greatest number and magnitude of differences
from low competence children in the home. This suggests that the
distinctiveness of high competence children probably is rooted in more
effective and demanding socialization in the home. Indeed, the observed

TABLE 3.2 Differences and Associated t-Values and Probabilities Between Pairs of Skill Areas Within Lifespheres for Competence Groups

| | | | | Skill Area Pairs $(X_1$-$X_2)$ | | | | | |
| | Functional Life/ Interpersonal | | | Functional Life/ Problem Solving | | | Interpersonal/ Problem Solving | | |
Lifespheres and Groups	X_1-X_2	t-Value	P	X_1-X_2	t-Value	P	X_1-X_2	t-Value	P
Home									
low group	1.48	.68	ns	-2.80	-1.78	ns	-4.28	-2.66	.014
high group	-.94	-.40	ns	-1.73	-1.80	ns	-.79	-.31	ns
Neighborhood									
low group	-8.12	-5.20	.001	-13.18	-7.29	.001	-5.06	-2.64	.015
high group	-8.36	-4.30	.001	-17.26	-8.38	.001	-8.90	-4.25	.001
School									
low group	-9.95	-3.26	.004	-6.43	-2.65	.015	3.51	1.44	ns
high group	-3.50	-1.47	ns	-1.82	-1.08	ns	1.68	.83	ns
All lifespheres									
low group	-3.89	-2.29	.032	-8.32	-7.08	.001	-4.42	-3.57	.002
high group	-4.04	-2.57	.018	6.92	-8.61	.001	-2.88	-1.88	ns

NOTE: Reported X_1 and X_2 values are mean scaled scores. Probabilities are for two-tailed test of significance.

TABLE 3.3 Differences and Associated t-Values and Probabilities Between Pairs of Lifespheres Within Skill Areas for Competence Groups

Skill Areas and Groups	Home/Neighborhood			Home/School			Neighborhood/School		
	X_1-X_2	t-Value	P	X_1-X_2	t-Value	P	X_1-X_2	t-Value	P
Functional Life									
low group	10.38	9.33	.001	3.35	1.17	ns	−6.85	−2.37	.028
high group	10.73	9.14	.001	1.99	.79	ns	−8.75	−3.26	.004
Interpersonal									
low group	.78	.41	ns	−7.50	−2.19	.041	−7.75	−2.35	.029
high group	3.31	1.45	ns	−.58	−.16	ns	−3.89	−1.45	ns
Problem solving									
low group	−6.79	−3.92	.001	−.38	−.13	ns	6.46	2.44	.024
high group	−4.79	−3.16	.005	1.90	.73	ns	6.69	2.42	.025
All skill areas									
low group	4.74	4.44	.001	−1.00	−.42	ns	−5.42	−2.37	.028
high group	5.64	6.04	.001	1.01	.45	ns	−4.62	−2.08	.050

NOTE: Reported X_1 and X_2 values are mean scaled scores. Probabilities are for two-tailed test of significance.

significant and negative association between overall competence of the high group and their home self-esteem ($r = -.55$, $p < .01$) may be rooted in the great number of demands placed on these children in the home.

CONCLUSION

The study's findings lend support to the proposition that the distinctiveness of Black children's development is at least partially rooted in the greater complexity and differentiation of their lifespace. In terms compatible with Siegel's (1979) Piagetian view of social competence, one might say that Black children must confront and integrate more new definitions and differences in order to conserve and maintain a sense of meaning and a perception of similarity in difference.

The study was guided by a research paradigm based on concepts of competence and ecology. Its findings suggest there is more involved in growing, coping, and surviving through a Black childhood than is indicated on a balance sheet of cognitive, language, and personality deficits. Developmental perspectives of a different tone and substance emerge through use of a research approach, which has at its core the social facts in which development is embedded. Knowledge of the what or content of Black children's behavior supports different perspectives from those associated with knowledge of the how or process of their behavior.

In this study Black children are revealed as acting upon complex social realities. All of these children are problem solvers. Differences between children with high and low competence are related neither to the characteristics of their home environments nor to the patterns of their behavioral skills. Instead, these groups are distinguished by the level and stability of their behavioral skills. High competence is associated with more demanding socialization in the home. But regardless of competence level, our data suggest these children experience discontinuity in the role demands of home and neighborhood and school. Because of such discontinuity and other characteristics of the school environment, these children's school experience tends to be problematic.

There are lessons to be learned from Black children.

REFERENCES

BRONFENBRENNER, U. (1979) The Ecology of Human Development. Cambridge, MA: Harvard Univ. Press.

COLE, M. and J. D. BRUNER (1971) "Cultural difference and inferences about psychological processes." American Psychologist 26: 867-876.

DAVIDSON, H. H. and J. W. GREENBERG (1967) School Achievers from a Deprived Background. New York: Associated Educational Services.

DILL, J. R. (1976) "Toward a developmental theory of the inner-city child," in R. C. Granger and J. C. Young (eds.) Demythologizing the Inner-City Child. Washington, DC: National Association for the Education of Young Children.

DOLL, E. A. (1947) Vineland Social Maturity Scale: Manual of Directions. Minneapolis: Educational Test Bureau.

DUSEK, J. B. (1974) "Implications of developmental theory for child mental health." American Psychologist 31: 19-24.

FOOTE, N. N. and L. S. CATTRELL (1955) Identity and Interpersonal Competence. Chicago: Univ. of Chicago Press.

FULLAN, M. and J. J. LOUBSER (1972) "Education and adaptive capacity." Sociology and Education 45 (Summer): 271-287.

GESTEN, E. L. (1976) "A health resources inventory: the development of a measure of the personal and social competence of primary-grade children." Journal of Consulting and Clinical Psychology 44: 775-786.

GLADWIN, T. (1967) "Social competence and clinical practice." Psychiatry 30: 30-43.

GLASER, E. M. and H. ROSS (1970) A Study of Successful Persons from Seriously Disadvantaged Backgrounds. Washington, DC: Office of Special Manpower Programs, Department of Labor.

GOLDFRIED, M. R. and J. D. D'ZURILLA (1969) "A behavioral-analytic model for assessing competence," in C. Spielberger (ed.) Current Topics in Clinical and Community Psychology, Vol. 1. New York: Academic.

GWALTNEY, J. L. (1981) Drylongso: A Self-Portrait of Black America. New York: Vintage.

HENDRIX, S. and P. DOKECKI (1973) The Personal-Social Competence Development of Low-Income Children. ERIC: ED 129-399.

HILLARD, A. G. (1974) "The intellectual strengths of Black children and adolescents: a challenge to pseudoscience." Journal of Non-White Concerns 2 (4): 178-190.

HUNT, J. McV. (1969) The Challenge of Incompetence and Poverty. Urbana: Univ. of Illinois Press.

INGLEBY, D. (1974) "The psychology of child psychology," in M. Richards (ed.) The Integration of a Child into a Social World. London: Cambridge Univ. Press.

LADNER, J. (1971) Tomorrow's Tomorrow: The Black Woman. Garden City, NJ: Doubleday.

LAMBERT, N., M. WINDMILLER, and L. COLE (1974) AAMD Adaptive Behavior Scale, Public School Version, 1974 Revision. Washington, DC: American Association of Mental Deficiency.

LEWIN, K. (1954) "Behavior and development as a function of the total situation," in L. Carmichael (ed.) Manual of Child Psychology. New York: John Wiley.

———(1951) Field Theory in Social Science. New York: Harper & Row.

MERCER, J. (1972) "IQ: the lethal label." Psychology Today (September) 44-47, 95-97.

———(1971) "Institutionalized Anglocentrism: labeling mental retardates in the public schools," in P. Orleans and W. H. Russell (eds.) Race, Change, and Urban Society. Beverly Hills, CA: Sage.

————and LEWIS, J. F. (1979) System of Multicultural Pluralistic Assessment (SOM-PA)—Adaptive Behavior Inventory for Children. New York: Psychological Corporation.

MURPHY, L. B. and A. E. MORIARITY (1976) Vulnerability, Coping, and Growth: From Infancy to Adolescence. New Haven: Yale Univ. Press.

OGBU, J. (1981) "Origins of human competence: a cultural ecological perspective." Child Development 52 (2): 413-429.

————(1974) The Next Generation: An Ethnography of Education in an Urban Neighborhood. New York: Academic.

PASSOW, A. H. [ed.] (1963) Education in Depressed Areas. New York: Teachers College Press.

PETERS, M. (1978) "Notes from the guest editor." Journal of Marriage and the Family 40: 655-658.

PHILLIPS, L. (1976) Human Adaptation and Its Failures. New York: Academic.

RIEGEL, K. F. (1976) "The dialectics of human development." American Psychologist 31: 689-699.

RIESSMAN, F. (1962) The Culturally Deprived Child. New York: Harper & Row.

RUTTER, M. (1979) "Protective factors in children's responses to stress and disadvantage," in M. W. Kent and J. E. Rolf (eds.) Primary Prevention of Psychopathology. Hanover, NH: University Press of New England.

SEARS, R. R. (1975) Your Ancients Revisited: A History of Child Development. Chicago: Univ. of Chicago Press.

SIEGEL, I. (1979) "Consciousness raising of individual competence in problem solving," in M. W. Kent and J. E. Rolf (eds.) Primary Prevention of Psychopathology. Hanover, NH: University Press of New England.

SLAUGHTER, D. T. (1977) "Relation of early parent-teacher socialization influences to achievement orientation and self-esteem in middle childhood among low-income Black children," in J. Glidewell (ed.) The Social Context of Learning and Development. New York: Gardner Press.

SMITH, M. B. (1968) "Competence and socialization," in J. A. Clausen (ed.) Socialization and Society. Boston: Little, Brown.

SPIVAK, G. and M. SHURE (1974) Social Adjustment of Young Children: A Cognitive Approach to Solving Real-Life Problems. San Francisco: Jossey-Bass.

STOTT, D. H. and L. G. SYKES (1967) Bristol Social Adjustment Guides. San Diego, CA: Educational and Industrial Testing Service.

SULLIVAN, A. R. (1973) "The identification of gifted and academically talented Black students: a hidden exceptionality." Journal of Special Education 7: 373-380.

TULKIN, S. R. (1975) "An analysis of the concept of cultural deprivation," in U. Bronfenbrenner and M. Mahoney (eds.) Influences on Human Development. Hinsdale, IL: Dryden.

WHITE, B. L. and J. C. WATTS (1973) Experience and Environment: Major Influences on the Development of the Young Child. Englewood Cliffs, NJ: Prentice-Hall.

WHITE, R. W. (1959) "Motivation reconsidered: the concept of competence." Psychological Review 66: 297-333.

WILKINSON, C. B. and W. A. O'CONNOR (1977) "Growing up male in a Black single-parent family." Psychiatric Annals 7 (7): 356-362.

ZIGLER, E. F. (1979) "The concept of competence and social policy," in M. W. Kent and J. E. Rolf (eds.) Primary Prevention of Social Competence. Hanover, NH: University Press of New England.

PART II

SOCIAL-ECONOMIC ENVIRONMENTS

4

THE SEA IS SO WIDE AND MY BOAT IS SO SMALL

Problems Facing Black Children Today

MARIAN WRIGHT EDELMAN

THE DECLINING QUALITY OF LIFE FOR CHILDREN TODAY

From the end of World War II to the early 1970s the world made great progress in improving the lives of children. This past decade, however, has witnessed a slow but significant decline in their quality of life, especially in the developing countries, where far too many children wage a daily struggle for existence or die at an early age.

Every day in 1982, more than 40,000 young children died from malnutrition and infection. For every child who died, 6 now live on in hunger and ill health (Grant, 1983).

The United Nations Food and Agriculture Organization estimates that a continuation of present trends until the year 2000 will result in a horrifying increase in the numbers of the seriously undernourished to some 600-650 million—an increase of about 30% (Grant, 1983).

Every minute, 10 children die as a result of diseases we know how to prevent: measles, polio, tuberculosis, diphtheria, whooping cough, and tetanus (Grant, 1983). Although vaccines have existed for decades and the cost is a mere $3 per child, only 10% of the 8 million children born yearly in the developing world are immunized (Grant, 1983). If efforts are not made to rectify this problem, a staggering number of children will continue to die each year, equivalent to the entire under-5-year-old population of the United States or to the combined child populations of the United Kingdom, France, Italy, Spain, and the Federal Republic of Germany (Grant, 1983).

Poverty and hunger are increasing for children and women in the United States, one of the wealthiest nations in the world. July 1983 Census Bureau figures (U.S. Bureau of the Census, 1983b) show that the poverty rate for children is growing faster than for any other age group in the population as a whole. More than 1 in 5 children now live in poverty. Since 1979 over a million American children a year have fallen into poverty.

Female-headed families with children are more likely to be poor. Census statistics reveal that 47.8% of female-headed families are poor. From 1981 to 1982, 391,000 children in families headed by women fell into poverty. The problem of poor women and children is such that the National Advisory Council on Economic Opportunity has made the following prediction:

> All other things being equal, if the proportion of the poor in female-householder families were to continue to increase at the same rate as it did from 1967 to 1978, the poverty population would be composed solely of women and their children before the year 2000 (Blaustein, 1982).

THE SPECIAL VULNERABILITY OF BLACK CHILDREN

While the status of the world's children in general is declining and increasing numbers of women and children in the United States are falling into poverty, the future of Black children looks even more bleak. Some Black children and families are thriving: Black young people are attending colleges and graduate schools and entering the professions in far greater numbers than ever before. Yet a large percentage of Black children still live in poverty, in dilapidated housing on squalid and crime-ridden streets, and have ill health as a result of inadequate nutrition and poor education.

Black children suffer disproportionately from downward trends in the economy and from the lack of commitment toward alleviating problems in health, education, housing, and employment. Today, for example, the poverty rate for Black American children is higher than it has been at any time since 1967. Almost 1 in 2 Black children is poor, compared to the poverty rate for American children in general of 1 in 5 (U.S. Bureau of the Census, 1983b).

After decades of systematic segregation and discrimination, the rising tide of opportunity brought by the Civil Rights movement was neither long enough nor strong enough to enable most Black children to gain the opportunities that so many white children take for granted. Today— at a time when unemployment levels are high and the federal government is cutting programs that aid children and their families—Black children, youth, and their families remain worse off than whites in every area of American life. Moreover, the gap is widening.

POPULATION

The Black population has been increasing slowly since the mid-1900s. In 1981 Blacks constituted 11.8% of the total population in the United States. This is the highest it has been since 1890.

The Black population is younger than its white counterpart. In 1981 the median age for Blacks was 25.2 years and for whites it was 31.2 years. Almost 35% of the Black population was under 18 years, whereas only 26% of the white population was that young (U.S. Bureau of the Census, 1983a). Because the Black community is "younger," its population will increase somewhat faster than that of the white community. Between 1983 and the year 2000, the number of Black children under 18 years of age is expected to grow by 20.3%, and the number of white children is expected to grow by less than 4.1% (U.S. Bureau of the Census, 1982a).

A greater percentage of Black children than white live in central cities. In 1980, 55.4% of Black children under 18 years lived in central cities compared to 20.4% of white children. The figures for the residence of poor children are even more striking: 27.1% of all poor white children lived in central cities in 1980, whereas 57.5% of all poor Black children lived in central cities. Only 26.2% of all poor Black children live in nonmetroplitan (rural) areas, whereas 42.8% of all poor white children lived in rural areas (U.S. Bureau of the Census, 1982b).

POVERTY

More than half of all Black infants born in 1982 were born into poverty. The poverty rate among all Black children under 18 years (47.3%) is higher now than at any time since 1967 (U.S. Bureau of the Census, 1983b).

In 1982, 51.5% of all Black children under the age of the 3 years were poor; 47.7% of all Black children 3 to 5 years old were poor; and 48% of all Black children 6 to 13 years old were poor (U. S. Bureau of the Census, 1983b). In 1980 almost two-thirds of all white children lived in families with incomes at *more than twice* the poverty level as compared to the 70.1% Black children who lived in families with incomes *less than twice* the poverty level (U.S. Bureau of The Census, 1982b).

The median family income among all Black children in 1969 was $14,580 (in 1981 dollars), or 56.4% of the white median. By 1981 it had fallen to $12,173, or 51.1% of the white median. The white median income of families with children also fell, but by only 7.9%, whereas the fall for Black families with children was 16.5% (U.S. Bureau of the Census, 1970; Bureau of Labor Statistics, 1982).

Among Black children living in female-headed families, the median family income fell from $8,326 in 1969 (1981 dollars) to $6,397 in 1981. This was a decline of 23.2% in real dollars. The median income of Black female-headed families with children in 1981 was only 30.7% of that of Black married couples with children. In fact, between 1969 and 1981, the real median income among Black intact families with children actually rose by 12.7% (U.S. Bureau of the Census, 1970; Bureau of Labor Statistics, 1982).

FEMALE-HEADED FAMILIES

More than half (55.3%) of all Black children are born to a single mother (National Center for Health Statistics, 1982). Three out of every 5 (59.9%) of all Black children under 3 years are not living with both parents. Black children under 3 years of age are four times as likely to live with only one parent and five times as likely to live with neither parent than are their white counterparts. Older Black children are more likely to live in intact families than are younger Black children (40.1% of the under 3 year-old group live with two parents, whereas 45.4% of the 15- to 17-year-olds do so). Among white children the pattern is the reverse; younger children are more likely to live in two-parent families than older ones (85.1% of those under 3 years, but only 77.7% of children 15 to 17, see U.S. Bureau of the Census, 1983c).

The great majority of Black children living in other than a two-parent family live with their mothers. In 1982, 81.9% of Black children who did not live with both parents lived with their mothers; 14.5% lived with neither parent (often living with another relative); and only 3.6% lived with their fathers. This is a considerable change from 1970 when, among Black children not living with their parents, only 70.0% lived with their mothers, 24.7% lived with neither parent, and 5.3% lived with their fathers (U.S. Bureau of the Census, 1983c). The tendency is now for the mother of a young Black child to remain with the child rather than place it with another relative.

Black female-headed families average the same number of children, and of the same ages, as Black married couple families. Each averages 2.0 children (U.S. Bureau of the Census, 1983d). Of Black children living in female-headed families, 43.2% live with a mother who did not graduate from high school. Of this same group, 64.2% live in central cities and 74.7% live in rented apartments (U.S. Bureau of the Census, 1983d). Of the Black children living with only their mothers in 1982, 44% had mothers who had never married; 20.3% had mothers who were divorced from their husbands; 27% had mothers who were separated from their husbands; 6.9% had widowed mothers; and 1.8% were there for other reasons (i.e., a father incarcerated or in military service; see U.S. Bureau of the Census, 1983c).

In 1969, 68.2% of the Black female-headed families with children living at home were poor. By 1979, the poverty rate had slowly fallen to 63.1%. From 1979 to 1982, the rate increased to 70.7%—higher than at any point since 1967. Most of the increases came during the recession of 1981 and 1982 (U.S. Bureau of the Census, 1983b).

In 1981, 23.9% of Black women with minor children were awarded child support payments from an absent father, but only 16.0% received them. These rates are less than half for those of similarly placed white women. When child support payments were made at all, they averaged less than $70 per month, per child (U.S. Bureau of the Census, 1983e).

Black children under 6 years of age are more likely to have their mothers working: 52.9% have working mothers against 44.8% of white children of the same age in 1982. Black mothers work longer hours: an average of 37.8% more hours per year. Black mothers also earn less money: In 1982 the median income of Black families with children under 6 years old with working mothers was only two-thirds that of similar white families (Shapiro and Mott, 1983). As a result, young Black children are far more dependent on full-time child care than are white children, and their parents are less able to pay for it.

HEALTH

A Black infant is almost twice as likely as a white baby to die during the first year of life. The Black infant mortality rate in 1980 was as high as the white rate in 1965. One out of every 47 Black infants died during the first year of life. Although both Black and white infant mortality rates have fallen over the last decade, there is no indication that the Black rate is falling fast enough to ever reach white levels (National Center for Health Statistics, 1983).

A Black baby is over three times as likely as a white baby to have a mother who dies in childbirth (National Center for Health Statistics, 1983). A Black infant is more than twice as likely to be born to a mother who received no prenatal care at all. In 1980, 20.7% of white infants were born to mothers who did not start prenatal care in the first trimester of pregnancy. Among Black infants, 37.3% lacked timely prenatal care (National Center for Health Statistics, 1982).

In 1980, 12.5% of Black and 5.7% of white live births weighed 2,500 grams or less (low birth weight, 5½ lbs.). These figures represent a slight decline from 1970 for both races. But among very low birth weight infants (1,500 grams, 3.3 lbs. or less) there has been no improvement— 2.4% of Black and 0.9% of white infants still have very low birth weights (National Center for Health Statistics, 1982).

In 1980, Black infants under one year of age were more than ten times as likely to die of nutritional deficiencies as were white infants (National Center for Health Statistics, 1981). In that same year, Black infants under 1 year of age were more than three times as likely to die of conditions related to low birth weight and to pneumonia than were white infants. They also were more than twice as likely to die of sudden infant death and of complications of pregnancy that afflicted their mothers. Their death rates were more than four times higher for gastritis and related disorders of the digestive system, and over three times as high for intestinal infections (National Center for Health Statistics, 1983).

One Black child under 6 years of age of every 8 has an elevated blood lead level. Black children are six times as likely as white children to show excessive exposure to lead (Public Health Service, 1982). Black children are five times as likely to contract tuberculosis as white children (National Center for Disease Control, 1982a).

Overall, in 1980 Black children were 68.6% more likely to die between ages 1 and 4 as were white children; 46.8% more likely to die between ages 5 and 9; and 22.8% more likely to die between ages 10 and 14. Only in the 15- to 19-year age group were white children slightly more likely to die than Black children—primarily because white children are far more likely to be killed in automobile accidents and by suicide in their late teens (National Center for Health Statistics, 1983). Black teenagers, however, are four times as likely to be murdered as white children their age (National Center for Health Statistics, 1981).

Black children have only two-thirds the number of routine infant and childhood health visits to physicians of white children (National Center for Health Statistics, 1980). In 1979, 1 out of every 10 Black children under age 17 had not seen a doctor in the last two years; and 1 out of every 8 Black children under age 6 had not seen a doctor each year (National Center for Health Statistics, 1981).

In 1974, 60% of all Black 1- to 4-year olds were immunized with three doses of DPT. By 1982, the proportion had fallen to 48.4%, fewer than half. Similarly, in 1974, 45% of Black 1- to 4-year olds had three doses of polio vaccine. By 1982, the proportion had fallen to 39.1%—fewer than 2 of every 5 Black preschoolers (National Center for Disease Control, 1982b).

In 1981, 1 out of every 6 Black children aged 6 to 16 had never seen a dentist. Black children under age 6 were 27.2% less likely to see a dentist than white children of the same age (National Center for Health Statistics, 1981).

EDUCATION

About half of all Black students end up at least one full grade behind the average white student of the same age in school. Moreover, the older the Black student, the further behind he or she is likely to be (U.S. Bureau of the Census, 1981). A Black student was 3.2 times as likely as a white student to be in an educable mentally retarded class, but only half as likely to be in a gifted and talented class during the school year 1979-1980 (U.S. Department of Education, 1982).

By the time they were 18, 1 out of every 5 Black students had dropped out of school before high school graduation in 1979. One out of every 3 was behind in grade level, although not yet a dropout (U.S. Bureau of the Census, 1981). In October 1981, 23.3% of all Black youth 20 and 21 years of age were high school dropouts. Although the percentage has decreased since October 1971, when it was 29.8%, almost 1 out of every 4 Black students drop out of school permanently (U.S. Bureau of the Census, 1983f). In the year prior to October 1982, there were 35 Black high school dropouts for every 100 high school graduates. There were only 19 white high school dropouts per 100 graduates (Bureau of Labor Statistics, 1983). Of the Black female high school dropouts age 18 to 21 surveyed in 1979, 40.4% gave pregnancy as their reason for dropping out of school (National Longitudinal Survey of Labor Force Behavior, n.d.).

In 1977, 50% of all Black high school graduates went on to college, compared to 51% of white high school graduates. By 1982, the proportion of Black high school graduates going on to college had fallen to 36%, whereas the white proportion remained almost the same at 52% (Bureau of Labor Statistics, 1983).

Unemployment levels for both Black high school graduates and dropouts are very high. As of October 1982, among Black youth who had graduated from high school that year (and were not enrolled in college), 30.7% were not in the labor force. Of those who were in the labor force, 58% were unemployed—in other words, only 29.1% (less than 1 out of 3) had a job in 1982. Among white high school graduates, the corresponding rate was 66.5% at work (Bureau of Labor Statistics, 1983).

Among Black high school dropouts (who had dropped out in the fiscal year ending October 1982), only 51.9% were in the labor force and, of them, 71.4% were unemployed. Thus, among Black high school dropouts, the proportion currently at work in October 1982 was 14.8% (only 1 in 7). The corresponding rate among recent white high school dropouts was 42.9% (Bureau of Labor Statistics, 1983).

MENTAL HEALTH

Although the mental health statistics are not as current, they also tell of a gap in the chances for adequate treatment between Black and white children.

Statistics for 1975 reported by the President's Commission on Mental Health (1980) show that Blacks under age 18 were over twice as likely to be admitted to state and county mental hospitals as whites, who were treated more often on an out-patient basis.

According to 1980 census data, Black children were placed in health, psychiatric, and foster care facilities at a rate about 75% higher than white children. They were found in correctional facilities at a rate 400% higher than white children (U.S. Bureau of the Census, 1984).

NATIONAL CHOICES

Governments throughout the world spend over $600 billion a year on arms while an estimated 1 billion people live in poverty and 600 million are under- or unemployed. World public expenditures average $19,300 per soldier per year and $380 per school-age child per year (Sivard, 1982).

Similar trends can be seen in the United States from 1981 to 1983; military spending increased by $55 billion while $10 billion was cut from federal programs that provided health care, nutrition, and education to poor and needy children (figures documented by Children's Defense Fund, 1983), programs depended upon by many Black children.

Some of the programs that have suffered severe reductions in their budgets and changes in regulations and eligibility requirements are as follows: Head Start; Chapter I (Title I of the Education and Secondary Education Act); Education for All Handicapped Children; Special Supplemental Food Program for Women, Infants, and Children (WIC); Title V Maternal and Child Health and Crippled Children's Program; Medicaid; Aid to the Families with Dependent Children (AFDC); Child Abuse Prevention and Treatment Act; Title XX Social Services Program; Adoption Assistance and Child Welfare Act; School Lunch Program; Summer Food Service Program; Child Care Food Program; Food Stamps; and the Job Training Partnership Act (replacement of CETA). As a result of cuts in these programs (A Children's Defense Budget):

- An estimated 1.5 million children have lost AFDC. Most have also lost Medicaid.
- 725,000 people, including about 290,000 children, have lost health services as a result of funding cuts affecting 239 community health centers.
- Over 200,000 children and mothers have lost preventive maternal and child health services.
- 1 million people have seen their food stamps eliminated or reduced.
- 1.1 million children of low-income families have lost free and reduced price lunches.
- 900,000 fewer children now receive school breakfasts.
- More than 1,000 schools have closed lunch programs, hurting the poorest children most.
- 500,000 poor children no longer get summer lunches provided through churches and other nonprofit organizations.

CONCLUSION

Over the last decade the status of the children in general, and of Black children in particular, has declined. Although the lives of some individual Blacks have changed for the better, Blacks as a group, especially Black children, continue to suffer disproportionately from poverty, ill health, inadequate education, and high unemployment.

It is more humane and cost-effective to prevent and combat the problems of Black children before they occur or become serious and require costly remediation. Children can grow into assets with a relatively modest investment in fairly administered and preventive measures. The 1980s, however, are witnessing a decrease in the nation's commitment to children. Concomitantly, millions of Black children are not getting a fair chance to lead healthy and productive lives. From birth to young adulthood, Blacks still face staggering obstacles as they struggle to achieve decency, dignity, and success in America.

REFERENCES

BLAUSTEIN, A. I. [ed.] (1982) The American Promise: Equal Justice and Economic Opportunity. New Brunswick, NJ: Transaction Books.

Bureau of Labor Statistics (1983) "Youth labor force marked turning point in 1982." Monthly Labor Review (August).

———(1982) "March 1982 Current Population Survey." Washington, DC. (unpublished)

Children's Defense Fund (1983) A Children's Defense Budget: An Analysis of the President's FY 1984 Budget and Children. Washington, DC: author.

GRANT, J. P. (1983) The State of the World's Children, 1982-83. New York: United Nations' Children's Fund.

National Center for Disease Control (1982a) Tuberculosis in the United States: 1979, Atlanta, Georgia. Washington, DC: author.

———(1982b) "Immunization survey, Atlanta, Georgia." (unpublished)

National Center for Health Statistics (1983) "Advance report of final mortality statistics, 1980." Monthly Vital Statistics Report 32(4).

———(1982) "Advance report of final natality statistics, 1978." Monthly Vital Statistics Report 31 (8).

———(1981) "Health Interview Survey, 1981." (unpublished)

———(1980) "The national ambulatory medical care survey, United States, 1979, summary." Vital and Health Statistics, Series 13, 66 (November 13).

President's Commission on Mental Health (1980) Task Panel Reports, Vol. 3. Washington, DC: Government Printing Office.

Public Health Service (1982) Health—United States—1982. Washington, DC: author.

ROSEN, B. (1979) "Distribution of child psychiatric services," in J. D. Nosphitz (ed.) Handbook of Basic Child Psychiatry, Vol. 4. New York: Basic Books.

SHAPIRO, D. and F. L. MOTT (1983) "Effects of selected variables on work hours of young women." Monthly Labor Review (July).

SIVARD, R. L. (1982) World Military and Social Expenditures 1982. Leesburg, VA: World Priorities.

U.S. Bureau of the Census (1984) "Persons in institutions and other group quarters." 1980 Census of Population, PC80-2-40. Washington, DC: Government Printing Office.

———(1983a) Statistical Abstract of the United States, 1982-83. Washington, DC: Government Printing Office.

———(1983b) "Money, income, and poverty status of families and persons in the United States: 1982, advanced report." Current Population Reports P-60 (140). Washington, DC: Government Printing Office.

————(1983c) "Marital status and living arrangements: March, 1982." Current Population Reports P-20 (380). Washington, DC: Government Printing Office.

————(1983d) "Household and family characteristics: March, 1982." Current Population Reports P-20 (381). Washington, DC: Government Printing Office.

————(1983e) "Child support and alimony: 1981, advanced report." Current Population Reports P-23 (124). Washington, DC: Government Printing Office.

————(1983f) "School enrollment—social and economic characteristics of students: October, 1981, advanced report." Current Population Reports P-20 (373). Washington, DC: Government Printing Office.

————(1982a) "Projections of the population of the United States: 1982 to 2050, advanced report." Current Population Reports P-25 (922). Washington, DC: Government Printing Office.

————(1982b) "Characteristics of the population below the poverty level: 1980." Current Population Reports P-60 (133). Washington, DC: Government Printing Office.

————(1981) "School enrollment—social and economic characteristics of students: October, 1979." Current Population Reports P-20 (360). Washington, DC: Government Printing Office.

————(1970) "Income in 1969 of families and persons in the United States." Current Population Reports P-60 (75). Washington, DC: Government Printing Office.

U.S. Department of Education Office for Civil Rights (1982) "Elementary and secondary school civil rights survey." Washington, DC. (unpublished)

PART III

EDUCATIONAL ENVIRONMENTS

5

RACIAL VARIATIONS IN ACHIEVEMENT PREDICTION

The School as a Conduit for Macrostructural Cultural Tension

MARGARET BEALE SPENCER

One of the important and central themes introduced by Brim in his presidential address to the American Orthopsychiatric Association pinpointed the need for national policies for child development. The perspective underscores the multiplicitous effects of the macrosystem on the life chances of children. According to Brim (1975), illumination of such policies would include the identification of "social indicators of the state of the child." The proposed social indicators would specify the effects of economics, cultural values, politics, law, and sociology as each relates to child development and would suggest new policies that serve the best interests of the child. Wynn (1978), Mackey and Appleman (1983), and Lerner (1979), however, imply that the "best interests of the child" generally are not at issue as children and youth are not valued and, in fact, lack a place in our society. Their assumption suggests that children represent a generally at-risk group when considered along with environmental influences as they are transmitted throughout levels of the ecosystem or social structure. Untoward experiences of minority status children become exacerbated in comparison when coupled with the daily, mundane, normative stress levels that accompany minority group status. This chapter and its empirical research explores the interfacing of social indicators (i.e., economics, cultural values) with an important aspect of Black children's growth—their achievement experiences and psychological development in desegregated school environments.

CONCEPTUAL FRAMEWORK

ECOSYSTEM RISK

Garbarino's (1982) systems approach to the environment follows upon the conceptual formulation of Bronfenbrenner (1979: 22), who sees the individual's experiences "as a set of nested structures, each inside the next." The most immediate level of the environment is referred to as the microsystem. Implied here are the contexts in which children have first-hand experiences: those situations wherein the child engages the environment. Although this level of the environment from a systems perspective was most notably commented upon by Bronfenbrenner, the issue had been raised during the previous decades by social psychologists of the Kansas tradition: Herbert Wright, Roger Barker, Paul Gump, Phil Schoggen. By tracking the experiences of children in small towns and communities in the Midwest and England, these researchers vividly demonstrated the impact of overlapping aspects of the physical environment on the lives and the educational experiences of children. As illustrated by Heber et al.'s (1972) intervention study, and as analyzed by Valentine (1971), when studying the minority child's microsystem experiences, a pathological context usually is assumed. Interestingly, unlike the mammoth study by Barker and Wright (1954), researchers have infrequently studied the minority child's microsystem in a manner that connotes adaptive, beneficial elements. A notable exception is Ogbu's (1974) research efforts. Components of the microsystem include the child's family, school, peer group, and church. Each has been associated with assumptions of deviance for minority children and family life. However, as demonstrated by Holliday's work (1984), the expectations of each system may differ significantly, which results in differential levels of perceived and demonstrated competence that vary as a function of the setting.

Moving outward from the child, the next level of the ecosystem is referred to as the mesosystem and serves to connect microsystems. As indicated, one of the most provocative analyses of this level for minority status families has been the research by Ogbu (1974), an ethnography of education in an urban community in Stockton, California. His careful analysis of the micro-, meso-, and exosystem levels demonstrates the accrued at-risk status of children who often lack a secure home-school link. Speculations concerning the home-school linkage for minority group families has been a well-discussed, infrequently researched connection. On one hand, the microsystem is concerned with the manner in which the child is perceived, accepted, engaged in reciprocal relationships, and reinforced for competent behaviors. On the other hand, the mesosystem concerns center around the nature of relationships between settings. (For example, in the case of Ogbu's work, do the settings trust and respect each other? Lacking trust, what are the implications for childhood experiences?)

The exosystem represents those contexts that lack the child's direct participation. However, decisions affecting the child's or adult's experiences at the microsystem level are determined at this level. Decisions made by school boards, corporate-level determined work schedules of employed mothers, and availability of child development resources and supports represent examples of decision-making levels of the exosystem that have profound effects on the child. Consistent with the views of Lerner (1979), Mackey and Appleman (1983), Elkind (1981), and others, programming decisions at the level of telecommunications also have had profound effects on the quality of life for this country's children and youth. The use of subliminals in advertising and programming that further influence unsuspecting viewers has only recently been discussed openly.

Finally, the most distant level of the ecosystem from the child's daily, first-hand experiences is the macrosystem. It represents the ideology, assumptive conclusions, and associated social policies concerning individual experience. Issues, values, and beliefs in the areas of racism, gender membership, morality, and the distribution of economic resources characterize this level of the ecosystem. All affect the Black community by impoverishing economic resources and limiting the availability of opportunities due to the fact of one's racial group membership. Concomitant values are communicated from the macrosystem to all other levels (i.e., exosystem, mesosystem, and microsystem), which results in an at-risk status of minority group members as a result of the institutionalization of negative assumptions. As suggested by Bronfenbrenner (1979), a microsystem should be a gateway to the world, not a locked room. The enhancement through reinforcement of a healthy conceptualization of self or identity allows a view of the environment as a challenge rather than as a source of threat. These notions have been suggested previously by symbolic interactionists (e.g., Smith, 1968). As a consequence of the child's evolving capacity "to read" or to make meaning of the environment, the lack of an at-risk status contributes to a sense of competence or personal causation (DeCharms, 1968).

COMPETENCE AND PSYCHOLOGICAL DEVELOPMENT

Competence generally is defined as "answering to all requirements: adequate, fit, capable." White (1959) has written extensively on the topic at the theoretical level and views humans as having an intrinsic motivation toward competence—that is, effective interaction with the environment. Foote and Cottrell (1955) conceptualize competence as generally synonymous with ability or as a satisfactory degree of skill for performing certain implied kinds of tasks. DeCharms (1968) uses an alternative term, but likewise suggests that individuals' primary motivational propensity is to be effective in producing changes in their environment. He calls this characteristic personal causation. The lack of environmental control has been described by Abramson et al. (1978) as the phenomenon of learned helplessness. However, irrespective of the rubric adopted, each label implies that the child's evolving sense of self (i.e., both personal identity and group identity), emerging cognitive structures, and broadening social experiences (both successes and failures) together serve a critical role for manifest competence. These abilities both affect and are affected by coping and adaptation by the child and the family.

Erik Erikson's epigenetic model demonstrates that, beginning with the infant, the perception of the environment as a predictable, responsive world results in a positive resolution of the initial trust versus mistrust identity crisis. The positive outcome results in the incorporation of two ego strengths: drive and hope. Similarly, resolving the second crisis in favor of autonomy versus shame and doubt likewise supports the incorporation of additional ego strengths: self-control and will power. The child's microsystem experiences appear inextricably linked to conflict resolution for each subsequent stage.

Research and theoretical contributions to the topic of competence have become increasingly salient in developmental psychology and psychopathology. The more recent research focuses on social adaptation and the relationship of competence to early attachment, socialization, parenting, and the development of prosocial behaviors (Garmezy et al., 1979: 23). As noted by Garmezy and his colleagues, the current focus on competence, from a developmental perspective, evolved from studies of children who are viewed as at-risk for future psychopathology. They suggest that the views of Robert White are significant of early signs of premorbid competence. Minority status children are at-risk given the fact of racial discrimination, its institutionalization, and the child's increasingly differentiated cognitive maturation. The latter, cognitive maturation, necessitates a progressive awareness of the group's unique status. The developmental product, then, given physical and cognitive maturation along with specific social experiences, is social cognition. The family serves a significant role in this process.

Parents often choose to rear their children "as human beings," as opposed to rearing them as children who remain the objects of often subliminally experienced racially biased beliefs (Spencer, 1983). Data suggest that, like gender awareness, the development of the self system and race awareness are cognitive processes. The latter is linked to racial attitudes and stereotypes (see Spencer, 1976, 1982a, 1982b). Because discordant value judgments concerning minority status permeate social structures and are transmitted from the macrosystem level to the microsystem level, parental intervention serves to offset or diminish potentially stressful encounters. Suggested, then, is a discordant relationship between macrosystem values concerning minority group status and own-group preferenced identity formation. There is an apparent inverse relationship between societal values and healthy psychological development for minority status individuals. The macrosystem's cultural values for Blacks are deficit at best.

Given the previously presented ideas, the child's acquisition of a healthy psyche requires an intervention between societally communicated cultural assumptions and the minority child's healthy psychological development. This lack of congruence or "fit" between societal values and healthy development is not ordinarily experienced by nonminority status children. Nonminority status children experience more linear development. The macrosystem transmits values and beliefs about the culture that are consistent with beliefs of worthiness transmitted at the microsystem level (e.g., religious images, assumptions of educability, attributions concerning the nature of the self, messages about the group's values as communicated by books, movies, popular periodicals, and advertisements more globally).

Active efforts to resolve stress and to create new solutions to the challenges of each developmental stage are described as coping by Erikson (1959). Adaptation is a broader concept that specifies the individual's adjustment to difficult conditions (White, 1974). The interaction between individuals and their social environments is emphasized by psychosocial theory. The individual is depicted as resourceful, competent, and motivated by changing needs throughout the life course. These issues are congruent with White's (1959) concept of mastery, which he conceptualizes as one aspect of the adaptation process. Resources are linked directly to mastery of specific tasks at each life stage. The environment supplies continuously changing expectations and evaluations while concomitantly stimulating the emergence of valued societal behaviors.

As suggested by Newman and Newman (1979), the environment must be viewed as a composite of immediate family members, peers, institutional cultural transmitters (e. g., the school), and the historical milieu within which development takes place. As noted, White (1974) views coping as the central adaptive mechanism that results in (1) the acquisition of new and appropriate information about situations, (2) the maintenance of control over one's emotional state, (3) the planning of a course of actions, and (4) the freedom to move in order to execute plans. Coping and adaptation serve key roles in the manifestation of competence. For children and families, the cooccurrence begins during infancy, proceeds through the enculturating experiences in the school milieu, and reflects an ongoing reciprocal interaction with the various layers of the ecosystem previously defined. Competence is the hoped for outcome. Parents and the school play critical roles in the process.

TRANSITIONS, CONTINUITIES, AND TRANSMISSION OF CULTURAL VALUES

As reported by Powell (1974), the Supreme Court's 1954 decision on school desegregation was responsive to the pioneering research efforts of two Black social psychologists, Mamie and Kenneth Clark (1939, 1940). Although critiqued subsequently on methodological and conceptual grounds, their research documented an important variable relationship that persists today: When offered a choice between black and white dolls, preschool-aged Black children frequently evaluate the color black and Black persons less positively than the color white and white persons. This variable relationship remains a provocative and perplexing research finding in the social science literature and continues to generate significant research efforts. Although more current research efforts offer alternative, more cognitive-developmental interpretations of the findings (e.g., Spencer, 1983, 1982a, 1982b), the Clarks' research remains salient in that it demonstrated empirically the relationship between macrosystem effects and children's psychological development. The research brought into focus the dire warning to the Western world offered by DuBois (1971) at the turn of the century. DuBois proposed that the problem of the twentieth century would be the problem of the color line, the relationship of the Western world with the peoples of color in Africa, Asia, and the islands of the seas.

My own research indicates that race awareness (that is, the child's understanding of race as a sociobiological category) is under way by age 3 and is related to the child's color concepts, racial attitudes, and race preferences (Spencer, 1983). In addition, the awareness of race represents cognitive structures that are related to the child's evolving knowledge of the social context: The awareness of race and social cognition appear inextricably linked (Spencer, 1982b).

As indicated previously, the child's evolving cognitive structures result from physical development along with specific social experiences. The family serves a critical role in this process. Research indicates that Black parents tend to view the crisis of the 1960s as an issue for their generation that "did make a difference." As a consequence, many report that their socialization efforts are geared toward rearing "human beings." It would appear that less emphasis is placed on child rearing as enculturation at the level of ethnicity (Spencer, 1984). It is suggested that the very "humanizing" position of such minority status parents serves as an accomplice to the dehumanizing effects of institutionalized racism. The physical fact of segregation appears to have crystalized an understanding of the nature of the sociopolitical system and the parental task of buffering its effect on children's psychological development. However, the illusion (delusion?) of desegregation, particularly in the school milieu where parents often feel more alienated (see Ogbu, 1974), exacerbates children's at-risk status. There is an absence of an advocate for the child between the negative belief-laden fabric of the school and the child's attempts at mastery. The same cognitive structures that are required for the acquisition of academic, school-related concepts and skills serve to illumine the school's lack of commitment to minority children's education and the belief of their ineducability. The dilemma takes on critical importance in that it has been speculated that by the year 2030 the majority of children in public schools in this country will be minority status children.

THE SCHOOL AS A SOURCE OF
SOCIOCULTURAL RISK OR RESILIENCE

Children spend considerable time and effort in classroom settings. Their ability to think in progressively more complex ways increases as a consequence of cognitive maturation. Consequently, their school experiences take on greater salience in the prediction of achievement. The phenomenon and its implications for more global competencies may be approached from several theoretical perspectives: Selman (see Muuse, 1982) and Shantz's (1975) view of social cognition; Cooley (1956), Mead (1934), and Sullivan's (1947) symbolic interactionism; or the social learning ("self-fulfilling prophecy") interpretation put forth by Rosenthal and Jacobson (1968).

However, irrespective of the theoretical perspective adopted, it would appear that the basic process of self-appraisal as inferred from salient others serves as the common theme throughout. As reported by Abbott (1981), race and others' perceptions of race also may play a role in the self-appraisal process and, thus, may affect children's achievement.

The study by Rosenfeld et al. (1981) is interesting in that it demonstrates the effects of the classroom structure itself on the prejudices of white intermediate school students. Their findings indicated that (1) the higher the percentage of minorities in a class, the more minority friends the white students had; (2) the greater the number of minorities in a class displaying hostility toward whites, the more negative were the whites' attitudes toward minorities in general; (3) the more equal the social class and achievement levels of the whites and minorities in a class, the more white students indicated having minority friends; and (4) the higher the self-esteem of the whites in a class, the more positive their ethnic attitudes. The findings suggest that the specific structure of desegregation plans have significant implications for the program's success.

The literature review of humanistic research by Roscoe and Peterson (1982) suggests specific characteristics of teachers and learning situations that facilitate the development of students as "total persons." They suggested that teachers should be interactive with students in a more genuinely accepting manner, which would facilitate and enhance the educational experience and academically beneficial nature of schooling.

Raspberry's quote of Kenneth Clark's solution to the needs of children "coming out of pathological environments" comes closer to the point when their experiences are compared with middle-income children. Clark states the following:

> What they require is a greater degree of acceptance of their humanity— and generally they get the opposite . . . they require the schools to be an oasis rather then a replica of the pathology of their environment. A ghetto child is, I think, more likely to be responsive to a teacher's hand around his shoulder than a suburban child. But the suburban child generally gets more human acceptance than the ghetto child . . . these children probably need some indication of human acceptance as a prerequisite to their being taught (Raspberry, 1973: A31).

The theme communicated is consistent with the notion put forward previously concerning the inverse nature of Black children's experiences. The issue generally concerning color, race, and acceptability of humanity had been articulated by DuBois (1971): "Most men in the world are colored. A belief in humanity means a belief in colored men. The future world will, in all reasonable possibility, be what colored men make it."

Washington (1980) states that advocates of integration have expected desegregated academic settings to be facilitative of academic achievement and self-perceptions of minority children. She notes that the results of research on such settings have not yielded the hoped for findings. Her research findings are revealing of the depth of the problem. She found that Black teachers had more favorable professional backgrounds, more favorable attitudes toward school desegregation and social distance, and more positive perceptions of Black children. Unfavorable attitudes, unfavorable perceptions, and unfavorable classroom behavior were directed toward Afro-American children. In addition, irrespective of teacher race, teachers have biased perceptions of Black children. Black teachers, who viewed desegregation and cultural diversity in a more positive manner than did white teachers, also had more favorable perceptions of Black children. The reverse was observed for white teachers. Similar findings were obtained in a subsequent study by Washington (1982). In this gender/race-focused study, her findings indicated that girls were perceived more positively than boys by both Black and white teachers. A more careful examination indicated that girls in general were not the objects of positive teacher perception. Rather, the evaluations of white girls were significantly more favorable; so much so, that the diminished unfavorable perceptions of Black girls were unaffected in the analyses of "females."

Kifer (1975) links the child's personality characteristics and academic achievement. Characteristics are depicted as responses to accumulated patterns of academic achievement: It is the student's history of consistent successes or failures that is linked to effective traits (Kifer, 1975: 193). His view integrates a model of competence similar to that proposed by White (1959, 1960), who views the child's performance as determined by years of experience in the academic setting. One child characteristic, race, has been shown to be deterministic of classroom interactional patterns.

This study explores differential predictive patterns of achievement for Black and white children in the third-, fourth-, or fifth-grade classrooms of desegregated schools in several southern school districts. The question explored was whether the predictive relationship between achievement (i.e., Criterion Reference Test and nationally normed achievement scores) and self-esteem, perceptions of teachers' perceptions, and school and teacher demographic characteristics would show a similar pattern irrespective of student race. The goal was to reject the null hypothesis of no differences in predictive achievement patterns by student race.

METHOD

SUBJECTS

The subjects in this study were a subsample of a larger, multicounty evaluation of children. The subjects were in the third, fourth, or fifth grades in one of 4 rural counties. The 22 classrooms represented 9 schools. The majority of children were from lower-income families. Eligibility for government-assisted programs indicated that there were no racial differences for socioeconomic status. Children were in desegregated schools and classrooms. All teachers were female and 2 of the 22 teachers were Black. The 445 children were near equally divided by gender (236 boys and 209 girls) and race (227 whites and 213 Blacks).

DESIGN OF THE STUDY

Separate measures of self-esteem (Hare, 1977) and perception of teachers' perceptions (Abbott, 1981) were obtained along with school achievement data. State Criterion Reference Test (CRT) data in math and reading and nationally normed achievement data in the areas of math, reading, language, spelling, and total score were used. When available, teacher demographic information was obtained along with teacher ratings of children's attitude and effort, attendance data, and information on whether or not a grade had been repeated. The student information was part of each child's permanent record. The Adjective Checklist by Abbott (1981) was a modification of a rating scale originally developed by Davidson and Lang (1960). As reported by Abbott, terms chosen for the checklist in its original form (i.e., by Davidson and Lang) reflected common word usage to describe "how people feel toward and how people think of others, especially how teachers feel toward and think of children." Children in the 10-16 year age range found the words chosen to be readable. Positive and negative feelings were equally represented. Each word was judged by teachers and junior high students as to favorability, unfavorability, or neutrality. Included were terms that were judged by 50% of teachers and 80% of pupils as representing favorable or unfavorable evaluations. The checklist by Davidson and Lang (1960) contained a total of 35 terms that met the criteria stated.

The follow-up study by Abbott (1981) modified the instrument to ensure its suitability for third-grade pupils. The more difficult words were changed to less difficult terms that approximated the meaning of the original words. The reliability obtained was similar to that originally reported by Davidson and Lang.

The Hare (1977) scale is a 30-item general self-esteem measure that combines items from the Rosenberg and Coopersmith scales with Hare's own items. The goal in creating a new measure was to obtain a scale that would be sensitive and both general and area-specific in content. Hare reports that the need to create a new measure derived from an ability to assess area-specific (i.e., school, home, peer) self-esteem from the Rosenberg general measure, and concern that the failure of the Coopersmith measure to detect differences in self-evaluation by children across different areas of experience might have been due to failure to emphasize the specific context.

The derived measure is both general and area-specific for the contexts of school, peer, and home. Ten-item subscales represent specific areas. The general esteem score is represented by the sum of the 3 area-specific scores. Data have been reported for fifth-grade students, although Hare reports that the instrument has been used successfully with younger children.

INSTRUMENTATION

The Adjective Checklist was scored on a favorable/unfavorable scale with averages of raw scores ranging from 35 to 105. The Hare General and Area-Specific Self-Esteem measure contained a 4-choice format. Range of scores possible for the general score was 30 to 120. Each area-specific subscore (i.e., peer, home, and school) ranged from 10 to 40.

PROCEDURES

Each class was introduced to the task by a well-trained female tester. Subjects were told that the tester was interested in how children think about themselves and school. As no one but the examiner would be reviewing the papers, each was asked to be truthful when responding. The Adjective Checklist and the self-esteem measure were group-administered. The Adjective Checklist was administered only once. The question format was as follows: "My teacher thinks ..." The options for response were the three phrases "all of the time," "some of the time," and "never," which were printed on the response sheet along with an example placed on the chalkboard. The tester would walk over to individual students to respond to questions asked.

For each of the 30 items of the Hare General and Area-Specific Self-Esteem measure, the following response options were printed on the response sheet and the chalkboard: "strongly disagree," "disagree," "agree," and "strongly agree."

STATISTICAL PROCEDURES

A series of stepwise multiple regressions were used that employed groups of independent variable clusters (i.e., teacher variables, school variables, child personality, family variables, academic teacher perceptions, social teacher perceptions, and personal/social teacher perceptions) and each of 7 dependent variable achievement scores (i.e., both State Criterion and nationally normed achievement scores).

A perusal of the intercorrelation matrix by race indicated that the items of the Adjective Checklist, self-esteem measure, and school variables (e.g., total absences, grades repeated, teacher ratings of attitude and effort) obtained a differential correlational pattern as a function of child race. Accordingly, for the Adjective Checklist items were grouped into three clusters: academic teacher perceptions, social teacher perceptions, and personal/social teacher perceptions. Items such as "my teacher thinks I waste time" or "don't want to learn" or "am a good thinker" were placed together in one (academic teacher perception) cluster. Items that rated social characteristics that had implications of self/other relationships were placed into a second cluster. Finally, items that focused on "self" or personal characteristics such as "my teacher thinks I am loud," "I am helpful," or "I am silly" were placed into a category. Teacher variables that constituted this cluster were represented by information such as teacher's age, degree, and years of experience. The child personality cluster was composed of the total score of the Adjective Checklist along with the Hare General and Area-Specific Self-Esteem scores.

Regression analyses were employed for the total sample and separately by race. Each independent variable cluster was used to predict each of the dependent achievement scores (i.e., State Criterion Reference Test scores in math and reading and the nationally normed achievement scores).

Conducted separately by race, independently derived or tailored regression analyses were introduced that used as the independent variable cluster those variables of the previously entered clusters that were most significant in predicting the individual achievement test scores. Thus, the content of the tailored variable clusters varied by race. Rural counties varied significantly in the achievement tests administered. At times, only the state Criterion Reference Test was employed. In other cases, only the nationally normed achievement test was used; occasionally both were used for children. As a consequence, pair-wise deletions were used to handle the problem of missing data in regression analyses.

RESULTS

As indicated from the t-test results listed in Table 5.1, there were significant differences by race for 5 of the 7 achievement scores. Only the language and spelling scores of the nationally normed achievement tests did not indicate significant differences by racial group membership.

There were no significant differences by race on the child personality measures. The Adjective Checklist was not significantly different when examined by the total scores for Black and white children. Similarly, the

TABLE 5.1 T-Test Results: Child Race by Achievement Score

Variable	Number of Cases	Mean	Standard Deviation	F Value	2-Tail Problem	T Value	Degrees of Freedom	2-Tail Problem
							Separate Variance Estimate	
CRT reading								
group 1	63	215.8	30.2	3.56	0.000	2.25	95.80	0.027
group 2	56	206.0	15.8					
CRT math								
group 1	60	213.5	17.4	2.35	0.002	3.65	91.58	0.000
group 2	55	198.0	26.7					
Ach. reading								
group 1	158	4.6	1.6	1.40	0.032	2.53	308.06	0.012
group 2	168	4.2	1.4					
Ach. language								
group 1	67	4.7	1.5	1.53	0.076	-0.66	126.90	0.510
group 2	77	4.9	1.2					
Ach. math								
group 1	158	4.5	1.7	2.03	0.000	2.23	249.33	0.027
group 2	169	4.2	1.0					
Ach. spelling								
group 1	22	6.1	4.1	2.23	0.041	0.21	33.75	0.839
group 2	32	5.9	2.8					
Ach. total								
group 1	158	4.6	1.9	2.59	0.000	2.61	256.76	0.010
group 2	167	4.2	1.1					

NOTE: group 1 (child race) = white; group 2 (child race) = black.

self-esteem score was not different, although the peer subscale indicated a trend: Black children obtained slightly higher scores (see Table 5.1). Only one difference by gender was observed on the child personality measures: Boys obtained a higher mean score on the peer subscale of the Hare Self-Esteem measure (t = 2.49, df = 421 and p = .01).

Teacher experience varied between 1 year to 21+ years. A chi-square analysis indicated that white pupils tended to have younger teachers who also usually had more advanced degrees. On the other hand, Black children more often had older teachers with entry level degrees (chi square = 12.9 with 3 df and p = .005). Older teachers, although having usually only an entry level degree, had more experience (chi square = 533 with 12 df and p < .001). Teacher degree and age were curvilinear. Teacher age ranged from 23 to 54 years. The majority had attended in-state schools. The youngest teachers and the oldest usually had only entry level degrees (i.e., B.A.). On the other hand, the two intermediate age groups of teachers usually had both the B.A. degree and an advanced degree (chi square = 65.3 with 3 df and p < .001).

The mean scores and variance on the personality measures obtained for the 4 counties were similar to one another and to the means and variances obtained for a larger, more urban, in-state county (N = 744). Accordingly, the data for the 18 classrooms representative of 9 schools and 4 counties were pooled.

TEACHER VARIABLES AS THE INDEPENDENT VARIABLE CLUSTER

The teacher variables included teacher age, degree, and experience. The predictive pattern was different for white and Black pupils. As indicated by Table 5.2, in the case of Black pupils 6 of the 7 achievement scores (both state criterion and nationally normed) were predicted by teacher characteristics. On the other hand, Table 5.2 indicates that teacher characteristics are less consistent in predicting achievement for white children. For Black children, who seem more sensitive to teacher characteristics, the amount of variance accounted for ranged from 21% to 43%.

SCHOOL VARIABLES AS THE INDEPENDENT VARIABLE CLUSTER

School variables (e.g., teacher ratings of attitude and effort, total number of children in classroom, and total absences) had varied predictive power by race. Only the number of children in a classroom

TABLE 5.2   Regression Results: Teacher Variables

Dependent Variable	Independent Variable(s)	Statistics		
		F	df	% Variance
Black subjects				
CRT reading	teacher age	16.95**	1,42	29
CRT math	experience	11.06*	1,41	21
Ach. reading	—	n.s.	—	—
Ach. math	teacher age degree (-)	24.7**	2,6	42
Ach. spelling	experience degree (-)	11.1*	2,29	43
Ach. total	teacher age	33.87**	1,70	33
White subjects				
CRT reading	—	n.s.	—	—
CRT math	—	n.s.	—	—
Ach. reading	experience	15.2**	1,82	16
Ach. language	teacher age	10.62*	1,31	26
Ach. math	—	n.s.	—	—
Ach. spelling	experience degree (-)	60.41	2,18	87
Ach. total	—	n.s.	—	—

*p < .01; **p < .001

was predictive of spelling on the normed test for white children: $F(1,17)$ = 4.75, p = .04 accounting for 22% of the variance. No other achievement score was predicted by school variables. For Black children, 5 of the 7 achievement scores were predicted by school variables. In fact, the state's own criterion reference test for reading ($F[1,14]$ = 12.59, p = .003, accounted for variance = 47%) was predicted by the teacher's rating of the child's attitude. The criterion reference test (CRT) for math was predicted by the teacher's rating of effort ($F[1,14]$ = 8.13, p = .01 and variance accounted for was 37%). The normed achievement test scores for math and the total achievement (performance) scores were predicted by ratings of effort, respectively: $F(1,45)$ = 11.80, p = .001 for 21% of the variance, and $F(1,43)$ = 5.18, p = .03 accounting for 11% of the variance. Achievement in spelling for the nationally normed test was predicted by total number of children in the classroom. Like the white pupils, Black children appear sensitive to the number of children in the classroom when considering spelling achievement: the fewer the pupils, the more improved achievement in spelling; the better the teacher's ratings of attitude and effort, the more improved the Black children's performance on achievement tests. As noted, a linkage between teacher ratings of attitude and effort and achievement was not significant for white pupils.

FAMILY DEMOGRAPHICS AS THE INDEPENDENT VARIABLE CLUSTER

For a subsample of children, family demographics were available: mother and father occupation, total parents in home, and total number of children in a family. Family characteristics were not predictive of student achievement irrespective of race. As noted previously, this study was a section of a larger desegregation study that had demonstrated no differences in participation of government subsidy programs as a function of race. It may be the case that when there is near homogeneity of social class, race takes on greater salience.

CHILD PERSONALITY VARIABLES AS THE INDEPENDENT VARIABLE CLUSTER

The child personality variables included the Adjective Checklist score and the general and area-specific scores from the Hare Self-Esteem scale. As noted from Table 5.3, home and school area-specific self-esteem were more often predictive of achievement for white students than for Black students. For each regression by race, the Adjective Checklist score obtained significance and was entered once. For this reason, the intercorrelation matrices for achievement scores and individual items of the Adjective Checklist were perused separately by race. A different pattern of significance emerged for Black and white pupils. Items that were academic-, social-, or personal/self-focused were entered jointly as a cluster of independent variables.

ADJECTIVE CHECKLIST ACADEMIC ITEMS AS THE INDEPENDENT VARIABLE CLUSTER

Examples of items included in this cluster were "my teacher thinks I waste time," "thinks I work hard." The child's perceptions of the teacher's academic attitudes toward him or her were more often predictive for Black pupils than for white pupils. In fact, the items did not predict achievement for 4 of the 7 achievement scores for white

TABLE 5.3 Regression Results: Child Personality Measures

Dependent Variable	Independent Variable(s)	Statistics		
		F	df	% Variance
Black subjects				
CRT reading	–	n.s.	–	–
CRT math	self esteem-school	14.03***	1,49	22
Ach. reading	self esteem-school self esteem-home	15.8***	2,49	18
Ach. language	self esteem-school	13.22***	1,70	16
Ach. math	self esteem-home self esteem-school adj. checklist (-)	13.4***	3,149	21
Ach. spelling	–	n.s.	–	–
Ach. total	self esteem-school self esteem-home	17.95***	2,148	20
White subjects				
CRT reading	self esteem-school	8.24**	1,57	13
CRT math	self esteem-school	12.85***	1,55	19
Ach. reading	self esteem-school self esteem-home	13.6***	2,147	16
Ach. language	self esteem-home	4.15	1,61	6.4
Ach. math	self esteem-home	7.26**	1,148	4.7
Ach. spelling	Adjective Checklist self esteem (-)	9.79**	2,19	51
Ach. total	self esteem-home	9.77**	1,148	6

$*p < .05; **p < .01; ***p < .001$

pupils. On the other hand, 5 of the 7 achievement scores were significantly predicted by perceived teacher academic values.

ADJECTIVE CHECKLIST SOCIAL ITEMS AS THE INDEPENDENT VARIABLE CLUSTER

Social items were those that described the child's behavioral interaction with others: "my teacher thinks I bother others," "I share things," "I love others." For white pupils, only 1 achievement score was predicted by social items (4% of the variance in the nationally normed reading achievement test score was predicted, $F(1,151) = 6.12$, $p = .01$.

For Black pupils, except for the spelling achievement score, all achievement test scores were predicted by a social category or a combination of items. The unique variance accounted for ranged from 7% to 15%. For Black pupils, the child's perceptions of the teacher's social evaluations of him or her consistently predicted achievement. This was not the case for white pupils.

ADJECTIVE CHECKLIST PERSONAL/SELF ITEMS AS THE INDEPENDENT VARIABLE CLUSTER

For Black pupils, personal characteristics significantly predicted achievement scores in 5 of the 7 assessment areas. However, 3 personal characteristics consistently were predictive: "My teacher thinks I am awake... nervous, and... sloppy." Variance accounted for ranged from 4% to 15%. On the other hand, for white pupils, all achievement score categories were predicted by personal/self characteristics, although twice as many items, either alone or in some combination, were predictive. For white pupils, variance accounted for ranged from 7% to 41%. However, as noted, a wider variety of personal characteristics were salient as predictors of achievement.

"TAILORED" INDEPENDENT VARIABLE CLUSTERS BY RACE

The data support the rejection of the null hypothesis of no difference. The pattern of independent variables predictive of achievement varied significantly by race. For the various analyses, those variables that obtained highest correlations with each of the 7 (achievement) dependent variable scores were entered as one cluster of independent variables for the specific achievement score. The variables that contributed significantly to the variance for each regression equation differed by race; accordingly, each tailored variable cluster, dependent on the pattern established by race from the previous, was representative for the specific (racial) group. The goal was to obtain the most salient cluster by race that would account for the greatest amount of variance in the dependent variable (i.e., each achievement score). As indicated by Table 5.4, for Blacks the amount of variance accounted for ranged from 16% to 95%. Similarly, for white subjects the variance accounted for ranged from 5% to 95%.

TABLE 5.4   Regression Results: "Tailed" Independent
Variable Clusters

Dependent Variable	Independent Variable(s)	F	df	% Variance
Black subjects				
CRT reading	attitude rating	12.59**	1,14	47
CRT math	effort rating	8.13**	1,14	37
Ach. reading	teacher age effort rating degree (-) attitude rating	132.5***	4,25	95
Ach. language	self esteem-school	5.1*	1,27	16
Ach. math	teacher age	16.1***	1,28	37
Ach. spelling	experience # children/class (-)	20.9***	2,26	62
Ach. total	teacher age attitude rating	63.94***	4,45	51
White subjects				
CRT reading	# children/class degree (-) self esteem-global adj. -not aware	11.5***	4,45	51
CRT math	self esteem-school # children/class experience (-) teacher age adj. -nervous (-) self esteem-home adj. -make mistakes	103.1***	7,39	95
Ach. reading	experience self esteem-global	14.84***	2,81	27
Ach. language	teacher age	10.62*	1,31	26
Ach. math	self esteem-home	4.02*	1,82	5
Ach. spelling	adj. -waste time teacher age	19.3***	2,18	68
Ach. total	adj. -not awake	5.48*	1,82	6

*p < .05; **p < .01; ***p < .001

To restate, variables entered for each achievement score by race included significant school variables, teacher variables, child personality variables, and items from the Adjective Checklist. For Black children it was ratings by the teachers of the child's attitude and effort that significantly accounted for the state Criterion Reference Test reading and math scores: variance = 47.4% and 37%, respectively. Consistent is the pattern from Table 5.4 that for Black children teacher and school characteristics predict achievement. On the other hand, data from Table 5.4 indicate that a variety of variables together most often are predictive of white children's achievement test performance.

DISCUSSION

The data suggest a different predictive pattern of achievement as a function of the students' race. Black children's sensitivity to school variables—for example, teacher ratings of the child's attitude and effort toward school—suggests both positive and negative elements in the area of intervention. The negative aspect has to do with the salience of teacher ratings (attitude and effort) and their permanence as part of the child's school record. As suggested by Rosenthal and Jacobson (1968), the pygmalion effect does produce significantly different patterns of expectation and interactional patterns. The fact that Black children more often had older, more experienced teachers might also mean that such teachers carry into the classroom milieu "more biased baggage," given their greater experience with the group. As indicated, teacher demographic information suggests that the majority of teachers had exclusively in-state experiences. The possibility of having been exposed to alternative perspectives was perhaps further diminished as a consequence of environmentally stable experiences and the lack of more advanced degrees.

The positive implications of the findings involve the obvious potential responsiveness to intervention. Furthermore, the total number of children in a class was predictive of achievement in spelling for both white and Black pupils. State and county boards of education can offer relief in the area of pupil density.

For white pupils the home-specific self-esteem score alone or in combination with the school-focused self-esteem score was most predictive of achievement. On the other hand, for Black pupils the school self-esteem subscore alone or in combination with the home-specific self-esteem score more often predicted achievement. Similar to the school independent variables (i.e., teacher ratings of attitude/effort), school-related self-esteem is an area in which its enhancement for Black pupils should be promotive of more general achievement on both State Criterion Reference Tests and nationally normed achievement test scores.

Totally unexpected was lack of a predictive relationship between home variables and achievement for pupils generally. It may be the case that the lack of socioeconomic status heterogeneity resulted in an enhanced salience of race in classroom interactional patterns.

The items on the Adjective Checklist, when divided into academic, social, and personal/self subcategories, proved illuminating. The child's perceptions of the teacher's academic attitudes more often were predictive of achievement for Black children than for white children. This finding appears consistent with the area-specific (school) self-esteem scores and achievement. The Black child's school self-esteem either alone or in combination with the home self-esteem predicted achievement. Similarly, the social items of the Adjective Checklist patterned more closely, for Black pupils, with the school variables (e.g., teacher ratings of attitude and effort). One item for a single achievement score was predictive for white pupils. However, a variety of social characteristics were predictive of achievement for 6 of the 7 achievement scores.

Also interesting is the finding that when one peruses the personal characteristics of the Adjective Checklist and achievement, there is twice the variety of characteristics that appear salient for the white child's achievement. A rather narrow group of characteristics are predictive for Black children.

The tailored regression analyses were significant for demonstrating the salience of teacher and school characteristics for Black children's achievement. The cluster of independent predictive variables are school linked and amenable to interventive strategies implementable through teacher training programs. The disproportionate number of Black children with older, more experienced teachers may infer something about the school's view of the Black child's academic needs. Younger teachers have less experience although more recent educational training and related cultural exposures. Although the older teachers make up in experience what they lack in advanced degrees, perhaps what they lack is an exposure to less traditional cultural values and assumptions concerning the learning capabilities of minority status children.

Children's understanding of the world and expectations for achievement are unavoidable consequences of increasingly more differentiated thinking. Cognitive maturation, physical development, and increasingly complex interactional experiences in desegregated rural settings may well place minority status children at a disadvantage unless an intervention occurs. Although school interventions have been discussed for the most part, as indicated initially, parental intervention may take the form of buffering the macrosystem effects as mediated through social institutions (e.g., the school and its administration). As suggested by previous research (Spencer, 1983) parents tend to intervene less often than is ideal. Too often they assume that the system works and conditions have changed for Blacks. They prefer to deemphasize race and encourage the illusion that participation in the turmoil of the 1960s made a difference. The Civil Rights Movement, they believe, has made a difference. Their societal values are consistent with reported child rearing strategies that foster the rearing of "human beings". These data suggest that parents and their perceptions are an untapped resource for intervention.

There is no reason to assume that the prediction of achievement should vary by race. It is the expectation that homogeneous communication and education occurs in educational settings.

The increasingly significant school dropout rate of minority children and youth might suggest an alternative interpretation of equality and homogeneous schooling experiences. Without an intervention at the microsystem level, high school dropout may well represent one method of adaptation, albeit in the short run. Although having deleterious consequences in the long run, it may serve to maintain ego integrity during the early, turbulent adolescent years. As suggested by the research reviewed, identity and competence appear inextricably linked. Their relationship is further supported by school dropout rates for minorities. The data reported offer a pattern for the history of school dropout rate statistics given the generally unexpected finding of positive self-esteem for Black adolescents. The individual's increasing ability to read the environment (i.e., its evaluation and expectations for self) along with an evolving awareness of inadequate academic experiences together imply specific recourses as perceived by adolescent "short-term" problem-solvers. One solution to maintaining a healthy ego as opposed to a pathological psyche might be to remove oneself from an environment in which the self is devalued (e.g., high teenage pregnancy and escalating school dropout rates). The solution is consistent with cognitive dissonance theory.

Because of the problem with sample sizes for some of the analyses, these data are indicative, at least, that more studies at the level of analysis presented may be helpful in unraveling the link between identity, competence, and the mediating effects of institutionalized bias.

The data suggest several questions in need of research efforts. Would differential predictive patterns for achievement vary if the degree of trust at the level of the mesosystem (e.g., school/home) was enhanced? As noted earlier, the macrosystem represents ideology, assumptive conclusions, and associated social policies (e.g., segregation). Because of the amorphousness of this level, should social indicators of child status be more effectively employed at state and county levels of government with federal-level enhancement, reinforcement, and accountability?

It would appear that consciousness must precede the introduction of alternative values. Younger teachers would be expected to have experienced heightened consciousness, perhaps, in comparison with more experienced (older) teachers. More precise information is needed to discern whether or not the value of greater teacher experience is offset by a lack of race consciousness. What kinds of incentives are effective in the race consciousness enhancing of older, more experienced teachers? What is the price for long-term changes in classroom interactional patterns between racially diverse teachers and students?

More cognitive processing-oriented research would help in ferreting out responses to school dropout related questions. It appears that the more differentiated cognitive organization influences and allows the "tuning out," "turning off," and "dropping out" of students in potentially growth-facilitating environments (i.e., the school).

The adaptation of children and youth, in the short run, suggests an error in the Abramson et al. (1978) model. Learned helplessness offers an overly simplistic analysis of cognitive processing and the attributional process. The Wortman and Dintzer (1978) model more correctly suggests that if one environment is unresponsive or untrustworthy, self-behavioral data are obtained from other environments. This analysis also is consistent with Holliday's (1984) research findings with young children. This latter model by Wortman and Dintzer (1978) helps to explain the often perplexing data of minority youth's positive self-regard.

The social indicators called for by Brim (1975), I believe, are in fact the tuning out, turning off, and dropping out behavior of many minority status children and youth. Bronfenbrenner (1979) has suggested that the microsystem should be a gateway to the world. The differential predictive patterns by race suggest that Black and white pupils are tuning in to very different messages, and solve problems accordingly.

REFERENCES

ABBOTT, A. (1981) "Factors related to third grade achievement: self perception, classroom composition, sex and race." Contemporary Educational Psychology 6: 167-179.

ABRAMSON, L. Y., M.E.P. SELIGMAN, and J. D. TEASDALE (1978) "Learned helplessness in humans: critique and reformulation." Journal of Abnormal Psychology 87: 49-74.

BANKS, W. C. (1976) "White preference in Blacks: a paradigm in search of a phenomenon," Psychological Bulletin 83, 6: 1179-1186.

BARKER, R. G. and H. F. WRIGHT (1954) Midwest and Its Children: The Psychological Ecology of An American Town. Evanston, IL: Row Peterson.

BRIM, O. (1975) "Macro-structural influences on child development and the need for childhood social indicators." American Journal of Orthopsychiatry 45, 4: 516-524.

BRONFENBRENNER, U. (1979) The Ecology of Human Development: Experiments by Nature and Design. Cambridge, MA: Harvard Univ. Press.

CLARK, K. B. and M. B. CLARK (1940) "Skin color as a factor in racial identification and preference in Negro children." Journal of Negro Education 19: 341-350.

——— (1939) "The development of consciousness of self and the emergence of racial identity in Negro preschool children." Journal of Social Psychology 10: 591-599.

COOLEY, C. H. (1956) Human Nature and the Social Order. New York: Free Press.

DAVIDSON, H. and G. LANG (1960) "Children's perceptions of their teachers' feelings toward them related to self-perception, school achievement, and behavior." Journal of Experimental Education 29, 2: 107-118.

DeCHARMS, R. (1968) Personal Causation: The Internal Affective Determinants of Behavior. New York: Academic.

DuBOIS, W.E.B. (1971) An ABC of Color. New York: International Publishers.

ELKIND, D. (1981) The Hurried Child: Growing Up Too Fast Too Soon. Reading, MA: Addison-Wesley.

ERIKSON, E. (1963) Childhood and Society. New York: Norton.

——— (1959) "Identity in the life cycle: selected papers." Psychological Issues Monograph Series 1, 1. New York: International Universities.

FOOTE, N. and L. S. COTTRELL (1955) Identity and Interpersonal Competence: A New Direction in Family Research. Chicago: Univ. of Chicago Press.

GARBARINO, J. (1982) Children and Families in the Social Environment. Chicago: Aldine.

GARMEZY, N., A. MASTEN, L. NORDSTROM, and M. FERRARESE (1979) "The nature of competence in normal and deviant children," in M. Kent and J. Rolf (eds.) Primary Prevention of Psychopathology, vol. 3. Hanover, MA: University Press of New England.

HARE, B. (1983) Personal communication.

——— (1977) "Racial and socioeconomic variations in preadolescent area-specific and general self-esteem." International Journal of Intercultural Relations 1, 3.

HEBER, R., H. GARBER, S. HARRINGTON, C. HOFFMAN, and C. FALENDER (1972) "Rehabilitation of families at-risk for mental retardation." University of Wisconsin. (unpublished)

HIGGINS, C., Sr. (1984) "The longest struggle." Tony Brown's Journal (January/March): 4-14.

HOLLIDAY, B. G. (1984) "Towards a model of teacher-child transactional processes affecting children's academic achievement," in M. B. Spencer et al. (eds.) Beginnings: Social and Affective Development of Minority Group Children. Hillsdale, NJ: Erlbaum.

KIFER, E. (1975) "Relationships between academic achievement and personality characteristics: a quasi-longitudinal study." American Educational Research Journal 12, 2: 191-210.

LERNER, B. (1979) "Children's rights in the United States." Lecture series for the Year of the Child, St. Patrick's College, Dublin, Ireland.

MACKEY, J. and D. APPLEMAN (1983) "The growth of adolescent apathy." Educational Leadership 40, 6.

McADOO, H. and J. McADOO (1973) "A different view of race attitudes and self concepts in preschool children." Presented at the annual meeting of the Association of Black Psychologists, Detroit.

MEAD, G. H. (1934) Mind, Self, and Society. Chicago: Univ. of Chicago Press.

MUUSE, R. E. (1982) "Social cognition, part 1: Robert Selman's theory of role taking," pp. 227-253 in Theories of Adolescence. New York: Random House.

NEWMAN, B. and P. NEWMAN (1979) An Introduction to the Psychology of Adolescence. Homewood, IL: Dorsey.

OGBU, J. (1974) The Next Generation. New York: Academic.

POSTMAN, N. (1983) "The disappearing child." Educational Leadership 40: 10-17.

POWELL, G. (1974) Black Monday's Children. New York: Appleton-Century-Crofts.

RASPBERRY, W. (1973) "The coping skills of ghetto children." Washington Post (March 23): A31.

ROSCOE, B. and K. L. PETERSON (1982) "Teacher and structural characteristics which enhance learning and development." College Student Journal 16, 4: 389-394.

ROSENFELD, D., D. S. SHEEHAN, M. M. MARCUS, and W. G. STEPHAN (1981) "Classroom structure and prejudice in desegregated schools." Journal of Educational Psychology 73, 1: 17-26.

ROSENTHAL, R. and L. JACOBSON (1968) Pygmalion in the Classroom. New York: Holt, Rinehart & Winston.

SHANTZ, C. (1975) The Development of Social Cognition. Chicago: Univ. of Chicago Press.

SMITH, M. B. (1968) "Competence and socialization." in J. A. Clausen (ed.) Socialization and Society. Boston: Little, Brown.

SPENCER, M. B. (1985) "Cultural cognition and social cognition as identity factors in Black children's personal-social growth," in M. B. Spencer et al. (eds.) Beginnings: The Social and Affective Development of Black Children. Hillsdale, NJ: Erlbaum.

———(1984) "Black children's race awareness, racial attitudes, and self-concept: a reinterpretation." Journal of Child Psychology and Psychiatry 24: 1-9.

———(1983) "Children's cultural values and parental child rearing strategies." Developmental Review 4: 351-370.

———(1982a) "Personal and group identity of Black children: an alternative synthesis." Genetic Psychology Monographs 106: 59-78.

———(1982b) "Preschool children's social cognition and cultural cognition: a cognitive developmental interpretation of race dissonance findings." Journal of Psychology 112: 275-286.

———(1976) "The social cognitive and personality development of the Black preschool child: an exploratory study of developmental process." Ph.D. dissertation, University of Chicago.

———and F. D. HOROWITZ (1973) "Effects of systematic social and token reinforcement on the modification of racial and color-concept attitudes in Black and white preschool children." Developmental Psychology 9, 2: 246-254.

SPENCER, M. B. and M. WAGNER (1984) "Differential effects of expressive and receptive language use on the inference task performance of middle and lower income children." Journal of Black Psychology.

SULLIVAN, H. S. (1947) Conception of Modern Psychiatry. Washington, DC: William Alanson White Psychiatric Foundation.

VALENTINE, C. A. (1971) "Deficit, difference and bicultural models of Afro-American behavior." Harvard Educational Review 41, 2: 137-157.

WASHINGTON, V. (1982) "Racial differences in teacher perceptions of first and fourth grade pupils on selected characteristics." Journal of Negro Education 51, 1: 60-72.

———(1980) "Teachers in integrated classrooms: profiles of attitudes, perceptions and behavior." Elementary School Journal 80, 4: 192-201.

WHITE, R. (1974) "Strategy of adaptation: an attempt at systematic description," in G.V. Eoelhu et al. (eds.) Coping and Adaptation. New York: Basic Books.

———(1960) "Competence and the psychosexual stages of development," pp. 3-32 in M. R. Jones (ed.) Nebraska Symposium on Motivation. Lincoln: Univ of Nebraska Press.

———(1959) "Motivation reconsidered: the concept of competence." Psychological Review 66: 297-333.

WORTMAN, C. B. and L. DINTZER (1978) "Is an attributional analysis of the learned helplessness phenomenon viable? A critique of the Abramson-Seligman-Teasdale reformulation." Journal of Abnormal Psychology 87, 1.

WYNN, E. (1978) "Behind the discipline problem: youth suicide as a measure of alienation." Phi Delta Kappan: 307-315.

6

BLACK PARENTAL VALUES AND EXPECTATIONS OF CHILDREN'S OCCUPATIONAL AND EDUCATIONAL SUCCESS

Theoretical Implications

JOHN SCANZONI

It often is observed that many whites hold the notion that Black families are significantly different from their own. One such example is that Black parents do not adequately prepare their children to participate effectively in the world of work. In contrast, my thesis is that in terms of socialization for achievement (as well as in all family aspects) Black and white families are basically more similar than divergent at the same social class levels. Consequently, whatever systematic racial differences in achievement that have existed are primarily the result of blocked economic opportunities.

THE STRUCTURE OF OPPORTUNITY

Numerous studies over the past two decades consistently have demonstrated the structure of a model that promotes optimum child achievement in a modern society such as the United States (Blau and Duncan, 1967). The model suggests that there are at least three broad elements (each containing numerous complex subfacets) contributing to educational and occupational achievement. The three broad elements are the socioeconomic (objective) position of the parents, the subjective orientations (including role modeling) to which parents expose their children, and, finally, the "community" influences to which children are exposed—community being defined broadly as environmental or socioecological influences emanating from kin, peers, school, church, and media. Until recently, most of the "achievement" studies contributing to the model were done largely with samples of white males. Nevertheless, the theoretical perspectives on which the model is based make it generalizable to white women, as well as to Black men and women. Furthermore, certain recent studies on disadvantaged collectivities such as white women also tend to support the basic validity of the model (Mott, 1982).

The theoretical underpinnings of the model have their roots in the conceptual frameworks currently prevailing in sociology: symbolic interaction, social exchange, and social conflict. Developmental notions (Hill and Mattesich, 1979) also are inherent in the model. Specifically, development can first be captured in intergenerational terms. That is, we can think of the offspring's achievements as being spawned (or hindered) by the previous generation's inputs. In effect, parental influences have consequences that persist over time, cross generational lines, and result in offspring achievements that are similar to or different than those of the parents. Second, development may be observed by studying intragenerational changes throughout the person's own life span.

An additional feature of the prevailing model is that when examining the parent generation, it has tended to focus on the father, assuming that it was his influence that is primarily responsible for his son's achievement patterns. But there is no inherent theoretical reason to limit parental influences to those of the father. In Black society the impact of women on their sons' and daughters' achievements has very likely been substantial for decades, even though sociologists have not assessed it in any systematic fashion (Rodgers-Rose, 1980). Moreover, given the steadily increasing labor force activity of white women, there is every reason to assume that in both races both sons' and daughters' achievements increasingly will be affected by both mothers' and fathers' influences. For these reasons, Figure 6.1 uses the label "Parental" rather than "Father" to depict the objective and subjective effects of parents on their offspring (of either sex).

BACKGROUND FACTORS

The segment of Figure 6.1 labeled "Structural Background Factors" covers at least three different elements (Scanzoni, 1977: 53). One of these elements is urban experience. In trying to understand contemporary Black families, Miller's (1964) distinction between the "underclass" versus relatively more advantaged families is useful. According to Miller, the underclass (or lower class) is made up of persons and households in which unemployment is more or less perpertual and, thus, annual income generally is at or below what the Census Bureau calls the "poverty line." Persons above that level are in various segments of what Miller calls the "working class" (i.e., persons who are employed full-time most of the year). Compared to lower-class persons, working-class (and middle-class) persons obviously have a greater level of what Miller calls "economic security." An underclass exists in both Black and white societies, but it is much larger in Black society (i.e., there is much more poverty).

One factor contributing to the large Black underclass has been the rural southern heritage of many Black persons. A recent study (Connecticut Mutual, 1981) reports that rural southern persons are significantly different (more traditional) from all other Americans (including southern urbanites) in terms of family values. According to other literature (Rainwater, 1970), Black parents who grew up in southern rural areas appear less likely to be able to socialize their children for effective achievement in urban society than are Black parents who grew up in the urban milieu.[1]

Background residence, however, cannot be disentangled from the second, and probably most vital, "structural" factor, the parents' social position. The larger the number of generations that Black families have been in the urban milieu, the more likely it is that those persons will have more education, higher job status, and higher incomes. These elements make up the social position of the household; and the higher the social position of the Black parents, the higher the social position of the offspring. Persons with a certain level of advantage tend to transfer that advantage in developmental fashion cross-generationally to their children.

A third background factor, which also has been embodied with social position, is household composition. That is, past literature (Rainwater, 1970) reports that Black children from female-headed households do not attain the same educational and occupational levels as do Black children from "intact" households (i.e., households in which both parents are present). The reason for that pattern, however, seems to lie

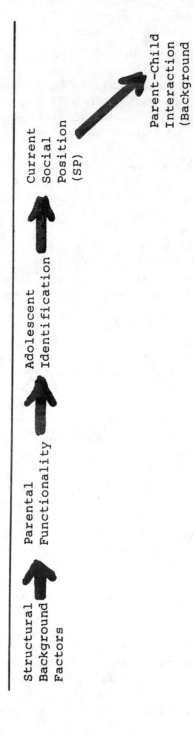

Structural
Background
Factors

Parental
Functionality

Adolescent
Identification

Current
Social
Position
(SP)

Parent-Child
Interaction
(Background
for Linkages
to Next
Generation)

SOURCE: Adapted from Scanzoni (1977: 22).

Figure 6.1 Family Linkages Affecting Children's Achievements

mainly with economic deprivation that Blacks experience in American society. Because of systematic discrimination against Black males, Black married women (with husbands present) have for many decades participated in the paid labor force to a much greater degree than white married women (Noble, 1964). Two incomes often were needed merely to survive economically, to stay out of the underclass. Complicating their efforts was the reality that working-class marriages (Black *and* white) were, during the recent past at least, more prone to separation and divorce than were middle-class marriages. When a Black working-class marriage dissolved, the woman and her children often were plunged near to or into the underclass, because of inadequate economic resources. Consequently, Black children from female-headed homes tended to lack economic resources, thus hindering their subsequent achievements. An additional factor contributing to continuing increases in Black female-headed households is the number of Black never-married adolescent women having live births (U.S. Department of Health and Human Services, 1980). These women tend to be concentrated in the underclass and, hence, to be poorly educated. Consequently, their capabilities of contributing significantly to the educational and occupational achievements of their children are problematic at best.

PARENTAL FUNCTIONALITY

Urban experience, social position, and household composition (the three elements of structural background factors that make up the "objective" dimension referred to earlier) exercise considerable influence on parental functionality. Winch (1962) defines functionality as the specific benefits or resources that parents pass on to their children. The greater the social position and the greater the occurrence of urban experience, along with intact households, the greater the level of "benefits" that parents pass on to their children. What are some of these specific benefits?

These benefits consist mostly of what I earlier called the subjective orientations parents pass on to their children. One such orientation involves urging their children to get as much education as they can, specifically because they are Black. Although education is critical to white and Black achievement alike, it may be more crucial to Blacks because of white economic discrimination and because other avenues of Black mobility (e.g., entrepreneurship) have been more restricted. In any case, one study (Scanzoni, 1977: 67) reported a substantial amount of that specific sort of parental functionality—Black parents stressing education to their children for racial reasons. Interestingly enough, Black women in the sample were more likely than Black men to report that their mothers were more insistent in stressing this particular orientation than were their fathers.

Alongside the emphasis on acquiring education there is evidence that Black parents in the study provided their children actual help or assistance in actually getting educated. On one hand, this help was intangible in the form of "continual reinforcement to go to school and to remain there as long as possible" (Scanzoni, 1977: 70). Moreover, Black (as do white) parents in the study explicitly encourage their children to "get ahead in life," and provided both "material help" and "counsel and example," to try to achieve that aspiration: "She had a value system that was a middle-class standard, not like poor people" (Scanzoni, 1977: 79). Another respondent stated, "He has given me the incentive to get ahead."

In addition to these tangible and intangible emphases on achievement for both sexes, there was some evidence that Black parents in the study made conscious efforts to socialize their sons not only to be "good providers," but also to be able to perform household chores as well. As one male put it, he was taught "all the ways of caring for a family—cook, wash, iron, sew, care for babies, wash diapers, and keep house" (Scanzoni, 1977: 83). Significantly, Billingsley (1968: 25) cites additional studies showing similar involvement of Black men in household chores, but notes that the researchers reporting these findings interpreted them to mean that the men were "henpecked or under the domination of their strongly matriarchal wives." By way of contrast, in today's climate those kinds of male behaviors are interpreted to mean greater marital egalitarianism. Thus, not only are white families becoming more like Black families with regard to female paid employment patterns, there also is an apparent growing convergence in the idea of the legitimacy of male participation in household chores (Pleck, 1982).

IDENTIFICATION WITH PARENTS

The greater the level of "functionality" (i.e., the tangible and intangible benefits provided by parents), the more likely it is for offspring to identify with parents. "Identify" here means that offspring draw upon parents as role models in order to shape their lives in some ways after their parents' lives. Some literature on lower-class Black families suggests that parent-child identification is highly problematic

(Schulz, 1969). If that is so, it is due in no small measure to the lack of benefits, or resources, that lower-class parents (Black or white) are able to supply their children. As resources are increased—as in families above the underclass—children reciprocate with stronger identification patterns. As several different respondents expressed it, "He was ambitious and so am I"; "I wanted to be reliable and dependable and have people trust in me as they did her"; "I wanted to be kind like my father—walk in his footsteps" (Scanzoni, 1977: 105-106).

SOCIAL POSITION OF OFFSPRING

Figure 6.2 explains in greater detail than does Figure 6.1 the social position of male offspring in the Scanzoni study. The father's occupation and education indicate the tangible resources supplied to sons. In other words, as fathers with resources share them with their offspring, sons try to shape their lives after their parents' lives. Next, as they identify with their parents, this tends to increase the level of education that sons seek and actually attain. Finally, the combination of son's own education plus parental tangible and intangible benefits enhance the occupationl prestige (and income) level of the son. Thus, in Black (and white) society the culmination of complex cross-generational and intragenerational influences lies with the kind of job the person attains, whether it is telephone installer, bricklayer, clerk, executive, bus driver, or factory worker. Furthermore, as I observed earlier, given the continuing family changes in our society, this sort of model can apply as much to daughters as to sons. As achievement eventually becomes as important to daughters as it has been to sons, and as parents come to socialize their daughters in the same ways they have been socializing their sons, we may expect women's and men's achievements to be explained by the same sets of factors (Mott, 1982).

CONTINUING GENERATIONS

Moreover, as Figure 6.1 indicates, the chain of resources, identification, and achievement continues beyond the offspring generation to their own children, both females and males. In the Scanzoni (1977) study, the offspring generation was the only one interviewed. They were asked about their parents' orientations and behaviors, as well as about their orientations and behaviors regarding themselves and their children. Responses regarding their children are the basis for asserting

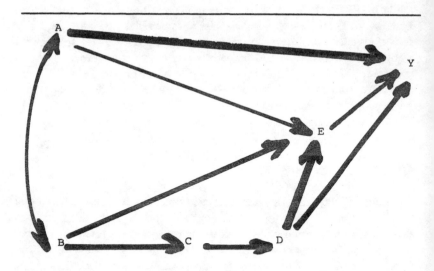

SOURCE: Adapted from Scanzoni (1977: 175).

NOTE: A = father's occupation; B = mother's occupation; C = parental functionality; D = identification with parents; E = son's (daughter's) education; F = son's (daughter's) occupation.

Figure 6.2   Chain of Influence on Son's (or Daughter's) Occupation

that many contemporary Black parents above the underclass want their own children to get ahead in life, and that they tend to believe the children's chances of actually doing so are reasonably good (Scanzoni, 1977: 276-281). And, as their parents did for them, they encourage their own children to become as well educated as possible and to choose their peers prudently based on the reasoning that peers can enhance or seriously hinder the child's life—both personally and in terms of subsequent achievements (1977: 284-286).

Of particular significance is the finding that the higher the job level of the parent (greater prestige and income), the more likely she or he is to state that the "most important thing a child can learn" in life is to "think for him/herself," that is, to be autonomous (Scanzoni, 1977: 292). Studies of American whites and Europeans reported the same positive relationship between social class and the kinds of contrasting values parents pass on to children (Kohn, 1978). Parents (Black and white) who have not attained as well as other parents state that children should learn to obey more than anything else. In a modern society, autonomy increases the child's chances for achievement, while mere obedience tends to reduce those chances. And the more advantaged Black parents are, the more likely they are to try to instill a sense of autonomy into their children. Hence, once more we find a basic convergence between Black and white families above the underclass. Whether consciously or not, those Black (and white) parents appear to sense the need to stimulate "independent thinking" in their children in the hope that autonomy can enhance their children's achievements.

SUMMARY

In terms of the patterns surrounding child achievement, Black families above the underclass appear to be more similar than dissimilar from comparable white families. Not that Blacks are merely imitating whites; instead they, like whites, simply are responding to the sorts of pressures and forces intrinsic to fostering child achievement in modern societies. Nevertheless, a basic distinction between Black and white families lies with their relative accessibility to tangible resources. As many Blacks continue to have less access than whites, and given the importance of those kinds of resources, their capabilities of preparing Black children to participate effectively in the world of work is correspondingly reduced. In spite of those externally imposed limitations, however, many contemporary Black parents continue patterns learned from their own parents in supplying both tangible and intangible resources requisite for their children's achievements.

NOTE

1. A recent report drawing on Census and other demographic data (Schneider, 1983) demonstrates continuing poverty and unemployment in a vast arc of rural (nonmetro) southern counties stretching from Virginia to Louisiana. The consequences for family-type issues in these counties are likely the same as those demonstrated years ago by Rainwater and others.

REFERENCES

BILLINGSLEY, A. (1968) Black Families in White America. Englewood Cliffs, NJ: Prentice-Hall.

BLAU, P. M. and O. D. DUNCAN (1967) The American Occupational Structure. New York: John Wiley.

Connecticut Mutual Life Report in the '80s (1981) The Impact of Belief. Hartford, CT: Connecticut Mutual Life Insurance Co.

HILL, R. and P. MATTESICH (1979) "Family development theory and life-span development," pp. 162-204 in P. B. Baltes and O. G. Brim, Jr. (eds.) Life-Span Development and Behavior, Vol. 2. New York: Academic.

KOHN, M. L. (1978) Class and Conformity. Chicago: Univ. of Chicago Press.

MILLER, S. M. (1964) "The American lower classes: a typological approach," pp. 9-23 in A. B. Shostak and W. Gomberg (eds.) Blue Collar World. Englewood Cliffs, NJ: Prentice-Hall.

MOTT, F. L. [ed.] (1982) The Employment Revolution: Young American Women in the 1970s. Cambridge: MIT Press.

NOBLE, J. L. (1964) "The American Negro woman," pp. 114-163 in J. P. Davis (ed.) The American Negro Reference Book. Englewood Cliffs, NJ: Prentice-Hall.

PLECK, J. H. (1982) "Changing patterns of work and family roles." Wellesley College. (unpublished)

RAINWATER, L. (1970) Behind Ghetto Walls. Chicago: Aldine.

RODGERS-ROSE, L. F. (1980) The Black Woman. Beverly Hills, CA: Sage.

SCANZONI, J. (1977) The Black Family in Modern Society: Patterns of Stability and Security. Chicago: Univ. of Chicago Press.

SCHNEIDER, K. (1983) "An arc of misery." Boston Globe (September 18): A3.

SCHULZ, D. A. (1969) Coming Up Black. Englewood Cliffs, NJ: Prentice-Hall.

U.S. Department of Health and Human Services (1980) "Selected demographic characteristics of teenage wives and mothers." Washington, DC: Public Health Service, Office of Health Research, Statistics, and Technology, 61.

WINCH, F. (1962) Identification and Its Familial Determinants. Indianapolis: Bobbs-Merrill.

7

EMPOWERING BLACK CHILDREN'S
EDUCATIONAL ENVIRONMENTS

JAMES P. COMER

Illiteracy in the Black population has been reduced from 95% in 1865 to 10% in 1940 and to about 4% today. School enrollment among Blacks and whites now is about equal. On the other hand, the quality of Black education leaves much to be desired. The Scholastic Aptitude Test scores for college-bound Blacks in 1982 were approximately 100 points below those of Whites. And the problem is equally, if not more, unsatisfactory for noncollege-bound students and dropouts.

Prior to the 1900s, a poor quality education and school dropouts were not problems. Even though Blacks worked primarily in the secondary job market—domestics, agricultural, and industrial laborers without training programs, upward mobility, and benefits—it still was possible without an education to earn a living, take care of a family, and experience the psychological and social sense of well being related to being able to do so. Workers, so affected, gave strength and stability to Black institutions such as the church, fraternal orders, and others and, in turn, received a sense of belonging, purpose, and worth from them.

Times have changed. Job and business opportunities have been greatly influenced by the course of the Industrial Revolution. From approximately 1900 to 1940, work changed from agriculture and early industry to heavy industry, and most workers needed moderate education and training to earn a living. Between the 1940s and the 1970s, scientific and technological development again changed the nature of work and the economy, and a worker needed a high level of education and training to be reasonably secure on the job market. In the period since the 1970s, the postindustrial age, even well-educated and trained people are not secure on the job market.

Thus, after the beginning of the twentieth century the educational and training demands needed to be successful on the job market began to change with each generation. Educational requirements for most jobs have increased, even when the specific skills needed to do the job do not require increased education levels. In short, education has become a ticket of admission to "living wage" jobs. Also, today's jobs—both service and the production of goods—require a high level of personal development needed for interaction with others and task performance. A disproportionate number of low-income Black children are disadvantaged here for historical reasons.

Heads of households who were able to obtain living wage jobs in the pre-1940s period had the best chance of caring for their families and experiencing a sense of well-being. They were in the best position to give strength and stability to their families and other institutions to which they belonged. Children in such an environment were best able to take advantage of school opportunities and participate in the job market of the next generation, and, in turn, prepare their children to participate in the job market of subsequent generations.

The immigration and development of the major body of Europeans and Asians (1865-1915) paralleled the course of the Industrial Revolution. Although they faced ethnic and racial discrimination, they were not denied political freedom. Ultimately, the latter led to political, economic, and educational opportunities that permitted large numbers of such families and communities to undergo the kind of three-generational development described above. Most settled in the North, East, and West, where industrial development and educational opportunities were most advanced. The situation was different for Blacks.

A large segment of the Black population found organization, belonging, worth, and purpose through participation in the Black church and other Black community-based institutions. And, as mentioned, they found work at the lowest level of the job market in the larger society. Nonetheless, many families enmeshed in this social network were able to undergo a three-generational family and community development similar to that of other Americans. But excluded from the political, economic, and educational mainstream, a disproportionate number of Blacks were not in a position to compensate for the effects of slavery.

A significant segment of the Black population was severely traumatized by a slave system that promoted dependency, self and group harmful passive-aggressive, here and now pleasure-oriented, rather than long-range achievement behavior, low self and group confidence and esteem, and other problems. This segment of the population was least able to create and participate in constructive Black community institutions or fully utilize the meager job and educational opportunities in the larger society.

The larger society made little effort to compensate for the trauma of slavery. Indeed, it did the opposite—excluded Blacks from primary wealth opportunities associated with land "giveways" in the nineteenth and early twentieth century, secondary wealth related to political and business activities, and tertiary wealth due to union programs and other social policies. The larger society spent 4 to 8 times as much money on the education of white children in primary and secondary schools—up to 25 times as much where Blacks were disproportionately large in numbers—in the eight southern states that had 80% of the black population. This was the case right up until the late 1940s. The endowment of two colleges for white women was more than that of all 100 Black colleges put together as late as the mid-1960s.

In addition, Blacks experienced social harassment, as extreme as frequent lynchings and as pervasive in nature as separate drinking fountains and toilets, right up until the 1940s. The psychosocial effects of all these conditions were extremely adverse. Thus, racist social policies and practices during and after slavery limited the development of the stable Black community and made it difficult to impossible for the traumatized Black community to compensate. Conditions only began to improve in the 1960s, and much subtle racism still remains and negatively affects Black families.

By the 1960s, the nation was already at the last stage of the Industrial Revolution, in which a high level of education and training was needed to be reasonably competitive on the job market. But as a result of past racist social policy, a significant segment of the Black community was undeveloped. In fact, many of the once stable Black families from the rural church culture prior to the 1940s destabilized in the industry-based urban communities and began a three-generational downward social spiral. This has led to a paradoxical condition in the Black community. Black families who managed to stabilize and obtain reasonably high levels of education and training are receiving better opportunities than ever before in the history of the country. Blacks who were traumatized, denied compensatory opportunities, and now are underdeveloped socially and educationally—and as a consequence psychologically troubled—are in more distress than any time since American slavery. The latter produce children at greater risk for social and educational underdevelopment, unemployment, and social and psychological problems.

At greatest risk are children born into female-headed households, particularly to teenage women. This primarily is because such families are more often poor. And, despite some exceptions, teenage mothers are themselves underdeveloped and less likely to promote optimal development of their children. Such parents are less often a part of supportive extended families and social networks today than in the pre-1940s period and, therefore, are under greater stress. They are more often out-of-wedlock, single-parent families.

The percentage of female heads of households among all Black families increased from 8.3% in 1950 to 31% in 1970 to 40% in 1981. The proportion of out-of-wedlock births to older (18 and 19 years old) and younger (15 to 17 years old) Black women rose to 79% and 93% respectively by 1979. Black women with four years of college education, and under less social and economic stress, have fertility and out-of-wedlock pregancy rates lower than those of their white counterparts.

Schools serving Black children from families under stress too often focus on the academic problems without understanding their relationship to the reality—past and present—of the Black experience. In addition to racial distrust and alienation, class and other issues must be taken into account. High mobility and mass communication have removed school people and other important role model authority figures from local school communities and brought increased information about the outside world into such communities. Differences are not attenuated by familiarity.

The hierarchical, authoritarian organization and mangement of the school makes it rigid and unable to respond to the challenge of modern times, particularly in schools serving low-income, minority group children. In a school in which there is distrust and alienation, class, racial, style, goal, and opportunity differences, the potential for conflict is high. It often is realized at the expense of quality teaching and learning, unless the school environment—interactions between parents, teachers, administrators, and students—is mutually supportive.

The Yale Child Study Center School Development Program was designed with an appreciation of the effects of racism and social and economic change. The primary mechanism to promote appropriate school change was a governance and management structure that could develop a supportive school environment, promote acceptable teaching and learning, and prepare children from low-income, minority group backgrounds for successful work and life performance in the world of today and tomorrow.

THE SCHOOL DEVELOPMENT PROGRAM

In 1968 two public schools were selected to participate in the School Development Program (SDP)—Martin Luther King, Jr. (K-4), about 240 students, and Simeon Baldwin (K-6), more than 300 students. The student population at both schools was 99% Black. Over 90% came from low-income families, with over 50% of the families receiving Aid for Dependent Children. Students at both schools had low scores on standardized tests in reading and mathematics. Both schools were faced with chronic and extensive behavior problems and poor attendance by both students and teachers. Initial work with the schools involved a four-person mental health team consisting of a psychiatrist (program director, Dr. James P. Comer), psychologist, social worker, and a mental health-oriented helping teacher from the Child Study Center.

The school intervention process developed by the SDP was a system-level primary prevention approach, which addresses all aspects of the school's operation, not a particular group of individuals or any particular pretargeted aspect of the school. The overall goal was to improve students' academic achievement by focusing on two subordinate goals: (1) students' psychological adjustment and skills and (2) the school climate—the attitudes and interactions of staff, students, and parents.

The mental health team did not attempt to directly modify the behavior of school staff, parents, or children. Instead, it facilitated successful program implementation through the application of mental health knowledge and skills to every aspect of the school programs. The critical program interaction was between the Child Study Center mental health team and the school governance and management body.

One member of the mental health team served on that body and assisted it in applying child development, behavior, and systems management knowledge, skills, and sensitivities to all of the programs it developed within the school. The mental health team person, as a member of the school governance and management group, helped to develop, implement, and evaluate programs within the school to address academic, behavioral, and psychological adjustment, parent participation, and staff development problems and opportunities. In this way, the school program brought previously distrustful and alienated groups together, was made sensitive to child development and relationship issues, was based on needs indicated by all program participants and not just the principal, and prevented problems rather than created them.

The four basic components of the program will be discussed below in greater detail. Although the critical interaction was between the mental health team and the governance and management body, the mental health team provided guidance and support to all three program components: the school governance and management body, the parents' program, and the curriculum and staff development program. These programs are described further as follows.

(1) *The Mental Health Team.* This team
    (a) worked with the governance and management body to enable it to base its academic, social climate, and staff development programs on mental health, child development principles;
    (b) facilitated the many interactions between parents and school staff to improve the social climate and cooperation throughout the school community;
    (c) worked with classroom teachers and parents to identify children who needed special services;
    (d) set up individualized programs for children with special needs, using the school's special education facilities and staff and other school-based or outside services as necessary and possible;
    (e) worked with classroom teachers to develop classroom strategies to prevent minor problems from becoming major;
    (f) offered ongoing consultation to all school staff to bridge the gap between special education and general classroom activities; and
    (g) provided consultation and training workshops to staff and parents on child development, human relations, and other mental health issues.

(2) *The School Governance and Management Body.* The school governance and management body included the school principal, a mental health team member, and representatives selected by teachers and parents. This group
    (a) met on a regular basis to carry out systematic school planning, resource assessment and mobilization, program implementation, and program evaluation and modification;
    (b) established policy guidelines in all aspects of the school program—academic, social, and staff development;
    (c) worked closely with the parent group to plan an annual school calendar to integrate social, academic, and staff development functions; and

(d) worked to facilitate social skill development and academic learning.

(3) *The Parents Program.* The parents program included one parent classroom assistant 10 hours per week in each classroom. Parents "graduated" from this position when their children graduated or left the school. This program assisted and encouraged parents to

(a) participate in the general parent-teacher membership group, which planned and implemented social and extracurricular activities (in cooperation with the governance and management group) in support of the school academic, social, and psychological development goals for students;

(b) select two or three members to serve on the governance and management group;

(c) assist classroom teachers for special events or field trips;

(d) become more closely involved in their child's education through parent-teacher conferences, home learning activities, or special classroom visits and through sponsoring teacher-led workshops for parents; and

(e) address issues of personal or family development through workshops or discussions on topics of importance to parents.

(4) *The Curriculum and Staff Development Program.* The curriculum and staff development program focused on the specific needs of teachers, although parents and mental health team members were included in the planning and implementation of the specific activities. This program

(a) integrated academic, arts, social, and extracurricular activities into a unified curriculum;

(b) encouraged teachers to develop special curriculum units in skill areas most needed in underdeveloped student populations—government, business, health and nutrition, and leisure/spiritual time activities;

(c) organized and facilitated periodic workshops (for teachers and parents) based on identified needs and program objectives at the building level rather than central office level; and

(d) developed new skills in areas such as teaching based on child development principles, positive teacher-student relations, teacher-parent cooperation, and innovative reading and mathematics teaching techniques and materials.

PROGRAM EVOLUTION

The program components and process described above were not created in a systematic and orderly fashion. The program emerged out of difficult and sometimes chaotic conditions in both schools. In the first year of the program, staff members were angry with one another and often worked at cross purposes. Cooperation and collaboration were not possible. Parents were angry and disappointed with the project. And in such an environment children were anxious and acted out or withdrew and became apathetic. A project director, and not our mental health team, was responsible for the day-to-day management of administrative matters. Thus, we had only our professional expertise to help us gain the parent-staff confidence needed to be able to improve the school environment. Several incidents gave us this opportunity.

In a fit of rage, a 10-year-old in the third grade smashed the window in the door of his classroom. He was withdrawn from the classroom temporarily to allow him and his teacher to cool off and to permit the staff to map a strategy to help him succeed in school. Our mental health team, serving as a pupil personnel service, helped his teacher and other staff members to examine the problem in the manner of clinicians in a case conference. Rather than labeling the youngster as bad or "slow," we explored the dynamics of the case. The student had a minor reading disability and there were serious family problems. His mother was depressed and separated from his father. The youngster lived with his mother and siblings and sorely missed the father. He was impulsive, emotionally fragile, and embarrassed and defensive about being two years behind in school. He exploded at the least suggestion that he was behind. Yet he was taunted by other students.

A plan was worked out based on the knowledge that impulsive children often cannot handle the stimulation of the average classroom. They become more disorganized and unruly as the day goes on. To the extent possible, the plan addressed his family problem and his impulsiveness and reading disability. In a meeting that included his teacher, father, the principal, the social worker, and the student, it was agreed that he would have to gradually work his way back into the classroom and school an hour at a time. Increasing the time would be based on his ability to manage the environment. Staff members were to assist him as needed.

Because he longed to be with a male figure and because he needed prestige and higher self-esteem, he spent the first hour assisting the male principal. When he was able to do this in a responsible way, a second hour with a reading teacher was added. When he felt he could tolerate additional time, a half hour in his regular classroom was added. And, finally, his classroom teacher spent a half hour with him while the helping teacher took her class for a special project. All of the adults involved helped him learn how to handle his feelings more appropriately and finally he indicated that he could make it an entire day, and he did.

An incident with a transfer student led to changing the entire process of bringing new students into the school. An orientation program was developed that reduced much transfer student anxiety and eliminated related fighting and other acting-out behavior. In another incident, the mental health team helped the staff discover why a child was mute in the classroom and provided assistance that eventually allowed the child and the family to fully participate in the school program. The child had set a fire that burned down the family home, but had not been able to tell his parents. Several different teachers had heard bits and pieces of the story. By talking together in a pupil service seminar, they were able to figure out what had happened and to assist the family. This confirmed and reinforced the need for communication, sharing of information, and collaboration among staff members.

The mental health team helped teachers develop strategies for helping angry children leave the classroom without embarrassing themselves and disrupting the school. A crisis unit was established that helped children learn how to express and manage their angry feelings in a less disruptive way. A program was established to keep children with the same teacher for two years. This came about when a child smiled at a teacher for the first time after eight months in her classroom. The teacher realized that the semester would be over in two months and there would be no way to carry over the trust just developing and use it to help a student be motivated to learn. With the understanding that many low-income children experience great discontinuity of adult figures in their lives, and more abuse, this program was established to increase continuity with a mature and trusted adult—the teacher. A number of students who made little to no academic gain the first year made up to two years of academic gain by the end of the second year with the same teacher.

IMPACT

Each one of these incidents and interventions increased the trust of the school staff and parents and the influence of the mental health team. The ability of the mental health team member serving on the school governance and management body to influence policies and programs was greatly enhanced. Each incident reduced the conflict among parents, teachers, and administrators in the school. The system management changes that occurred increased the sense of orderliness and direction. Staff energy, which once was tied up in anger and conflict, now was released and available for the academic tasks.

As the climate of the school improved and the students appeared more interested in learning, parent participation in the program increased. In addition to the two or three parents serving on the governance and management body, a large number of parents began to serve on the general membership group and put on activities in support of the school programs. This was in a cooperative effort with the school staff. Parent participation and shared sponsorship led to the development of programs that were consistent with, and reflective of, the best aspect of the community culture outside of the school. There were potluck suppers, school dances, fashion shows, and a variety of other activities. Some of these programs raised money to support trips for the youngsters and other academic programs.

The good climate of relationships allowed the staff to develop positive attitudes about the students and to develop an academic program that recognized many as underdeveloped but able. They set high-level goals for the students. Better feelings about themselves as teachers allowed them to acknowledge that they had areas of weakness. They planned and developed building-level staff development programs based on their academic goals for the children and their own needs. All of these activities led to an environment that facilitated teaching, learning, and child growth and development. This new atmosphere created higher levels of confidence and expectation among all involved and, in turn, an upward spiral of staff, parent, and student performance.

PROGRAM ASSESSMENT AND MODIFICATION

At the end of the first five years of the program there was a careful assessment of what worked and what did not. It was clear that didactic lectures about child development and human relations did not work, but the application of child development and behavioral and social science principles to every aspect of the school through various program components did work. It also was clear that as students developed social and interactional skills, aggressive and troublesome behavior declined.

The overall improvement in school climate or environment also was important.

The program was discontinued in Baldwin School. But observing the improved social and academic performance of the students in Baldwin and King over the first five years, the staff argued that the students should be able to perform as well as many middle-income students. It was felt that many of the students came to school underdeveloped in certain skill areas, but that these skills could be taught; that many of the students felt undersupported, but that the school environment could be modified to be supportive. It was decided that a program that more consciously and systematically provided the youngsters with the skills that middle-income children gain simply by growing up with their parents should result in the expected grade level academic performance for our low-income students. The program was entitled, "A Social Skills Curriculum for Inner-City Children." This program was initiated in 1975 and carried out in King School and field-tested in Katherine Brennan (K-5) school.

The process of developing this program began with asking parents and staff what aspirations they had for the children and what skills they would need to accomplish them. It was determined that they would need social and academic skills in several performance areas—politics and government, business and economics, health and nutrition, and leisure/spiritual time. In addition to carrying on the unsual academic program, activity units were developed geared to these performance areas. Units, which integrated the teaching of the basic academic skills, the arts, and social skills, were developed for each activity area. The first activity unit developed is illustrative of the process.

The politics and government unit was developed just before an election in the city. Third- and fourth-grade students involved in the unit wrote letters of invitation and follow-up "thank you" notes to the candidates. These were language arts, social science, and social skills activities. The parents and teachers—using funds raised from parent program activities—rented a bus and took the children around the town. During the ride the adults pointed out various conditions and the students and adults discussed their relationship to politics and government. This was a social science lesson. They returned to the school and wrote papers about their trip, a language arts and social science lesson.

The teachers and parents taught the children how to raise questions with the candidates in a direct but responsible fashion. They also taught the children to be hosts for visiting parents and the candidates. These all were social skills lessons. The students created and practiced a dance drama program to present to their parents and the candidates on this occasion, the involvement of the arts and self-expression. The activity was highly successful and all involved experienced a sense of achievement and belonging within the school and to the larger political process.

An evaluation of the activity showed that a number of unregistered parents then registered and voted. Youngsters had significantly higher knowledge of the political process and knew the names of many more officials at the local, state, and national levels. All of the four activity area units had similar outcomes. Students and parents were stimulated and motivated by this program. Indeed, many of the parents most involved in the project eventually left the school and took jobs they would not have had the confidence to apply for before being involved in the program. Six parents that we know of returned to and completed high school and then college and now are professional people. Three of these parents, and many of the nonprofessional working parents, were receiving Aid for Dependent Children prior to their involvement in the school program.

It is the impression of middle and high school staff that children from our project elementary schools perform better academically and socially than students from the same socioeconomic background who did not attend the project schools. We now are doing a systematic study to determine whether this is the case.

RESULTS

As planned, our Child Study Center mental health team has been out of the school buildings since 1980, and now provides indirect support as indicated. The intervention techniques have been internalized by school staff and the program is being carried on by them.

Brennan School serves a low-income housing project and King School ranks approximately twentieth of 25 schools on the New Haven school system "affluence indicator." Since 1975, King School has not had a voluntary teacher transfer. One teacher was recruited away for a new program and returned, at her request, the next year. Two teachers have been promoted to positions outside the school. Brennan School has not had a voluntary transfer since 1975. A teacher lost to Brennan because of a temporary decline in the school population requested and received a transfer to King and replaced one of the teachers promoted out of that building.

The same principal was at King for 14 years, until he went on a sabbatical leave to become a fellow at the Child Study Center. He now is

TABLE 7.1   Mean Grade Equivalent Scores in Reading and
            Mathematics Graders at King and Brennan Schools

Year	Date	Expected Score	Reading	Math
King School				
1969-1970	Oct. 1969	4.2	3.0	2.9
1977-1978	Oct. 1977	4.2	3.4	3.7
1978-1979	Oct. 1978	4.2	3.6	3.9
1979-1980	Oct. 1979	4.2	3.9	4.0
1980-1981	April 1981	4.8	4.5	4.8
1981-1982	April 1982	4.8	4.4	4.9
1982-1983	April 1983	4.8	5.2	4.9
1983-1984	April 1984	4.8	5.5	5.5
Brennan School				
1969-1970	Oct. 1969	4.2	3.1	3.5
1977-1978	Oct. 1977	4.2	3.2	3.2
1978-1979	Oct. 1978	4.2	3.4	3.6
1979-1980	Oct. 1979	4.2	3.5	3.7
1980-1981	April 1981	4.8	4.2	4.3
1981-1982	April 1982	4.8	4.2	4.2
1982-1983	April 1983	4.8	4.8	5.1
1983-1984	April 1984	4.8	5.4	5.9

SOURCE: Data compiled by Dr. Martin Klotz, Coordinator of Research and Evaluation, New Haven Public School and Dr. Muriel Hamilton-Lee.
NOTE: 1969-1970 scores are from the Metropolitan Achievement Test; all other scores are from the IOWA Test of Basic Skills.

attempting to utilize the principles of our model in another school without our direct support. The same principal was at Brennan School from 1975 to 1980. He spent a fellowship year at the Child Study Center in 1980-1981 and now is a regional director in the New Haven school system with responsibility, in part, for disseminating the principles of our model. Achievement improvement under the new principal continues.

Both schools use texts, equipment, and the curriculum utilized throughout the city. According to Census track data, the socioeconomic level of the communities has remained the same over the last 10 years. It is the subjective impression of the staffs that it has, in fact, declined.

DISSEMINATION AND DISCUSSION

Evidence of program success made dissemination of our project model a logical next step. Two events facilitated this effort. First, a new

TABLE 7.2   Standardized Test Scores for King School, Grade 4

		Number of Months Below National Grade Level Norms	
Year	Text Administered	Reading	Math
1969-1972	Metropolitan Achievement Test	19*	18*
1973-1976	no testing		
May 1977	Metropolitan Achievement Test	9	5
May 1978	Metropolitan Achievement Test	8	3
Oct. 1978	IOWA Test of Basic Skills	6	3
Oct. 1979**	IOWA Test of Basic Skills	2	2

NOTE: In 1979 a total language score was computed on the IOWA best of Basic Skills. King fourth-grade students scored at grade level.
*Average based on scores during the three years indicated.
**For results since 1979, see Table 6.1.

TABLE 7.3   Average Percentage in Attendance: M. L. King and K. Brennan Schools, 1975-1983

Year	All Elementary Schools	M. L. King	(Rank)	K. Brennan	(Rank)
1975-1976	90.3	92.9	(6)	91.1	(14)
1976-1977	91.2	94.5	(2)	92.6	(8)
1977-1978	90.3	93.0	(4)	91.7	(11)
1978-1979	91.0	93.8	(3)	93.3	(7)
1979-1980	90.8	93.6	(4)	93.7	(2)
1980-1981	90.6	94.2	(1)	91.3	(13)
1981-1982	88.6	94.1	(2)	93.5	(4)
1982-1983	88.8	95.0	(1)	93.0	(5)

SOURCE: Office of Research and Evaluation, New Haven Public Schools.

school superintendent, Dr. Gerald Tirozzi, in 1977 encouraged us to participate in his effort to improve all New Haven elementary schools. Second, in connection with a school desegregation settlement, the Benton Harbor, Michigan school system expressed interest in our model and proposed dissemination methods.

We were aware that our model—an outside mental health team made up of a psychologist, social worker, psychiatrist, and a helping teacher—was too expensive for most school systems. Also, we had evidence from our practical experience that our knowledge, skills, and sensitivities were being picked up by educators with whom we were working. This was reasonable in that there was nothing magical or profound about what we were doing. We simply were applying basic social and behavioral science concepts to school programs through the system management vehicle—the governance and management group. To our knowledge, this approach had not been used before, but we believed that it could be taught.

To this end, the Yale Child Study Center established a fellowship for educators (also called the "Leadership Development Program") of one-year duration. Educators are immersed in a mental health environment through five seminars, including one that provides the theoretical framework for our intervention approach. A second aspect of the fellowship is a special project, of interest to them and their respective school systems, in which educators apply mental health knowledge, skill, and sensitivity to project management. And, third, they participate in selected aspects of the New Haven school system program, particularly the New Haven Urban Academy.

The Urban Academy is the major school system improvement effort. It is governed by a representative body—the superintendent, central office administrators and principals, teachers, Yale Child Study Center and the University of Connecticut, pupil personnel service representatives, and parents—similar to the governance and management body operating at the building level. It developed a two-tiered program. Tier 1 is a monthly series of lectures designed to introduce all New Haven school system principals to school improvement possibilities. The initial six Tier 2 schools included our two project schools and four others. The number of Tier 2 schools increases each year as Tier 1 schools show a readiness and there is sufficient support for them. There are now ten schools at the Tier 2 level, eight elementary and two middle schools. The Tier 1 schools utilize an "instructional plan for improvement," developed largely by the University of Connecticut, and the Tier 2 schools integrate this plan into the more comprehensive school development plan worked out in our initial project schools.

Four educators have completed work in our leadership development program. Two are involved in helping other principals implement, and one is directly involved in implementing, the Tier 2 model in New Haven schools. Two currently are participating in the fellowship. The educator from Benton Harbor is serving as a change agent in the Benton Harbor school system. With the support of the superintendent, Dr. James Hawkins, she has established an Urban Academy. Four elementary schools are involved at the Tier 2 level. During the 1982-1983 academic year, the four schools met their first-year academic goals, ten months of achievement in reading and mathematics during a ten-month period of school.

Thus, there is evidence in New Haven and Benton Harbor that the Yale Child Study Center School Development Program is an effective way to improve the academic performance of low-income, minoity group children. In addition, improved attendance and social performance on the part of teachers, parents, and students suggests that the program meets the social and psychological needs of all involved. The program provides children with skills that they can use as adults. There is initial evidence that educators, as well as mental health personnel, can provide the knowledge, skill, and sensitivity necessary to create a good school environment and, in turn, improve teaching and learning.

Obviously, school programs cannot compensate for the economic and resultant family stress conditions experienced by too many Blacks. But schools attuned to Black community history and needs represent one of the best opportunities to prepare more Black youngsters for successful performance in school and life. Good schools can provide support for families of current students and, in turn, the families of these students in the future.

8

REEXAMINING THE
ACHIEVEMENT CENTRAL TENDENCY

Sex Differences Within Race and
Race Differences Within Sex

BRUCE R. HARE

Among the most pressing needs of the newly emergent concerns with the specific development of research in Black psychology is the necessity to develop a body of literature specifically directed toward the forwarding of information regarding the cognitive and achievement status of Black children. The necessity for such a development derives not so much from a lack of literature on Black children in general but, rather, from the failure of the existent literature to pay adequate attention to such diversities as might exist across racial and/or cultural lines. Furthermore, this is not to suggest that Black children have not been treated in the normative literature but, rather, that when they have been included in such studies, normative assumptions regarding their status relative to white children have created a literature in which their differences from such children generally have been defined as pathological deviations from the norm (Hare, 1977a). The prejudice of the existent literature thus leads us to require not just the consideration of alternative lines of explanation of such differences as might be found generally between Black and white children, but also to engage in subanalyses that, for example, might demonstrate patterns of sex differences among Black children that may differ in significant ways from the patterns that exist among white children (Hare, 1977a). Rather than reinvestigating the general race and sex differences that have been reported in the literature along cognitive and performance dimensions, this chapter specifically addresses two subareas of investigation.

First, given that the general sex literature (Maccoby and Jacklin, 1974) is based largely upon white, middle-class children and adults, it offers us limited information with reference to the possibilities of differences in patterns of sex differentiation across ethnic and cultural groups. Thus, this gap in our knowledge suggests the necessity to separately compare boys and girls within each racial group on dimensions of sex difference in order to investigate whether or not the general patterns of sex difference that have been reported hold, as well as whether the patterns within racial groups are similar or different. The second concern will be the subanalysis and comparison of race differences within sex groups. Thus, both the comparative analyses of white and Black boys and the comparative analyses of white and Black girls will be included in order to assess whether the general literature on race differences can be seen as an appropriate territory from which to generalize across sex lines.

The dimensions upon which the comparisons will be made are general self-esteem, area-specific (i.e., school, peer, and home) self-esteem, self-concept of ability, achievement orientation, anxiety, sense of control, importance of social abilities, and performance on standardized reading and mathematics achievement tests. The sample consisted of 582 10- and 11-year-old fifth-grade children who were surveyed in 1977.

The study raises four general questions for investigation: (1) Do Black boys and Black girls differ significantly in self-perception and achievement with socioeconomic background controlled? (2) Do white boys and white girls differ significantly in self-perception and achievement with socioeconomic background controlled? (3) Do Black boys and white boys differ significantly in self-perception and achievement with socioeconomic background controlled? (4) Do Black girls and white girls differ significantly in self-perception and achievement with socio-economic background controlled? Because of the sparsity of literature directed to the study of Black children, this chapter will be presented within the context of what is known about sex and race differences in general.

OVERVIEW

SEX DIFFERENCES

As previously stated, Maccoby and Jacklin (1974), in a massive review work on sex differences, indicated that the bulk of psychological work on sex differences has been done with middle-class, white American children and adults. The consequence of this analysis has been a sparsity of literature that would be specifically geared toward telling us the nature of such differences as may exist by sex among Black children. Nevertheless, the authors reported no significant sex differences in general self-esteem, confidence in task performance and achievement orientation, sense of control, or verbal reading and mathematics ability, although they report a tendency for girls to score higher in verbal abilities than boys at earlier ages. They also reported boys to be more independent, to have more positive peer interaction, to possess a higher self-concept of strength and potency, and to have lower anxiety scores than girls. There is little comparative sex data on area-specific (school, peer, and home) self-esteem. Some recent area-specific research by Hare (1977b) with a pooled sample of Black and white children of varying socioeconomic status (SES) backgrounds, however, reported no significant sex differences on these dimensions when race and SES were controlled. Although we would expect generally to find similar sex differences among Black boys and girls, we are concerned here with the possibility of varying patterns of sex difference across racial groups, perhaps as a function of cultural variations in sex role socialization.

Some researchers have hypothesized fewer sex differences among Black children and adults, arguing an egalitarian character to Black culture (Lewis, 1975). For example, Lewis posited, "the Black child to be sure distinguished between male and female, but unlike the white child, is not inculcated with standards which polarize expectations according to sex. Many of the behaviors which whites see as appropriate to one sex or the other, Blacks view as equally appropriate to both sexes or equally inappropriate to both sexes." Simmons and Rosenberg (1975) further reported, in discussing adults, that there is evidence that white females have lower self-esteem than white males, whereas Black females are at no disadvantage relative to Black males. The analysis will further allow us to ascertain whether the patterns of sex difference reported in the literature are applicable to our separate comparison of the white boys and girls in this sample.

RACE DIFFERENCES

Most studies of race differences have involved comparisons of white and Black children that have failed to test for sex differences. Thus, it becomes necessary to base our discussion on what is known about race differences in general, although the objective of this investigation will be to assess the degree to which patterns of race difference may vary within sex groups. There is a strong tradition reporting lower general self-esteem among Black children than white children (Clark and Clark, 1947; Kardiner and Ovesey, 1951; Grier and Cobb, 1968). The theoretical premise of this school of thought was succinctly stated by Kardiner and Ovesey (1951: 297) when they postulated, "the basic fact is that in the Negro aspiration level, good conscience and even good performance are irrelevant in face of the glaring fact that the Negro gets a poor reflection of himself in the behavior of whites, no matter what he does or what his merits are." The foundation of this assumption is that, as a people in a predominantly white culture, Blacks are incapable of rejecting the negative images of themselves that are forwarded by whites. This tradition typically was based on interpretive analyses of the reasons why Black children chose white dolls over Black dolls, the use of psychiatric patients, and other questionable projective and sampling techniques. Such studies additionally tended to operate under the normative assumption that whatever the white felt, or however they scored, was the standard. Thus, any deviations that Black subjects made from the presented white standard were characterized as pathological deviations from the norm, whether they scored lower or higher on such measures (Hare, 1975, 1980).

In contrast, more recent studies with larger, more representative samples and social class controls have ranged from finding no significant differences to finding Blacks scoring higher. There has been little cross-race research on area-specific self-esteem. Coopersmith's (1967) major work in this area used a restricted sample of white, male, middle-class preadolescents. More recent research by Hare (1977b), however, reported significant race difference only in school self-esteem, and a subsequent study by Hare (1980) reported no significant racial differences on any of the area-specific or general self-esteem measures. Significant race differences have been reported on other variables germane to this chapter. Blacks have been reported as having higher self-concepts of ability than whites (Hare, 1980), lower achievement orientation (Hare, 1980), lower sense of control (Coleman et al., 1966; Hare, 1980), higher concern with social abilities (Hare, 1980), and lower scores on standardized achievement test scores (Coleman et al., 1966; Hare, 1980). Again, it should be emphasized that these findings are from studies that did not compare the white and Black subjects within sex. That is to say, these were general comparisons of white and Black children that did not take into account the possibilities that patterns of race difference may differ among Black and white girls from the patterns that may be found among Black and white boys.

METHODS

SAMPLE

This study was conducted in the Champaign, Illinois school system in the spring of 1977. The city's population size is approximately 50,000 persons. Of the school district's children, 23% are Black. The system was desegregated in 1967, primarily through busing Black children and through a plan requiring each school building to be within 15% of the school district's minority population as well as within guidelines for desegregrated classrooms. The completed sample of over 500 subjects included all fifth graders in the district who consented to participate with parental approval and were in school on the days of the survey. I was able to obtain questionnaires from over 90% of the total fifth-grade population. In controlling for age, the sample was limited to 10- and 11-year-old fifth graders. The decision to choose fifth-grade students was based on a desire to select a population old enough to comprehend the measures, while still preadolescent and, therefore, theoretically, not likely to experience fluctuations in levels of esteem that may accompany changes in body image in adolescence. The literature supports the position that in ability and stability, children at this age are an ideal sample for this kind of study (Simmons et al., 1973).

INSTRUMENT

In order to investigate the self-esteem questions, a 30-item self-esteem scale was used. The scale combines ideas from the Rosenberg (1965) and Coopersmith (1967) models to create a measure that is sensitive and both general and area-specific. For additional information concerning the validity, reliability, and factor loading of this scale, the reader is referred to Shoemaker (1980) and Hare (1975). This 30-item general self-esteem scale consists of three 10-item subscales, a school self-esteem scale, a peer self-esteem scale, and a home self-esteem scale. A 7-item general self-esteem scale by Rosenberg also was included as an additional general self-esteem measure. Self-concept of ability was assessed by 5 of Brookover et al.'s (1965) items; academic achievement was measured by performance on the mathematics and reading sections of a standardized metropolitan achievement test administered district-wide in the fall of 1976; and sense of control was measured by Coleman et al.'s (1966) items measuring internal/external control. Highest scores on this measure are indicative of greater internality. Finally, achievement orientation was measured by Epp's (1975) 13-item scale, and social abilities by a series of items concerned with such factors as being good at sports and games, being popular, being popular with the other sex, which were developed by Hare in 1975. The following are sample items from the measures. General self-esteem was measured, for example, by the respondents being asked to strongly agree, agree, disagree, or strongly disagree with such statements as the following: "I feel I am a person of worth" and "I feel I do not have much to be proud of." School, peer, and home self-esteem were measured by responses to the following statements: "My teachers expect too much of me," "I often feel worthless in school," "Other people wish they were like me," "I have at least as many friends as other people my age," "My parents are proud of the kind of person I am," and "I often feel unwanted at home." Self-concepts of ability were measured by responses to such items as "How do you rate yourself in school ability compared to those in your classes?" and "Do you think you have the ability to go to college?" Sense of control was measured by response to such items as "Good luck is more important than hard work for success" and "People like me don't have much of a chance to be successful in life." Achievement orientation was measured by agreement or disagreement along the 4-point scale with such items as "It's mostly luck if one succeeds or fails" and "Nothing in life is worth the sacrifice of moving away from your family." Finally, social abilities were indicated by having the subjects rate such abilities as being good at sports and games, popular, and pretty or handsome.

Socioeconomic divisions were developed from the Blau and Duncan (1967) index of occupational status. The index was divided into thirds to categorize the occupation of head-of-household; thus, subjects from families falling below the index value of 34 are categorized as lower class, those between 34 and 64 were categorized as middle class, and those above were categorized as upper-middle class. The index was divided so that the first point approximated separation of manual from nonmanual labor and the second division approximated the point two-thirds of the way up the index.

ANALYSES

In order to investigate the questions, a series of 2 by 3 analyses of variance were used to control for SES when looking at race and sex effects as well as to test the significance of their interaction. It should be noted that this Statistical Package for the Social Sciences (SPSS) program adjusts for unequal cell size. Furthermore, the test reported here for each main factor effect (race or sex) is equivalent to the test for the unique proportion of the variance accounted for each factor in a hierarchical multiple regression analysis. As such, it is a conservative test of the importance of race and sex as the variance accounted for by race and SES or sex and SES is removed before assessing the significance of race and sex.

RESULTS

DIFFERENCES BETWEEN BLACK BOYS AND BLACK GIRLS

Whereas the literature reviewed on sex comparisons between white children or children in general revealed few differences, Black boys and girls in the sample differed on a variety of important dimensions (see Tables 8.1 and 8.2). The results are consistent with the literature on whites in this age group in reporting no significance sex differences among Blacks in general self-esteem or sense of control. The results also are consistent with the literature on whites in reporting Black boys scoring lower than Black girls in anxiety and reading achievement and in showing Black boys to trend toward a higher peer self-esteem and significantly higher ratings of the importance of social abilities. The results, however, differ significantly from the prior literature on white children in that Black boys scored significantly lower than their female counterparts in mathematics ability and achievement orientation and displayed a trend toward lower school self-esteem. Finally, there were no significant differences between Black boys and girls in home self-esteem or self-concept of ability. It should be noted that none of the sex by SES interactions was significant. In short, the data suggest some important sex differences between Black boys and girls, particularly with regard to the school-related dimensions of achievement orientation on which the girls hold clear advantage. The only dimension on which

TABLE 8.1 Significance of F Values from Two by Three ANOVA's for Compared Groups

Variables	1 Black Girls vs. Black Boys — Sex differences from Sex by SES ANOVA	2 Black Girls vs. White Girls — Race differences from Race by SES ANOVA	3 White Girls vs. White Boys — Sex differences from Sex by SES ANOVA	4 Black Boys vs. White Boys — Race differences from Race by SES ANOVA
Rosenberg Gen. Self-Esteem	0.354	0.720	0.007**b	.196
Hare General Self-Esteem	0.768	0.912	0.270	.275
Hare School Self-Esteem	0.082	0.779	0.542	.060
Hare Peer Self-Esteem	0.067	0.875	0.116	.789
Hare Home Self-Esteem	0.654	0.493	0.084	.397
Self-Concept of Ability	0.194	0.000**bl	0.509	.183
Achievement Orientation	0.042*g	0.012*w	0.127	.000***w
G. Anxiety	0.042*g	0.361	0.050*g	.691
Sense of Control	0.713	0.011*w	0.169	.031*w
Social Abilities	0.012*b	0.216	0.675	.000***bl
Read Ability	0.004**g	0.000***w	0.412	.000***w
Math Ability	0.026*g	0.003**w	0.294	.000***w
	n = 117	n = 291	n = 465	n = 291

NOTE: g = girls higher; b = boys higher; bl = Blacks higher; w = whites higher;
$*p < .05$ $**p < .01$ $***p < .001$

the Black boys scored higher than their female counterparts are the nonschool dimensions of social abilities and slightly higher peer self-esteem.

**TABLE 8.2 Means and Standard Deviations for All Groups
on All Measures**

Variables	Black Girls		Black Boys		White Girls		White Boys	
	Mean	S.D.	Mean	S.D.	Mean	S.D.	Mean	S.D.
Rosenberg Gen. Self-Esteem	20.87	4.02	21.20	3.37	21.69	3.99	22.63	3.53
Hare General Self-Esteem	88.85	12.05	88.40	11.39	90.55	14.00	91.86	11.59
Hare Peer Self-Esteem	27.42	4.36	29.04	4.53	28.04	4.99	28.76	4.94
Hare Home Self-Esteem	31.99	5.01	31.66	5.54	32.18	5.71	33.05	5.13
Self-Concept of Ability	19.39	3.06	18.54	3.85	18.25	3.72	18.52	3.19
Achievement Orientation	34.55	5.21	32.82	5.28	38.19	5.62	37.49	5.74
General Anxiety	14.54	6.89	11.84	6.54	12.25	7.19	10.38	11.44
Sense of Control	8.76	1.68	8.98	2.04	9.65	1.65	9.88	1.70
Social Abilities	31.43	5.05	33.66	3.89	30.85	4.68	31.06	4.41
Reading Ability	34.31	18.72	25.90	15.23	52.20	24.96	51.40	26.24
Math Ability	31.96	18.22	24.48	13.87	46.43	26.26	48.70	26.46
	n = 67		n = 50		n = 224		n = 241	

DIFFERENCES BETWEEN WHITE BOYS AND WHITE GIRLS

Consistent with the literature, white girls showed significantly higher anxiety than white boys. However, despite the existence of a traditional literature that also suggested that white girls might show some significantly higher reading and/or mathematics achievement, the results of this study indicated no significant differences by sex within the white group on standardized reading or mathematics achievement. An additional and rather surprising finding, given the literature that suggests no difference in general self-esteem among white children at this age, is that white boys showed significantly higher general self-esteem than their female counterparts at this age as measured by the Rosenberg scale. All other comparisons along the sex dimension among white children were found to be nonsignificant. Specifically, the white boys and girls did not differ significantly in school self-esteem, peer self-esteem, home self-esteem, achievement orientation, sense of control, or concern with social abilities.

DIFFERENCES BETWEEN BLACK BOYS AND WHITE BOYS

Consistent with more recent studies of race differences in general and area-specific self-esteem the results indicated no significant differences on any of these measures between Black and white boys with SES controlled. Nevertheless, as previous studies of race differences have reported, the Black boys scored significantly lower than white boys on sense of control, achievement orientation, and performance on standardized reading and mathematics achievement tests. The Black boys, however, scored significantly higher than the white boys on their concerns with such social abilities as being good at sports and games, being popular, and being popular with the opposite sex. It should again be noted that none of the race by SES interactions was significant.

DIFFERENCES BETWEEN BLACK GIRLS AND WHITE GIRLS

Consistent with the literature, white girls showed significantly higher standardized reading and mathematics achievement test performance than Black girls, as well as significantly higher achievement orientation. Also consistent with the literature, white girls showed a higher sense of control, that is, a greater sense of internality, than their Black counterparts. A surprising finding here, not consistent with previous literature, indicates that Black girls have a significantly higher self-concept of their ability than their white counterparts. Again, it should be noted that, consistent with the previous literature, the Black girls and the white girls did not differ significantly on any of the general or area-specific self-esteem measures. It also should be noted that none of the race by SES interactions was significant.

DISCUSSION

As the primary concern of this study is to look underneath the central tendencies, I will discuss the findings of the study within the context of the meaning of sex differences within race and race differences within sex. The objective is to provide additional information regarding the degree to which the findings are consistent or inconsistent with the general literature, as well as to theorize as to possible causes for such within-group deviations from this central tendency.

The reported findings from the comparison of Black boys and Black girls generally are consistent with the literature as reported by Maccoby and Jacklin (1974) on white children and adults. The absence of esteem differences either in general or in specific areas, as well as the absence of differences in self-concept of ability and in sense of control among Black children, suggests that the general sex difference pattern is applicable to Black children. However, given the absence of significant differences in standardized reading or mathematics achievement reported among white children, the presence of significant differences in reading and mathematics achievement among Black children takes on added meaning. The findings suggest a performance hierarchy on standardized achievement tests, with the whites at the top, undifferentiated by sex, followed by the Black girls, followed by the Black boys. The additional finding of a significant difference in achievement orientation among Black children that is inconsistent with the literature and favoring the Black girls is an additive indicator of the possible differences between Black boys and girls in the achievement area. When we also consider the trend toward a higher peer self-esteem among Black boys and their significantly higher concern with social abilities, these findings suggest that Black boys may be indicating a lower preoccupation with academic performance than Black girls and a higher concern with peer-related and socially related abilities. These sex differences, it should be noted, were not found to exist among the white children.

The reported findings between Black boys and white boys also are generally consistent with the race literature; particularly given the recent studies indicating no significant differences in general or area-specific self-esteem among such boys. Also consistent with previous studies, the white boys are shown to have higher reading and mathematics ability, higher sense of control, and higher achievement orientation than the Black boys. There was, furthermore, a significantly higher concern with social abilities favoring the Black boys.

Analyses of the relationships between Black and white girls indicated a consistency with the literature on race differences in indicating no differences in general or area-specific self-esteem, but significant differences in reading and mathematics achievement test performance favoring the whites. The findings also are consistent with the general literature in indicating that Black girls have a lower internality—or, to put it differently, that white girls showed a greater sense of control than their Black counterparts. Consistent with the general literature, which reported a significant racial difference in self-concept of ability favoring the Blacks, the Black girls show a significantly higher self-concept of ability rating than their white counterparts. Given this significantly higher self-concept of ability of the Black girls in the face of their significantly lower reading and mathematics achievement test scores than their white counterparts, one might theorize that their higher self-concept ability may be related to their higher standardized achievement test performance than the Black boys (Hare, 1979). One might consider their higher self-concept of ability a problematic question, given their lower performance than their white female counterparts. But as Rosenberg (1973) has suggested, it is possible that these Black girls are using same group members as their point of reference when estimating their academic ability. Therefore, their differences in achievement orientation, reading, and mathematics performance from Black boys may be the source of this particularly surprising finding. The comparison of sex differences among white children, although expected to be most consistent with the traditional literature—given that they have been most represented in the traditional sampling technology—prove to be most inconsistent with the existent literature. For example, whereas Maccoby and Jacklin (1974) and others reported no significant differences in general self-esteem among this age group of preadolescents, the white boys were found to have a significantly higher general self-esteem than their female counterparts. It should be noted that in none of the other comparisons was there found any difference in general or area-specific self-esteem.

A second surprising finding was the absence of significant differences in either the more expected reading or the less expected mathematics ability territories as measured by standardized reading test performance. That is, there were no significant differences by sex among the white children on standardized test performances, despite the fact that the literature suggested that at these early ages girls would tend toward higher verbal and reading test performances than boys. Consistent with existent literature, the white girls were found to have significantly higher anxiety than their male counterparts. But once again, the absence of significant differences in concern either with social abilities or in peer self-esteem by sex within the white group is inconsistent with the previous research that suggests that those differences should exist among such children.

These general findings, at the very least, suggest that the patternings of differences among white boys and girls may well be changing. Overall, the analyses of these four groups indicate some clear patterning differences. For example, it appears that the differences that were found within race by sex among the Black boys and girls are clearly related to achievement dimensions. The significant differences in achievement orientation and reading and mathematics ability among the Black children by sex are indicative of this presumption. On the other hand, the absence of differences along these achievement dimensions among white children, but the presence of differences in general self-esteem by sex among the white children, suggests that the differences existent among them are along the cognitive rather than the performance plane. On the other hand, the patterning of race differences within sex seem to remain relatively stable. That is, the Black boys share with Black girls a lower standardized reading and mathematics achievement test performance than their white counterparts of the same sex, as well as a lower achievement orientation and sense of control than their white counterparts of the same sex. The Black boys additionally showed a higher concern with social abilities than their white counterparts, and the Black girls showed significantly higher self-concept of ability than the white girls. Generally speaking, however, it appears that the pattern of similarity and difference that was assessed for racial groups holds up equally as well within sex groups when the sex groups are analyzed separately. Some additionally interesting pattern findings suggest that sense of control is clearly race-related in that there were no significant within-race differences, but there were significant across-race differences, even when the boys and girls were analyzed separately with the whites scoring higher. On the other hand, general anxiety appears to be a clearly sex-related dimension in that the girls scored significantly higher in anxiety, even when they were analyzed within racial group.

IMPLICATIONS

DISCUSSION

The findings of the study suggest a number of territories that are in need of further investigation. The general existence of a pattern of sameness among white children, particularly with reference to the achievement dimensions, indicates that certain movement in the educational system and in child socialization practices among white children may have reduced sex differentiation. On the other hand, the finding of significant difference in general self-esteem among white preadolescent children suggests the need to explain why esteem differences should come into existence among such children, at such an early age, at the same time that the ability dimensions appear to be undifferentiated.

A second concern, given both the importance of the ability dimensions and the absence of distinctions along the ability dimensions by sex within the white group, is the prime issue of the continued existence of standardized achievement test performance differentials across racial groups, even when sex is held constant. Although we have blamed a piece of the standardized test performance differential on cultural bias, which in my opinion is a legitimate concern, the existence of a significant sex difference among Black children on these very same dimensions raises a third issue in need of investigation. The existence of significant differences in reading and mathematics performance among Black children, as well as the existence of an achievement orientation differential, suggests the necessity of exploring the possible variations in sex role socialization within Black families that may be partially causal both to the achievement differences reported and to the differences in concern with peer abilities and other social abilities. It is clear that the pattern is one in which the Black girls hold academic advantage while the Black boys appear to hold a social abilities and social concern advantage. The fact that Black boys and Black girls do not differ significantly in self-esteem from one another or from their sex counter-parts of other race suggests that their psychological well-being along the places of esteem is based potentially on different dimensions of competency. The capacity of Black children in general and Black boys in particular to maintain higher levels of esteem in the face of lower test performance may be applauded on one hand as proof that they maintain the capacity to differentiate between how a potential alien structure may treat them in the academic sense and how they feel about themselves generally. Nevertheless, the ability of the Black boys to feel as good as they appear to about themselves relative not only to their white counterparts but to the Black girls suggests the possibility that esteem ratings among Black boys may be based more on their interactions with their peers and less on their performance in the academic area. To the extent that differential treatment in the area, perhaps through sex bias within race, is responsible, we should certainly pursue territories for alleviating the problems of sex discrimination within race within the schools.

On the other hand, to the extent that we may possibly be getting indicators of some differences in sex socialization that allow Black boys to compute their concepts of worth in territories that are nonacademic, the data leave open the possibility of increasing the power with which, or the generating energy with which, they would approach such academic tasks. The point here is that although the information regarding esteem is clearly positive, the fact that we continue to manifest patterns of sex role differentiation among Black children favoring Black girls while the gap previously favoring white girls has been closed by the white boys has important implications for future success in the academic area. As was pointed out by Hare (1980), two counseling strategies may well be necessary if this kind of achievement information is both active and potentially reflective of differential sources of esteem among these children. Although we are familiar with the problems of low self-esteem as the preponderance of literature suggests, for example, along social class lines, we have been negligent in the amount of attention that we pay to the generating sources of self-esteem. That is, the capacity of different groups of children to differentially score and differentially perform in the academic area, but simultaneously to be able to manifest patterns of general esteem that are equal to or higher than their counterparts who are doing well or better in the academic area suggests the necessity of emphasizing counseling strategies that might be directed toward altering the sources of esteem, rather than attempting to raise the level of self-esteem. Within the context of the school, this strategy, needless to say, would necessitate parental cooperation as well as higher expectations and nondifferentiated treatment regardless of sex, race, or social class (Hare, 1977a) if it is to be effective as a strategy. Hand in hand with such a strategy, however, would have to come a pattern of child socialization that, in theory, would not allow for high levels of self-esteem in the absence of adequate academic effort. Although the data are not available to tell us whether or not these pattern differences among Black children are a consequence of discrimination along sex lines within the school area, there also is the possibility that we are seeing some consequences of differential sex socialization within Black families. We must attempt to develop strategies and to identify the mode and the elements with which we may possibly be transmitting differential messages to Black boys and Black girls.

As previously indicated, some authors have begun to theorize about differences in sex role socialization among Black children. For example, in a survey of Black women it was reported that they felt that Black boys were raised differently, were given more leeway, and that when parents told Black girls what was expected of them, the girls were expected to toe the line. However, Reid (1972) reported an ambivalence in child rearing practices toward the boys, indicating a willingness to allow them more space. We are not concerned with the possibilities of more space as preparation for competition in the adult world but, rather, with the possibility that too much space could result in the transference of energies that might be directed toward academic success but instead are directed toward nonacademic pursuits, such as being good at sports and games and popular. I would further emphasize that I would in no way, by suggesting the necessity of investigating this issue, remove from the school the burden of proving that it is not responsible for creating these differences in patterns. There also is a body of literature that suggests that teacher expectancies vary along sex lines, such that Black girls may show a pattern differential that is more acceptable to the schooling circumstance. It has been reported that Black girls tend to behave more "passively" in the academic situation, which may be a code way of acting more acceptably. The patterns of aggression that normally are attributed to Black boys and the general cultural bias that is anti-Black male in the American social structure may, in effect, create a circumstance in which the caretakers of the school system are most afraid of, least competent in handling, and most likely prejudiced against Black boys. If that is in fact the case, then the capacity of these Black boys to maintain high self-esteem even with low academic performance is indicative of their capacity to cognitively and adequately read the environment and protect their self-images by transferring their territories of accomplishment to areas over which they feel they have a greater sense of control. The existence of significant racial differences in sense of control is consistent with this possibility. Furthermore, the existence of patterns of social abilities interaction in which the Black boys show not only greater concern with peer relationships and social abilities than Black girls, but also greater concern than their white male counterparts, may also be consistent with this possibility. Finally, it is hoped that this study was successful, not in just generating interest in subanalyzing such groups, but in demonstrating that if one does go beneath the central tendency and begin to subanalyze the groups, one may find differences in performance, cognitive perceptions, and, ultimately, variations across race within sex and across sex within race that would not be visible if one were to remain at the undifferentiated aggregate.

REFERENCES

BLAU, P. and O. DUNCAN (1967) American Occupational Structure. New York: John Wiley.

BROOKOVER, W., J. LAPERE, T. HAMMACHER, and E. ERICKSON (1965) Self-Concept of Ability and School Achievement. East Lansing: Michigan State Univ. Press.

CLARK, K. and M. CLARK (1947) "Racial identification and preference in Negro children," in T. M. Newcomb and E. L. Hartley (eds.) Readings in Social Psychology. New York: Holt, Rinehart & Winston.

COLEMAN, J. S., E. Q. CAMPBELL, and C. F. HOBSON (1966) Equality of Educational Opportunity. Washington, DC: Government Printing Office.

COOPERSMITH, S. (1967) The Antecedents of Self-Esteem. San Francisco: Freeman.

EPPS, E. (1975) "Impact of school desegregation on aspirations, self-concept, and other aspects of personality." Law and Contemporary Problems 39 (Spring): 300-313.

GRIER, W. and P. COBB (1968) Black Rage. New York: Bantam.

HARE, B. R. (1980) "Self-perception and academic achievement variations in a desegregated setting." American Journal of Psychiatry 137, 6: 683-689.

——(1979) Black Girls: A Comparative Analysis of Self-Perception and Achievement by Race, Sex, and Socioeconomic Background: Report 271. Baltimore: Johns Hopkins University, Center for the Social Organization of Schools.

——(1977a) "Black and white self-esteem in social science: an overview." Journal of Negro Education 46, 2: 141-156.

——(1977b) "Racial and socioeconomic variation in preadolescent area-specific and general self-esteem." International Journal of Intercultural Relations 1, 3: 31-51.

——(1975) "The relationship of social background to the dimension of self-concept." Ph.D. dissertation, University of Chicago.

KARDINER, A. and L. OVESEY (1951) The Mark of Oppression. New York: Norton.

LEWIS, D. K. (1976) "The Black family: socialization and sex roles." Phylon 36, 3: 221-237.

MACCOBY, E. and C. JACKLIN (1974) The Psychology of Sex Differences. Stanford, CA: Stanford Univ. Press.

REID, I. (1972) Together Black Women. New York: Okpaku Communications.

ROSENBERG, M. (1973) "Which significant others?" American Behavioral Scientist 16 (July): 829-860.

——(1965) Society and the Adolescent Self-Image. Princeton, NJ: Princeton Univ. Press.

SHOEMAKER, A. (1980) "Construct validity of area-specific self-esteem: the Hare self-esteem scale." Educational and Psychological Measurement 40 (July): 495-501.

SIMMONS, R. and F. ROSENBERG (1975) "Sex, sex roles, and self-image." Journal of Youth and Adolescence 4, 3: 229-258.

SIMMONS, R., M. ROSENBERG, and F. ROSENBERG (1973) "Disturbance in the self-image of adolescence." American Sociological Review 38: 553-568.

PART IV

**PARENTAL ENVIRONMENTS:
RACIAL SOCIALIZATION**

9

RACIAL SOCIALIZATION
OF YOUNG BLACK CHILDREN

MARIE FERGUSON PETERS

Regardless of their particular economic circumstances, Black American families live their lives under continuous and varying degrees of oppression because of racism. Because of their racial identity, the normal, everyday life of Black people in this country encompasses a reality, both subtle and overt, of prejudice, discrimination, and devalued and depreciated status and opportunities (Pierce, 1975; Powell, 1973). Prejudice and discrimination affect the kind of jobs and income of Black heads of household as well as the standard of living, such as their housing, neighborhood, quality of schools, and medical care of the whole household. For Black families this is a fact of life, taken for granted in the world they know. It is a 450-year legacy Black parents cannot and do not ignore. Although they may hope for a better future world of fairness and racial equality, Black parents understand that they face an extraordinary challenge—to raise children who will be able to survive in a racist-oriented society.

Only Black families and certain other minority families in America live and socialize their children under conditions that are glaring contradictions of our national beliefs and ideals. Keniston (1978: xiii-xiv) described children in Black families as "the most endangered

AUTHOR'S NOTE: Special acknowledgment must be given to the late Jean V. Carew, who was coprincipal investigator of this study until her untimely death. Support for this research was provided by the Minority Center at the National Institute of Mental Health, Grant 7 RO1 MH35785-01 MN.

EDITORS' NOTE: *Marie Ferguson Peters died on January 6, 1984. She had a profound influence on many of us working in the areas of Black children and families. We will miss her.*

children in our society. . . . Although our national creed insists that all children should have equal chances, from the start the deck is systematically stacked against [Black children]." Many Black children must overcome obstacles caused by poverty, unemployment, and crowded city ghetto living, and all Black children must learn to cope with ubiquitous deterrents and roadblocks that inhibit their access to mainstream American life.

Black families make resourceful and creative adaptations as they cope with discrimination and low income (Hill, 1972; Stack, 1974), and their supportive child rearing strategies buffer some of the cruel and demeaning messages Black children receive from a hostile world beyond the Black community (Taylor, 1976; Richardson, 1981; Nobles, 1974; Willie, 1976). In a study of racism and child rearing, Richardson (1981) wrote as follows:

> Historically, the survival of Black Americans depended on certain strategies which were necessary for their continuing existence in a hostile society. It has been the responsibility and the task of black parents and the black community to prepare and condition black children for such a world. *Black mothers are required to mediate the hostile external society for their children* (Richardson, 1981: 99; italics added).

It is clear that the reality, racism, and response to racism must be included in any interpretation of parental behavior in Black families. In order to understand the dynamics of child socialization in Black families, the racism factor must be considered. Although the classic stress theories of Hill (1963) and others (Hansen and Hill, 1964; Hansen and Johnson, 1979; McCubbin et al., 1980) do not incorporate a racism factor in their stress formulations, when research involves Black families, the theories can be modified to incorporate the influence of racial identity on both the cause and subsequent reactions to a stress/crisis event. A theoretical conceptualization for adapting Hill's classic formula for stress/crisis events in the lives of Black families has been presented in detail elsewhere (see Peters and Massey, 1983). Basically, this perspective views Black families, because of their constant exposure to overt or concealed racism, as living under mundane extreme environmental stress (Pierce, 1975) and suggests that research that examines Black family functioning must incorporate this fact.

RACIAL SOCIALIZATION:
DEFINITION AND INQUIRY

The socialization of children in Black families, then, occurs within the mundane extreme environment of real or potential racial discrimination and prejudice. The tasks Black parents share with all parents—providing for and raising children—not only are performed within the mundane extreme environmental stress of racism but include the responsibility of raising physically and emotionally healthy children who are Black in a society in which being Black has negative connotations. This is racial socialization.

What racial experiences do Black parents and their children have? What do Black parents do about it? What do they say? Through questions such as these, the impact of race on child rearing was explored in a sample of Black families who participated in a two-year longitudinal field study of the social development and rearing of young children. The study was entitled the Toddler Infant Experiences Study (TIES). The TIES respondents talked about discipline, management, and other aspects and problems of child rearing that concern parents. As Black parents, however, they could not escape including how racism, discrimination, and prejudice affected their lives, their children's lives, and their thinking about their children's future. This chapter will describe some of the experiences parents had involving racial discrimination and prejudice and will describe how being Black affected the way the parents viewed their children, their racial identity, and their behavior as Black parents of Black children.

THE TODDLER INFANT EXPERIENCES STUDY

The Toddler Infant Experiences Study was an ecologically oriented descriptive study of the socioemotional development of young Black children and the child rearing behaviors, attitudes, and goals of their parents. For two years, beginning at 12 months of age, 30 Black children were observed and their parents interviewed once a month for two to three hours in their natural home environment. There were two different foci: the child and the parent. Children's behaviors, their transactions with the physical (home) environment, and their interactions with parents and others were examined to reveal the patterns of parent-child behavior. At the same time, extensive interview data were gathered to explore in depth parents' interpretations and inputs on their children's development. In addition, about half of the mothers (16) participated in a lengthy interview concerning the racial socialization of their children—their attitudes, behaviors, and goals as parents who were raising minority children in a majority culture.

SAMPLE

The study population consisted primarily of two-parent working-class and middle-class Black families, each of whom had a child born between September and December of 1977. Thirty families participated; all were principally caring for their children at home. A few also had a babysitter or used day care on a part-time basis for less than twenty hours a week. Although the study families were self-selected, recruited from many sources, and cannot be considered representative of Black families in the city in which they live, their state, or the nation, the families can be considered viable examples of the ordinary, average-income, law-abiding, hardworking, working-class Black families that are the backbone of America. Similar to the majority of Black families, the majority of the study families were two-parent, nonwelfare families with children at home. A minority were single parents. All were urban. Although all now live in the Bay area of California, similar to the majority of Black Americans they have family roots in the South. At the beginning of the study in September 1978, the family income ranged from below $500 per month to over $2,000 per month. Family size ranged from one to six children, although most had only one or two children. Seven families had a baby during the two-year study.

RECRUITMENT

Families were recruited for TIES via radio announcements, television interviews, newspaper articles, signs in supermarkets, and through friends. Many people were attracted to a project on Black children. The constraints of the research design, however, which required cohorts of infants born within a specific three-month period, at least one parent home with the child during the day, and willingness to participate monthly in a two-year long study, quickly narrowed the field to 30 families over the two-year period.

PROCEDURE

Data were gathered via monthly observations and interviews. An observer/interviewer visited each family at home once a month and spent two to two and a half hours observing the child, recording and videotaping the child's behavior, and interviewing the mother or other caregiver home with the child. The parenting and race interviews, which took four to five hours, were reserved for the end of the two-year field observations. These special interviews were conducted at the research office. Sixteen mothers volunteered to participate in these interviews.

The parenting and race interviews consisted of two sections. First, respondents were interviewed concerning how they were rearing their young children. We probed about their general worries, concerns, and problems as parents of active toddlers. These findings have been reported elsewhere (Peter and Massey, 1981). The second section of the interviews focused specifically on issues Black parents face as they socialize Black children. We talked about their child rearing goals and behavior as Black parents raising Black children. We explored the situations they encountered in which their Black identity created a problem and we discussed the stress families experience that can be attributed to racism.

REARING BLACK CHILDREN
IN A BLACK/WHITE WORLD

Raising Black children in a society in which blackness often is devalued may seem to some to be a difficult task for Black parents, who themselves experience prejudice. The TIES parents understood that they were not simply raising an American child but that they also were raising an Afro-American, a Black American child, whose culture, background, and present situation differ from other American children. As we talked to parents about the problems of parenting, many recounted experiences they had had with racism, discrimination, or prejudice. In general, parents tended not to initiate a racially oriented discussion concerning their parenting. However, in response to our probes it became clear that racial identity was an important factor in their lives and in how they were raising their children.

In order to ascertain how Black parents conceptualize their roles as the first and, for the first few years, the prime socializers of their children, and in order to understand how they perceive the impact of racism on their children's lives, a series of open-ended questions focused on the values and attitudes Black parents hold concerning rearing Black children.

TEACHING CHILDREN TO SURVIVE

As Richardson (1981) found in her study of Black mothers, the mothers in TIES understood the nature of the mundane extreme environment in which they lived. She concluded as follows:

> Black mothers know that their children will ultimately experience racism. They believe that racism experiences can be devastating and destructive if the child has not been prepared to recognize or develop techniques and strategies for coping with these experiences. The mothers also know that black children will ultimately have to know that they are black and understand what a black identity means in a racist society (Richardson, 1981: 168-169).

The TIES sample of young Black mothers expressed similar views and they felt strongly a responsibility not only to provide and care for their children but to teach their children how to survive the harsh world of prejudice and discrimination. Parents conceptualized survival in terms of coping. They expressed this in many ways; for example, a mother whose immediate response to a question concerning what Black parents should teach their children was "to be able to cope with whatever it might be." A mother of two small boys added, "It's most important for me to teach my sons how to deal with society as it is—to let them know they're protected as long as they're at home, but when they get out there in the world, *they're not protected anymore.*" A young mother of a 2½-year-old daughter explained simply, "I have to teach her to cope."

Parents are explicit when stating why the reasons for teaching children "how to cope" are so important. A mother of two boys put it bluntly: "I've got to teach them that in a white society they're going to get pushed around and be used." A mother of two older children and a 3-year-old daughter said that it was important for her to give her daughter a "good foundation—something to fall back on when the going gets rough so she won't have to turn to dope when she has problems." Another mother explained, "I think my sons are going to have to have a little tougher skin or a little more tolerance to be able to make it."

THE IMPORTANCE OF SELF-RESPECT AND PRIDE

Children must not only know about racism. Parents specify qualities they encourage in the development of their children. Parents mentioned that it is important that their children "be positive about themselves." They want a daughter to "have respect for herself" or a son to "get respect for being himself." Pride and self-respect often are seen as having practical value for Black children. As one mother pointed out, "I'd like them to have enough pride, because if you have enough pride or self-confidence in yourself, you'll let a lot of things roll off your back"; or, as another parent expressed it, "so nobody can put them down." A mother of two said that she wanted her children "to feel sure of themselves. They need this to be able to make the best of their future."

On a more subtle level, building self-respect and pride concerning their racial identity undergirds every parent's child-rearing philosophy. Parents expressed this in very direct terms:

> I want them to be proud of the fact that they are Black.
>
> I tell my child, "you're Black, we're all Black in this family; be proud of it!"
>
> I've told my daughter many times, "you're a pretty little Black girl and I'm proud of you!"
>
> I tell them to hold their heads up and not to be ashamed to be Black.

Parents are careful to put pride in racial identity in proper perspective so that it becomes neither an obsession nor a crutch. For example, a parent of a precocious 3½-year-old explained:

> I want her to know that she's Black, but I don't want her to put Black in front of everything she does. She's going to put herself right up there and her color isn't going to have anything to do with her success.

UNDERSTANDING THAT FAIR PLAY MAY NOT BE RECIPROCAL

Parent encourage honesty and fair play, but at the same time some parents warn their children that they cannot necessarily expect fair play in return. For example, a mother of a 3-year-old girl who attended nursery school part-time while her mother attended classes at the local community college stated:

> I want my daughter to be aware that there are differences between Blacks and whites. She can't do certain things white kids can. She can do them,

but she won't get away with them. She's got to understand that they'll get a break faster than she will.

A mother of two boys agreed:

Just the fact that they are Black means that they may be treated differently sometimes and they're going to have to put up with a lot more. If your white boss calls you "nigger," he's not going to get in as much trouble as if you turn around and call him a "honky." You're likely to get fired, even if it's the other way around and you're his boss. They come down a lot heavier on you when you're Black. He's going to have to know that there are some things that he's going to have to let shine on—just for his own survival.

Parents emphasized the importance of getting along with others. They stated that children must know how to "live in this world with other people" and "fit into society"; or, as a mother of a pretty 3-year-old child with very dark skin explained, "I have to teach her to get along with everybody because they're going to down her one way or the other, sometimes, just because she's dark. Some people—Black, white, or Mexican—are going to treat her differently because she's dark."

A GOOD EDUCATION: A TOP PRIORITY

Parents were asked, "Are there any special coping strategies you feel that are especially important to teach a young Black child?" A number of parents replied immediately, "Yes, a good education!" Like most American parents, they felt that it was most important for their children to have a good education; but these parents shared a compelling and culture-specific reason. As a mother of three boys explained, "When you're Black, you've got to get a little more education than whites have."

A number of parents, in addition, viewed obtaining a good education as somewhat problematic for Blacks. "I have to get her a good education," said a mother of two teenagers and a preschooler, "but I'm finding it to be a hard problem when so many teachers don't really care about little Black kids these days." Another mother of three feared her children might be discouraged from venturing into occupations outside the Black community: "I don't want them to be afraid of going into professions because only white people are in them."

BUT MOST OF ALL—LOVE

Parents were asked, "What is the most important thing you do for your children?" Most parents mentioned love first:

What I do is give mine love.

I try to give them love and security. I feel they need this most of all.

I love her so she'll love others. I don't want her prejudiced against any other race.

I give her a lot of love.

To me, it's love. We give them security and love. They're the same.

Love and security is the prescription these parents believed provided their children protection from potential emotional scars from onslaughts of bigotry and duplicity by detractors.

DO PARENTS PERCEIVE RACISM AS STRESS?

The parents in this study, as do parents in every society, socialize children according to the norms of their culture and the validity of the environment in which they live. Black parents experience the American phenomenon of racism in varying degrees and every parent has a philosophy or theory regarding how to best survive as a family now, and how their children will be able to survive as adults. The interviews with these parents revealed dramatically that these Black families lived their lives in the everyday ubiquitous environment of the mundane extreme environmental stress described earlier in this chapter.

Family crises often were precipitated or exacerbated by racism on the part of an employer, institutions, or individual. Parents cited instances of poor medical care, trouble in a job situation, problems with the law, and many minor unpleasant, more subtle incidents with racial overtones. Parents often were concerned about how these situations affected their children. Although it is difficult to prove direct linkages between family crisis, event, racism, effect on child, and child response, a number of parents clearly saw the connections in their particular situation. Table 9.1 illustrates five situations that linked a racially caused family event to child behavior. For each event, the table shows the racially connected cause, effect on child, and child's observed coping behavior. It is interesting to note that in one of the examples the young child does not exhibit an adverse response to the family stress situations that involved

**TABLE 9.1   Examples of Racially Caused Events in Black Families
and the Effect on the Children**

Event	Racially Related Cause	Effect on Child	Child's Observed Coping Behavior
Father's loss of job.	Being last hired, Blacks are first fired on this job.	Father bored, short-tempered; leaves home to "hang"; child misses father.	Avoids father or demands attention from father.
Surgeon's negligent handling of mother's hospital abortion.	Blacks receive poor clinical/doctor care in this hospital.	Mother becomes depressed and neglects child.	Amuses self when mother appears to be preoccupied or demands attention from mother.
Death of three young children close to the family.	Inadequate nutrition and health care—prenatal and postnatal	Coping with absence (death) of companion/playmate.	Ask a few questions; seems to accept fact that playmates are gone.
Mother unable to leave job when ill.	Racist attitude of employer who treated Blacks unsympathetically.	Exacerbated mother's health problem, mother tired and ill when home and has little energy or time for child.	Whines for mother's attention.
Death of mother's sister.	Childbirth complications not properly monitored in hospital.	Child must share family resources with cousin who now resides in child's home.	Accepts and enjoys having older "sister" who was already living in family when child was born.

death. Two situations, the death of three cousins/playmates and the death of child's aunt, were seen as affecting the young child directly. The father's loss of a job, the mother's negligent abortion, and the mother's working although ill were believed to affect the child indirectly through the behavior of a parent. In three cases the child's coping behavior in reaction to the family stress/crisis event placed an added strain on the parent by the child's making excessive demands for attention.

Discrimination was not necessarily experienced in concrete situations, as seen in Table 9.1. Often it was the subtle prejudice Blacks sensed in the behavior of whites they met in the course of their daily activities. Blacks never know when a store clerk, bank teller, a waiter in a restaurant is going to show overt prejudice that is not only insulting but difficult to ignore. An ordinary business transaction, shopping excursion, or pleasure outing suddenly can be transformed into a source of anger and emotional stress.

One mother, for example, who had taken her two little girls to their favorite ice creamery, became "fed up" and walked out because the waitress not only ignored their table and served customers who came in after them, but was "nasty" when the mother finally requested service. "I had a difficult choice to make," this mother said, "walk out and face the kids' howling because they didn't get their ice cream, or sit there and sizzle."

TABLE 9.2   Where Parents Have Met Discrimination

Where	Number of Respondents
By a salesperson	14
In seeking a job	12
In a restaurant	12
On the job	11
In a hospital or clinic	9
In school	8
In seeking housing	7
By a bank	6
At a recreational facility	4
At a bar or disco or night club	3
By a public service agency, such as the telephone or the light companies	1

NOTE: N = 16.

Another parent described even more graphically how she felt. "You keep sitting there," she said, "wondering when you're going to get waited on, watching everybody else being waited on, and it just makes you feel bad and then it makes you want to be violent, you're wondering if you should get up and do something. All these things go through your head."

A third mother talked about the more subtle attitudes of some waitresses: "They ask, 'Can I help you?' But you know they don't really want to help and you wonder about the food they bring out."

Twelve, or three-fourths, of the mothers volunteered stories about discrimination in restaurants. Even more (14) had experienced discrimination by a salesperson. Typically, they mentioned that sales clerks waited on others before coming to them. A mother who had worked as a sales clerk added that white customers sometimes ignored her and waited for the white salesperson. A number of parents described incidents, such as going into a bank to transact business with an officer or shopping in a store that featured high-priced merchandise, only to be suspected of being too poor to be a serious customer. Table 9.2 lists the places parents mentioned in answer to the questions, "Have you ever been discriminated against? Where?"

As we have seen, it is evident that racism affects important aspects of the daily lives of the Black families in our study, and these experiences influence the parents' perceptions of the external world their children someday must enter. However, parents "don't dwell on it," as one mother said.

Because mundane extreme environmental stress is a normal environment for Blacks in this country, the phenomenon of racism may not be perceived as stress by Black parents. We therefore said to each respondent during the interviews, "Some people feel that being Black places an added stress in the lives of children. What do you think about this?" Opinions were divided: A little over half (9) of the 16 parents who participated in the racism interview agreed. For example, one mother answered in the following manner:

> Yes, I certainly do agree about that, because your children have to act better, be smarter, perform better than somebody comparable who is white. Then they get the idea that they are being resented just because they're acting better, performing better, and are smarter than whites are.

A mother whose older children attended a racially mixed school agreed:

> Because they have to learn to deal with our culture as Black people and also deal with the mainstream culture at the same time, it's hard trying to relate, trying to intermingle the two and come up with a good understanding of what life should be all about.

A parent whose oldest daughter is in second grade replied simply, "This is the problem I'm having at my daughter's school. I can't see her teachers—who are whites—relating to her culture. So my daughter has a problem!"

On the other hand, almost half (7) disagreed. They did not feel that children were necessarily stressed by racism. One mother of two boys said, "I disagree. It depends on how you bring up the child. If parents bring up their children so that they know how to handle things, then there's no stress."

A mother of two preschoolers, considering the question in terms of her children's situation now, replied, "Kids don't know what's happening. They can't do anything about discrimination and it really doesn't bother them at this age, less their parents want to carry on about it." A number of parents expressed the view that if children feel stressed, it is because their parents subject them to their own feelings of stress. As a mother of five pointed out, "When Black children feel stressed it's because they're getting it from their parents."

A mother of two daughters and a son explained that stress is avoided because children learn "about how it is." She added,

From the time you're a kid, your mother and father tell you about discrimination; brothers and sisters, aunts and uncles, they all tell about it. So when you grow up and put in for a position but don't get it, you'll say, "Hey, I knew I wasn't going to get it." So you don't feel too bad about it. You've accepted the possibility of rejection before you put in for the position. You really know you're not going to get it, but you put in for it anyway.

When the question turned from stress on children to stress on adults, most parents (13) felt that being Black placed an added stress in their lives. A mother of a 3½-year-old, connecting stress of parents with stress on children (see Table 9.1), said, "If we can't deal with situations, it causes stress and we give that stress to our children."
Another mother commented as follows:

I strongly agree. It's harder to get a job even when you're qualified, and when you do get a job, you don't get the promotions that are due you. I know, it happened to my husband, and it just happened to my sister a little while ago.

Another mother, emphasizing the effects of the stresses of discrimination and prejudice, noted, "It makes some Blacks have a chip on their shoulders, be mad all the time, even hate white folks."

SUMMARY

In conclusion, the general consensus of the 16 parents was that being Black brought a different dimension to the way they were raising their children. They recognized that being Black brought an added stress into the lives of children as well as into their own lives. However, there were "special things" parents did to prepare their children for being Black in this society. We term these special things "racial socialization." Although a majority of the respondents believed that their 2½-to 3-year-old children did not know the difference between the races and did not understand their own racial identity, about half of the parents already had explained to their preschoolers that they were Black and the other half planned to talk about race to their children later. Incidents of racial discrimination or prejudice had occurred to *all* adults in the study, but most of the preschoolers had not yet experienced it. Finally, although parents felt that it is important to prepare their children to "deal with racism," a number of parents felt that they were not necessarily "prepared" by their own parents for coping with the racial prejudice and discrimination they had experienced.

This study has explored in some detail the experiences of a group of Black parents raising their young children in the unpredictably hostile environment of racial discrimination and prejudice that Pierce (1975) has called both mundane and extreme. Respondents were pragmatic and unflappable in their awareness of the persistence of racism in the real world their children must experience, and they were especially concerned about the racial socialization of their children. They appeared to be racially socializing their young children in individual yet similar ways. Although this was not a representative sample of Blacks in America, there is no reason to believe that the TIES respondents were any more thoughtful, articulate, or concerned about racism than other Black parents anywhere in this country discussing the various ramifications in their lives.

In her study of Black mothers, Richardson (1981: 318) suggested three propositions: (1) that racism acts as an intervening variable in the socialization process of Black children; (2) that the sociocultural/racial environments and experiences of mothers influence their perception of social reality; and (3) that the perception of social reality and adaptations parents make affect their child rearing values and behavioral strategies. Not only were these three propositions supported in the present study, but parents understood these connections and influences. The socialization of Black children takes place in a unique environment. Attempts by child development experts to modify the parenting styles of Black parents must be based upon an understanding of the functional value of racial socialization—the culture-specific child rearing values, attitudes, and behaviors Black parents have developed.

REFERENCES

BELL, C. (1980) Personal communication.
CAREW, J., M. F. PETERS, and G. C. MASSEY (1979) "Socialization and childrearing in Black families: innovative approaches in research strategies and methodologies." Presented at the annual meeting of the Society for Research in Child Development, San Francisco.
DIXON, V. J. (1971) "Two approaches to Black-white relations," pp. 23-66 in V. J. Dixon and B. Foster (eds.) Beyond Black or White. Boston: Little, Brown.
DOHRENWEND, B. S. (1973) "Life events as stressors: a methodological inquiry." Journal of Health and Social Behavior 14: 167-175.
DuBOIS, W.E.B. (1907) The Souls of Black Folks. Chicago: A.C.M. McClurg.
ELLISON, R. (1947) Invisible Man. New York: Random House.

HANSEN, D. A. and R. HILL (1964) "Families under stress," in H. T. Christensen (ed.) Handbook of Marriage and the Family. Chicago: Rand McNally.

HANSEN, D. A. and V. A. JOHNSON (1979) "Rethinking family stress theory: definitional aspects," pp. 582-603 in W. R. Burr et al. (eds.) Contemporary Theories about the Family. New York: Free Press.

HILL, ROBERT (1972) The Strengths of Black Families. New York: Emerson Hall.

HILL, RUEBEN (1963) "Social stresses on the family," pp. 303-314 in M. B. Sussman (ed.) Sourcebook on Marriage and the Family. Boston: Houghton Mifflin.

HOLMES, T. S. and R. H. RAHE (1967) "The social readjustment rating scale." Journal of Psychosomatic Research 11: 213-218.

KENISTON, D. (1978) "Forward," pp. xii-xvi in J. Ogbu (ed.) Minority Education and Caste. New York: Academic.

KUHN, T. S. (1970) The Structure of Scientific Revolution: International Encyclopedia of Unified Science, Vol. 2 (2). Chicago: Univ. of Chicago Press.

LEWIN, K. (1938) A Dynamic Theory of Personality. New York: McGraw-Hill.

McADOO, H. P. (1977) The Impact of Extended Family Variables Upon the Upward Mobility of Black Families: Final Report. Contract 90-C-631 (1). Washington, DC: Department of Health, Education and Welfare, Office of Child Development.

McCUBBIN, H. I., C. B. JOY, A. E. CAUBLE, J. K. COMEAU, J. M. PATTERSON, and R. H. NEEDLE (1980) "Family stress and coping: a decade review." Journal of Marriage and the Family 42, 4: 855-871.

NOBLES, W. (1974) "Africanity: its role in Black families." Black Scholar 5 (June): 10-17.

PETERS, M. F. and G. C. MASSEY (1983) "Mundane extreme environmental stress in family stress theories: the case of Black families in white America," in H. L. McCubbin et al. (eds.) Advances and Developments in Family Stress Theory and Research. New York: Hayworth.

———(1981) "Black beginnings: childrearing patterns in a sample of Black parents and children age 1 to 3." Presented at the annual meeting of the Society for Research in Child Development, Boston.

PIERCE (1975) "The mundane extreme environment and its effect on learning," in S. G. Brainard (ed.) Learning Disabilities: Issues and Recommendations for Research. Washington, DC: National Institute of Education.

POWELL, G. (1973) Black Monday's Children: A Study of the Effects of School Desegregation on Self-Concepts of Southern Children. New York: Appleton-Century-Crofts.

RICHARDSON, B. B. (1981) "Racism and child-rearing: a study of Black mothers." Dissertation Abstracts 42, 1: 125-A.

STACK, C. (1974) All Our Kin: Strategies for Survival in a Black Community. New York: Harper & Row.

TAYLOR, R. (1976) "Black youth and psychological development." Journal of Black Studies 6 (June): 353-372.

WILLIE, C. V. (1976) A New Look at Black Families. Bayside, NY: General Hall.

WRIGHT, R. (1957) White Man, Listen. Garden City, NY: Doubleday.

10

THE BLACK FAMILY'S
SOCIALIZING ENVIRONMENT

Self-Esteem and Ethnic Attitude
Among Black Children

ALGEA O. HARRISON

Over the past four decades social and behavioral scientists have investigated and written extensively on self-esteem, ethnic attitudes, and their interrelations. The major issue in the earlier works was the phenomenon of "Negro self-hatred." Research paradigms were designed to give Black children a preference between a Black or white peer as a social object. Studies reported findings of Black children selecting white peers as compared to Black peers and it was assumed that they were rejecting themselves and their race. In contrast, some studies found that Black children preferred members of their own ethnic group. Social movements, socioeconomic status (SES), geographical regions, and ethnic mixture of schools were found to influence the subject's decision. Simultaneously, empirical investigations of self-esteem among Black and white children reported inconsistent findings. The mixed findings suggested that Black children had higher, lower, or similar levels of self-esteem when compared to white children. The findings from these series were provocative and generated numerous studies, critiques, and reviews. For important reviews, see Banks (1976), Brand et al. (1974), Hraba and Grant (1970), Nobles (1973), Proshansky (1966), Proshansky and Newton (1968), Stephen and Rosenfield (1979), and Wyne et al. (1974). Inadvertently, these two problematic areas of study were linked and generated some of the strongest criticism of research studies using

Black children as subjects. The major criticisms were the lack of a well-defined conceptual and theoretical linkage between ethnic preference and self-esteem and serious methodological shortcomings among the research studies in the accumulated body of knowledge.

Nevertheless, the reported findings had implications for the home environment of Black children. The family setting is assumed to consist of influential elements for shaping the self-concept: warm, nurturing, and supportive adults who model and reward and punish behaviors. Given the child's internal mechanisms, this early nurturing home environment is assumed to foster positive self-esteem. Furthermore, one of the developmental tasks that is crucial for Black children is the development of an attitude toward their ethnicity, given systematic, institutionalized racism in America. The early home environment is postulated to be the important socializing setting for the development of ethnic attitudes. The attitudes and behaviors of adults, who usually are members of the ethnic group, in the home environment are important to this developmental task.

There are a limited number of valid assessments of Black family life that are sensitive to the social roles and family functions from the perspective of the Black culture. Fewer yet are investigations attempting to delineate the aspects of the family environment that directly and indirectly affect the development of ethnic attitudes among Black children. Nevertheless, we can safely assume that Black family life affects the acquisition of an ethnic attitude among Black children.

This chapter is a selective review of the self-esteem and ethnic attitudes and Black family environment. The focus of this review is on three themes: (1) conceptual issues, (2) methodological issues, and (3) a description of the family socializing environment.

CONCEPTUAL ISSUES

The accumulated body of knowledge on the relationship between self-esteem and ethnic attitudes among Black children has been severely criticized for the conceptualized approaches. The two major issues are the conceptualization of "Black self-hatred" and "Black self-concept."

BLACK SELF-HATRED

One of the major issues in the existing body of literature on the relationship between self-esteem and ethnic attitude is the conceptual definition of Black self-hatred or self-rejection. Critics have posed the question of whether there is an attitudinal or behavioral manifestation of self-rejection among Black children, as proposed by social scientists. The sociosystem reasoning for the existence of Black self-hatred is based on a postulated linkage between social structures and personality traits. Blacks have been discriminated against, rejected by society, and exposed to systematic institutionalized racism. It has been proposed that Blacks internalize society's negative view of their ethnic group and, as a black person is simultaneously a member of the ethnic group rejected, he or she rejects him- or herself. This descriptive reasoning was based on observations of experimental studies that used mostly Black children and adolescents of low socioeconomic families as subjects (e. g., Kardiner and Oversey, 1951; Pettigrew, 1964; Rainwater, 1968). Studies tended not to be made on families that reflect the diversity of Black income levels.

The major shortcoming of this sociosystem perspective is the unidirectionality of its causal explanation. It erroneously assumes that children are passive in their interactions with the environment. Children do not incorporate information from larger social systems in an unfiltered manner; rather, the information is processed by internal mechanisms and external mediators. A number of intervening mediators have been identified as operating between Black children and larger social systems: for example, family socialization techniques (Peters, 1981; Slaughter, 1983), religious institutions (Hill, 1971), and kinship systems (McAdoo, 1978; Stack, 1975). Thus, although the conceptualized linkage between social structures and personality traits has some merits, as utilized by these social scientists, it falls short of a credible conceptualized linkage between society's view of an ethnic group and a person's view of him- or herself and his or her ethnic group.

The majority of the experimental studies cited to support the conceptualized Black self-hatred have used peer preference research paradigms. According to Stephen and Rosenfield (1979: 708), the inferential chain "assumed that black and white stimuli, respectively, represent black people and white people; second, it is assumed that choosing the white stimuli implies a rejection of the black stimuli and thus the 'rejection' of black stimuli can be taken as evidence of rejection of black people; and, third, it is assumed that this failure to prefer and identify with black people implies rejection of the self." Implicit and explicit shortcomings of this inferential chain have been expounded in professional publications.

The major criticisms of the inferential chain are as follows: (1) using behavior of whites as the norms (Nobles, 1973); (2) absence of definitive evidence of a white preference among Black subjects (Banks, 1976); (3)

global assumptions that fail to consider differencing variables, for example, socioeconomic status and geographical region (Brand et al., 1974); (4) indirect measures of Black self-rejection (Proshansky and Newton, 1968); (5) lack of empirical linkage between the assumed attitude and behavior (Brand et al., 1974; Hraba and Grant, 1970); (6) lack of supportive empirical research for the assumed linkage of Black subjects' evaluations of their ethnic group and self-evaluation (McAdoo, 1977); and (7) lack of an empirically demonstrated link between racial preference behavior and direct measures of low self-esteem (Cross, 1978). These valid criticisms of the inferential chain and supportive experimental studies force a "no" answer to the question of whether there is a behavioral manifestation of self-rejection among Blacks.

On the other hand, Jackson et al., (1981) argue for a compartmentalization of group and personal identity rather than an assumed overlap between the two. Within this proposed conceptual framework, the individual's racial preference under specific conditions does not necessarily reflect a unitary trait; rather, it is a more situationally determined characteristic influenced by the developmental level of the subject. A person's view of self and ethnic group develops along different paths with connections being aroused under varying conditions. In other words, Black subjects can prefer whites rather than Blacks in some situations and still maintain a high sense of individual self-esteem and a positive view of their ethnic group. A nonpreference for Blacks under some conditions does not mean a rejection of self or ethnic group.

In summary, the inferential chain and proposed social system and personality trait linkage lack a well-defined conceptual and empirical underpinning in the majority of the writings on "Black self-hatred."

BLACK SELF-CONCEPT

The psychological construct of self is a well-researched concept from Western theoretical approaches, which are challenged as limited when used as a conceptual framework for understanding self-concept among Blacks (Nobles, 1973). The three theoretical models that have served as an analytical framework for discussions of the issue of Black self-concept are Mead's, Cooley's, and Erickson's. Thus, the "generalized other" (Mead, 1934), the "looking glass" (Cooley, 1956), and the "internalized prototype" (Erickson, 1968) have been proposed as structuring ethnic attitudes and self-esteem among Black children (Ziajka, 1972).

The theoretical positions noted advocate the importance of society's view of an individual's reference group in the multifaceted and multidetermined formulating process of the individual's self-concept. In other words, it is assumed that Blacks develop self-images that are peculiar to their historical and contemporary conditions in American society (Wyne et al., 1974) and are different from any other ethnic and nonethnic group in the United States. It has been postulated by Wyne and colleagues (1974: 4) that "there is a unique blend of biological, psychological, and sociological conditions which combine to form the black self-concept." Nobles (1972, 1973) suggests that the Black self-concept can best be understood with an incorporation of African philosophical view into the perspective (e.g., Abrahams, 1962; Mbiti, 1970).

Nobles (1972, 1973) cogently describes the African view of self as distinct from Western theoretical positions in the degree of emphasis placed on the self as "I," the self as "me," and the self as "we." Persons of African descent would attempt to maintain a strong positive unit relation between their "I," "me," and "we." Hence, the Black self-concept exists and it is more extended or inclusive than the self-concept of persons of European descent. Although Nobles's ideas have not received extensive empirical investigation, logically they do have merit. The degree to which adult Blacks identify with other Blacks, express their ethnicity, and reflect the Black experience in their values, socializing goals and techniques, cultural artifacts, and so on molds their self-concept. The boundaries of the self-concept are more flexible and incorporate the "we" to a larger extent than the self-concepts of non-Blacks, as frequently in environmental interactions the individual is not differentiated from the ethnic group: for example, "they all look alike" instances, in which the black person is forced to react first as a member of an ethnic group rather than omit an individual reaction. The process is expressed further among Black adults in the behaviors they model and behaviors they reward and punish in their children. The role of models and socializing agents has been accepted as part of the processes involved in determining and shaping the developing self-concept and ethnic identity of persons.

At this point, clarification of terms is needed. The terms self-concept and self-esteem are related but not identical concepts. "Self-esteem is based on evaluations and judgments about one's perceived characteristics; self-concept does not imply positive or negative feelings about the self" (Mussen et al., 1984: 318). The terms have been used interchangeably in the literature on self-esteem and ethnic attitude. The majority of the studies have measured self-concept among Black children and if it is lower than a white normative group, it is assumed that Black childen have low self-esteem. The self-concept is a set of ideas about oneself that is descriptive rather than judgmental (Mussen et al., 1984: 356). The fact that children are aware that they are Black is part of the self-concept; their evaluation of their racial characteristics is part of their self-esteem. Furthermore, children's attitudes or evaluations about their ethnic group and selves as members of that group appear at approximately the age of 7, as it is difficult if not impossible to measure self-esteem before that age in any meaningful manner (Mussen et al., 1984.).

The controversy has centered around which cultural group, Black community or white society, has served as the major source of attitudes and perceptions internalized by Black children in ethnic membership evaluations. There are social scientists who postulate that the white culture's views of Blacks are internalized by Black children, and this is reflected in experimental findings of low self-esteem and negative attitude toward their racial group (e.g., Clark and Clark, 1939). On the other hand, others postulated that the Black community is the major source of values and attitudes internalized by Black children (e.g., Barnes, 1972; Nobles 1973). Furthermore, as Blacks became more overtly verbal in advocating their group attitude, a trend toward higher self-esteem and positive feelings toward their ethnic group was noted in studies examining these variables among Black children (Hraba and Grant, 1970; Ward and Braun, 1972). Concomitantly, others assumed that self-esteem and racial attitudes were compartmentalized and situational. Self-esteem varies for different domains of behavior, and children rate themselves differently in different areas (Mussen et al., 1984). Thus, it is possible for children to separate society's view of their ethnic group from their view of themselves (McAdoo, 1977) and to flex their self-esteem depending upon the situation; self-esteem measures vary according to home, peer, or school settings (Hare, 1977).

SUMMARY

The relationship between self-esteem and ethnic attitude has been described as "self-hatred" by many social and behavioral scientists. The concept of "self-hatred" has been criticized for numerous reasons, most noted is the lack of a well-defined theroretical framework incorporating the inferential chain. As previously used, the postulated linkage between society's view of the ethnic group and an individual's perception of his or her ethnic group and self is faulty because it fails' to consider mediating social systems (e.g., family, religious institutions). Generally, there is agreement concerning the existence of a Black self-concept or an attitude toward in-group or reference group. The controversy is over which social system is the dominant source of information used by Black children to make evaluative judgments regarding their own ethnicity and their ethnic group. Some writers postulate that the Black community is the major source of content regarding the self and ethnic group. Others, however, postulate that the dominant determinant is the view of the wider society. Both positions cite supportive empirical findings. Currently, the prevailing view is that Black children compartmentalize the information from various sources and develop a strong preference for their own ethnic group.

METHODOLOGICAL ISSUES

Critiques and reviews of the proposed relationship between self-esteem and ethnic attitudes have been the concern of numerous writers (Banks, 1976; Banks et al., 1979; Brand et al., 1974; Cross, 1978; Jackson et al., 1981; Williams and Morland, 1979). Several methodological issues have been selected for review: These are validity of measures of the concepts, chance responses, attributes of the stimuli, and ethnicity of examiner.

VALIDITY OF MEASURES

Ethnic attitudes have been measured by an operationalization of the concept as ethnic identification and ethnic preference. It has been assumed by some that there is a societal norm that dictates that one prefer persons of the same ethnic group to which society says one belongs (Williams and Morland, 1979). Whether this is a desirable or acceptable characteristic has been questioned (Banks, 1976). This perspective has the possibility of fostering a negatively oriented ethnocentrism toward out-groups and a preference for in-groups under all conditions. Furthermore, it has not been demonstrated that this is a universal propensity of societies or a position unique to American culture, as most white American adults and children exhibit an excessive own-group preference in the experimental studies of reference group preferences. Nevertheless, social and behavioral scientists have accepted these findings as the norm and whenever an ethnic group does not exhibit a similar pattern of preferences, the concluding statements of the research have referred to that group's pattern as deviant or less than normal.

Brand and colleagues (1974) have provided the most extensive review of the methodologies of the research studies on ethnic identification and preference. They surmise that eight basic designs have been used for investigating ethnic attitudes. All of the various methods have short-comings and, hence, interpretations of findings from research studies should be accepted with caution and within the shortcoming of the assessing instruments.

The shortcomings highlighted for each measure are briefly presented. *Surveys of verbalized attitudes* are highly subject to response and cultural bias, have very little predictive power, and present difficulties in interpretation of the points of the scale. The choice of *ethnic dolls* as a measure has some merit; however, the earlier studies failed to consider the unfamiliarity of Black dolls as a possible reason for subjects' failings to select their own ethnic doll. Altering the physiognomy, color, and other attributes of the dolls has produced different results in various studies. Therefore, caution should be exercised in accepting the findings of studies employing doll choice unless the experimenter has given consideration to the important attributes of the stimuli. Studies using *personality assessment devices* reveal limited information as there are so many uncontrolled stimuli variabilities in the instruments. Research designs that analyze *sociometric interaction* do not illuminate the relationship of choice to various personal attributes and may tap differing and unrelated attitudes and behaviors related to ethnic preference.

To continue, studies employing behavioral observations and atti-tudinal measures are limited; however, these studies have a stronger theoretical framework than other methods. Within present knowledge these designs offer promise for increasing the understanding of ethnic preferences. The *disguised measure of attitude biases* have yielded consistent information about the societal stereotypes, but are limited in insightfulness regarding the development of ethnic attitudes. Moreover, there are serious ethical implications involved in deception research. *Measures of autonomic change* are of value in verifying dichotomized attitudes of prejudice and nonprejudice. This, however, provides little insight into the process of acquisition of these attitudes. Experimental designs employing a preference measure exhibited in *photographs or line drawings* show a lot of promise. Yet they need concurrent validation with other measures and the criteria on which photographic stimuli were selected should be explicit.

CHANCE RESPONSE

The most serious challenge to the methodology of the ethnic preference research design was set forth by Banks (Banks, 1976; Banks et al., 1979). As Banks so cogently argues, the proposed white preference among Blacks is a "paradigm in search of a phenomenon." In other words, the commonly employed research paradigm designed to elicit ethnic preferences among subjects has failed to elicit preference responses above chance. Banks reviewed and reanalyzed the data from the most noted studies of ethnic preference, including the famous Clark and Clark (1947, 1950) study. His analysis revealed that the dominant pattern of choice behavior among Blacks toward white and Black stimuli alternatives has conformed to simple chance.

These series of studies give the most compelling and strongest argument against the proposed idea of Black self-rejection. If the phenomenon is apparent only if the scoring pattern of whites (who exhibit high own-group preference) are considered as norms and contrasted with Blacks, this speaks to strong threads of ethnocentric bias among social and behavioral scientists. Rather than label Blacks as expressing self-hatred/rejection, the more appropriate conclusion is that young white subjects exhibit a strong sense of in-group bias in their selection of choices in peer preference measures, and young Black subjects exhibit very little preference. Nevertheless, it is apparent that in-group and out-group attitudes do emerge in the behavioral repertoire of individuals, and this makes the issue a viable concern to social and behavioral scientists.

ATTRIBUTES OF STIMULI

Series of studies have noted how certain attributes of the stimuli are potential determinants of children's peer preferences. Attributes that have been found to be significant are skin color and physiognomy (Gitter et al., 1972), sex (Doke and Risley, 1972), physical attractiveness (Langlois and Stephan, 1977), and bias toward the color white (Williams et al., 1975).

Skin Color and Physiognomy. Gitter et al. (1977) demonstrated that the physiognomy and skin color of photographs and dolls were relevant determinants of choices in ethnic preference studies. A number of previous studies failed to control for these attributes of the stimuli in the research designs. In their study, the researchers presented 4- and 6-year-old subjects with a series of slides depicting three of a set of nine dolls. The dolls differed in three levels of physiognomy. Levels of physiognomy were defined in terms of thickness of lips, width of nose at base, and texture of hair. Subjects were judged to have misidentified if there was a difference between self-ratings of their skin color and physiognomy when compared to judges' ratings of their skin color and physiognomy. A subject also was given a verbal misidentification score based on whether the subject responded correctly to the question, "Are you white, Negro, Colored, or Black?"

Although the interviewers in this research study were of the same ethnic group as the subjects, it was not clear from the procedural description in the publication whether the four judges rating the physiognomy of the Black subjects were Black. If not, this poses the possibility of shortcoming in the research design as the extent to which the subjects were labeled as misidentifying was how close their self-rating of their thickness of lips, width of nose, and texture of hair agreed with the perceptions of someone who was white. Conversationally, it is difficult to get whites and Blacks to agree on a label for shadings of color and description of facial features of Blacks.

Nevertheless, the findings were that Black children whose skin was judged darker, as compared to those with lighter judged skin, misidentified significantly more. Hence, it is suggested that the skin color and physiognomy of the subjects and the photograph and doll stimuli may affect the scoring pattern in racial preference studies.

Sex of Ethnic Stimuli. Doke and Risley (1972) investigated the determining effect of race and sex of stimuli in photographic representation of children among 4- and 6-year-old subjects. The data indicated that the sex dimension exerted predominant control over responses of young children. The findings were consistent with previous research that featured individuals differing in both sex and race, and inconsistent with studies featuring racially different individuals of the same sex. In the later studies the racial aspects were dominant. Yet these findings suggest that the race of the stimuli person diminishes in importance if other dimensions are salient. Brand and colleagues (1974: 881) surmise in their review of the issue: "In general, sex of experimental stimuli develops as a critical variable at an earlier age than ethnicity of experimental stimuli." They also noted that the importance of the sex of the examiner as a determinant in this type of research needs to be clarified by future investigations.

Physical Attractiveness of Stimuli. It has been reported that children develop stereotypes regarding physical attractiveness and this influences how peers are perceived and the personality traits with which they are attributed (Dion et al., 1972). Langlois and Stephan (1977) investigated the interface between stereotypes of ethnicity and physical attractiveness among Black, Anglo, and Mexican American elementary school children. It was found that children from all three ethnic groups responded primarily on the basis of physical attractiveness rather than ethnicity. Thus, the authors concluded that stereotypes associated with physical attractiveness were stronger determinants of peer preferences and behavioral attributes than ethnic stereotypes.

Bias Toward Color White. Williams and his colleagues (1975) have advocated that there is a tendency to evaluate the color white more positively than the color black. It was proposed that prowhite/antiblack color bias may be related to the child's status as a diurnal animal and to his or her experiences with the light of day and dark of night. Subsequently, they conducted a series of experiments to explore the possibility that color bias may act as a determinant and/or support of the racial bias observed at the preschool and early school age levels. In the series of studies support was found for the tendency of preliterate Euro- and Afro-American subjects to have a prowhite/antiblack bias. This suggested that the color of the stimuli in and of itself, without an evaluative statement regarding ethnicity of person, is an important determinant of the responses for studies in the body of knowledge regarding ethnic attitudes.

ETHNICITY OF EXAMINER

The findings on the effects of ethnicity of the examiner on the subjects' choice in ethnic preference studies are inconsistent. Some researchers have reported no effects (e.g., Hraba and Grant, 1970; Morland, 1958) and others have noted significant effects (Sattler, 1970; Solkoff, 1972). The impact varies with the nature of the questions investigated, characteristics of the experimental population, and surrounding social factors (Brand et al., 1974; Solkoff, 1972).

The nature of the question interacts with the ethnicity of the examiner and influences the response of the subjects. Directional effects of emotionally laden questions were mixed with movement sometimes toward other or own ethnic group, depending on the nature of the question (Brand et al., 1974). For example, less militancy was noted in Black subjects' responses to white examiners than to Black examiners (Pettigrew, 1964). In contrast, Black and white adolescents' reactions to a questionnaire concerning social relations and engagements did not vary with examiner ethnicity (Bryant et al., 1966). On standardized measures of intelligence, children have obtained higher IQs with examiners of their own and other ethnic groups. Importantly, prowhite bias was significantly lower for higher levels of cognitive development when the examiner was black (Clark et al., 1980).

The characteristic of the experimental population also is important in influencing the effect of the ethnicity of the examiner. Whether subjects attend segregated or integrated schools (Porter, 1971) and subjects' reactions to reinforcement conditions, age, and socioeconomic levels (Sattler, 1970) have a differential impact. Currently, few well-controlled studies have manipulated the variable of ethnicity of examiner so that predictive statements can be issued. The concluding position for a number of researchers is to recommend that in future studies using Black children as subjects the examiner should be a member of the ethnic group.

SUMMARY

The format of the major research paradigm used to support the proposed relationship between self-esteem and ethnic attitude has been peer preference studies. Critics have documented several methodological flaws in the accumulated body of knowledge generated by these and similar studies. Brand et al. (1974) have provided the most critical review of the methodologies. Socioeconomic status, geographical region, ethnicity of school environment, ethnicity of examiner, and attributes of the stimuli have a differential impact on subjects' responses in peer preference studies. Few studies have controlled for these factors simultaneously. The most damaging evidence against the accumulated findings was set forth by Banks (1976), who critically noted how the data from the majority of studies only demonstrated that Black children's preference for white peers were scores at the level of chance. Generally, white children exhibit greater own-group preference than most other ethnic children. The value judgment attached to these findings are a reflection of the ethnocentrism of social and behavioral scientists who assume that the behavior of white children is the norm. Thus, the more appropriate conclusion is that young Black children exhibit no preference between Black and white peers. The trend of Black children regarding ethnic preference is an early awareness of ethnic differences (Horowitz, 1936), a lack of peer preference based on ethnicity alone, and increase in preference for members of own ethnic group with age (Stevenson and Stewart, 1958).

FAMILY SOCIALIZING ENVIRONMENT

The cumulated societal perspective of Blacks and the psychological needs of Black children interface in the home environment around the developmental tasks of acquisition of an intergroup attitude or an attitude toward one's ethnicity. One of the most important developmental tasks for Black children is the acquisition of an attitude toward their ethnic group. This developmental task is more complicated for Black children than other children because of the uniqueness of Blacks as a group to the larger social systems. The historical legacy of slavery, reconstruction, postreconstruction, World War II, civil rights movement, and postcivil rights movement have crystallized the position of Blacks in the sociopolitical and economic social systems in America. Yet the social positions of Blacks as a group are both static and fluid regarding larger social systems.

It is within this fluid relationship of Blacks to larger social systems that a Black child develops an attitude toward blacks as a group, group identity, ethnic reference group, or in-group attitude. One of the most stable and influential social systems that affects the developing construct is the family environment. A focus on the family environment as a primary socializing agent does not exclude the effects of other socializing agents, for example, peers, schools, media (Zigler et al., 1982). The home environment is a primary source, however, of the content of an ethnic attitude for the developing child. The sociocultural determinants of intergroup or ethnic attitude take the form of significant and relevant individuals, situations, practices, and events that are immediately and directly experienced by the child (Proshansky, 1966). The discussion of the impact of the family environment on the development of an ethnic attitude will follow a description of the developmental trends of ethnic attitudes.

DEVELOPMENTAL TRENDS

There is empirical support for the developmental trend of ethnic attitudes that postulates an interaction between the child and the environment (Hess, 1970; Horowitz, 1936; Morland, 1962; Proshansky, 1966; Radke et al., 1950; Spencer, 1982; Stevenson and Stewart, 1958). The developmental sequence is ethnic awareness, ethnic orientation, and an emerging ethnic attitude (Clark et al., 1980). Clark and colleagues (1980: 332) summarize the stages as follows:

> Stage 1, *ethnic awareness*, is characterized by the child's development of an ethnic identity during the third or fourth year. This process stems from the child's ability to recognize racial identity and to categorize people by ethnic groups. Stage 2, *ethnic orientation*, refers to increased racial awareness as well as a tendency to describe and judge individuals in ethnic terms. Roughly, this stage occurs between the ages of 4 and 7. Finally,

Stage 3, *ethnic attitudes*, is characterized by the differentiation and integration of the child's beliefs, feelings, and behavioral tendencies regarding different ethnic groups.

The developmental trend proceeds as a function of the interaction between the developing cognitive and perceptual abilities of the child and the environment (Clark et al., 1980; Dollard and Miller, 1950; Katz, 1973; Katz and Zalk, 1978; Lewis and Brooks-Gunn, 1979; Spencer, 1982). The rationale assumes that perceptual categorization of racial groups is a prerequisite for subsequent attitude development. The perceptual processes of "acquired distinctiveness" and "acquired equivalence of cues" (Dollard and Miller, 1950) are the mechanisms used for the development of group differentiation. Briefly, group differentiation involves an increase in attention to perceptual cues marking between-group differences and simultaneously a decrease in attention to perceptual cues marking individual differences within a group (Katz, 1973, Katz and Zalk, 1978). In other words, perceptual cues that distinguish persons by ethnic groups become more salient, and perceptual cues that personalize individuals within ethnic groups become less salient. These perceptual processes combine with verbal labels, social stereotypes, and other external information from social systems to foster evaluative attitudes concerning one's own and others' ethnic group. Support for this rationale has been demonstrated by modifying children's attitudes with increasing perceptual individuation of other group faces (Katz and Zalk, 1978); children finding it more difficult to learn to discriminate faces of another racial group than those of their own (Katz, 1973); and presence of perceptual correlates with racial attitudes (Katz et al., 1973). Consequently, the ethnic attitude of Black children can be partially explained by the interaction between their perceptual processes and information from external social systems regarding their ethnic group.

Consistent with the conceptual focus on internal structures of the child, social scientists also explored the interaction between the child's developing cognitive structures and ethnic attitudes. Theoretically, children construct their knowledge concerning ethnic groups from the impetus of developing internal cognitive stuctures interacting with environmental stimuli. The ability to conserve, to attribute causality, to develop a level of language, and to decentralize are cognitive prerequisites for developing an attitude toward one's ethnic group. Therefore, it was predicted that Black children's ethnic preference patterns would exhibit a developmental hierarchy and shift to a less stereotypic view of one's ethnic group. Support for this rationale has been indicated by data showing an increase with age of in-group preference (Hess, 1970; Spencer, 1982; Stevenson and Stewart, 1958), lower prowhite bias with higher levels of cognitive development (Clark et al., 1980), and a significant relationship between children's understanding of the origins of race and measures of physical conservation and physical causality (Clark et al., 1980).

The perceptual and cognitive process interacting with environmental stimuli shape the child's early perceptions of self and others as members of an ethnic group. With increasing age (after age 6-7 years) the cognitive, affective, and behavioral components of an ethnic attitude become more differentiated and integrated. Thus, it is possible for an ethnic attitude to manifest itself differentially, depending on the child's level of cognitive maturity, emotional dynamics of situations, and type of behavior required. The content of the ethnic attitude has been acquired also in various environmental settings. The early home environment has been accepted as an important area for the child's acquisition of an ethnic attitude or attitude toward one's ethnic group. Aspects of the home environment that are important for the process are discussed.

FAMILY ENVIRONMENT

The conceptual framework for the importance of family environment as a major socializing setting for the development of ethnic attitude is indicated by the proposed linkage among social structure, social values, and socialization. The assumption among social scientists is that social values are linked closely to the aims and structure of a particular society, and these values determine socialization goals and techniques (Harrison et al., 1984). A review of scientific writings on Blacks suggests that generally the cultural and social values important to the acquisition of ethnic attitudes are bicultural adaption (Peters, 1981; Staples, 1971), religious orientation (Hill, 1971), and strong family ties (McAdoo, 1978; Stack, 1975). A child's orientation to these values would occur primarily in the home environment, and these social values inadvertently would stress a positive orientation to the ethnic group. The majority of Black parents want their children to function effectively in both the ethnic and nonethnic cultures (Harrison et al., 1984). The emphasis on strong family ties assures that the child is attentive to and models adults of their ethnic group; and religious organizations give supplemental support for the role of parents and the values espoused in the home. According to Williams (1979: 410): "Values to a great extent, shape child-rearing practices. Parents who belong to minority subcultures socialize their young into some of the dominant group value patterns characteristic of the larger society, but also seek to imbue their young with other values particular to their ethnic subculture." Recognizing the heterogeneity among Black families, a positive orientation toward the ethnic group is a common socialization goal among Black families.

The parenting style of Black families fosters positive orientation toward the ethnic group because of its techniques of making the parents and family members salient figures in the life of the child for information regarding ethnicity. Black parents emphasize rearing their children to be comfortable with their blackness—to be secure, to be proud, and to grow up being and feeling equal to anyone (Harrison-Ross and Wyden, 1973). They provide a buffer for the negative message that may be transmitted to their children by a society that perpetuates stereotypic images of Black people (Peters, 1981). Black parents are aware of the necessity of imparting a message regarding ethnicity and self-esteem to their children in preparation for the expected encounters with racism (Nobles, 1981; Peters, 1981). The socialization techniques of focusing on interpersonal relationships, respect for authority figures, and obedience (Allen, 1978; Young, 1970) assure that ethnic members' views are listened to and internalized by the child.

Kinspeople also play an important role in the socialization of Black children (Allen, 1978; McAdoo, 1978; Stack, 1975). The involvement of other adult members of the ethnic group in the socialization process underscores the importance of interpersonal relationships. Members of the kinship system share childcare responsibilities and consider the importance of child mastery of the physical environment secondary to child mastery of the interpersonal environment. Contrary to earlier misinterpretation of the role of Black fathers, they seek to maintain warm, nurturing relationships with their children (Allen, 1978; Cazenave, 1981; McAdoo, 1981), and have mentioned that race has an impact on their parenting (Peters, 1981). Black mothers have been found to use a supportive personal-subjective style with emphasis on individualism in their approach to child rearing (Bartz and Levine, 1978; Hess, 1970; Nobles, 1981; Peters, 1981; Schacter, 1979). These socialization patterns foster an attachment to the family system among Black children and strengthen the probability of the child being orientated toward family members for messages regarding ethnicity. It is through the family that a culture is transmitted (Staples, 1971).

CONCLUSIONS

Social scientists have investigated extensively the relationship between self-esteem and ethnic attitude with implications for the family environment among Black children. The accumulated body of knowledge has been severely criticized for conceptual shortcomings and methodological flaws. The relationship between self-esteem and ethnic attitude has been conceptually defined as Black self-hatred. Critics have posed the question whether there is an attitudinal or behavioral manifestation of the proposed self-rejection among Black children.

A review of the existing literature fails to substantiate the proposed inferential chain used in racial preference research designs to document Black self-hatred. Controversy has centered around which social system—the Black community or mainstream society—is the dominant source of information regarding Blacks internalized by Black children. Currently, most social scientists conclude that Black children compartmentalize the information from various sources and develop preference for their own ethnic group.

Critics also have noted methodological flaws in the peer preference studies that have been cited to support a negative ethnic attitude among Black children. The major criticism has focused on the validity of measure of the concepts, chance responses, attributes of the stimuli, and ethnicity of the examiner as problem areas among the studies. Few studies have controlled for these factors simultaneously.

The developmental trend of Black children regarding ethnic preference is an early awareness of ethnic differences, a lack of peer preference based on ethnicity alone, and an increase in preference for members of own ethnic group with age. The warm, nurturing, supportive family environment assures Black children of developing a positive view of their ethnicity and ethnic group.

REFERENCES

ABRAHAMS, W. E. (1962) The Mind of Africa. Chicago: Univ. of Chicago Press.

ALLEN, W. (1978) "Black family research in the United States: A review, assessment and extension." Journal of Comparative Family Studies 9, 2: 167-189.

BANKS, W. C. (1976) "White preference in Blacks: a paradigm in search of a phenomenon." Psychological Bulletin 83, 6: 1179-1186.

———G. V. McQUATER, and J. A. ROSS (1979) "On the importance of white preference and comparative difference of Blacks and others: reply to Williams and Morland." Psychological Bulletin 86, 1: 33-36.

BARNES, E. J. (1972) "The Black community as the source of positive self-concept for Black children: a theoretical perspective," in R. L. Jones (ed.) Black Psychology. New York: Harper & Row.

BARTZ, K. W. and B. S. LEVINE (1978) "Child rearing by Black parents: a description and comparison to Anglo and Chicano parents." Journal of Marriage and the Family 40, 4: 709-720.

BRAND, E. S., R. A. RUIZ, and A. M. PADILLA (1974) "Ethnic identification and preference: a review." Psychological Review 81: 860-890.

BRYANT, E. C., I. GARDNER, Jr., M. GOLDMAN (1966) "Responses on racial attitudes as affected by interviewers of diffferent ethnic groups." Journal of Social Psychology 70: 95-100.

CAZENAVE, N. (1981) "Black men in America: the quest for manhood," in H. McAdoo (ed.) Black Families. Beverly Hills, CA: Sage.

CLARK, A., D. HOCEVAR, and M. H. DEMBO (1980) "The role of cognitive development in children's explanations and preferences for skin color." Developmental Psychology 16, 4: 332-339.

CLARK, K. and M. CLARK (1950) "Emotional factors in racial identification and preference in Negro children." Journal of Negro Education 19: 341.

————(1947) "Racial identification and preference in Negro children," in T. M. Newcombe and E. C. Hartley (eds.) Readings in Social Psychology. New York: Holt, Rinehart & Winston.

————(1939) "The development of consciousness of self and the emergence of racial identification in Negro preschool children." Journal of Social Psychology 10: 591-599.

COOLEY, C. H. (1956) Human Nature and the Social Order. New York: Free Press.

CROSS, W. (1978) "Black family and Black identity: a literature review." Western Journal of Black Studies 2 (Summer): 111-124.

DION, K. K., E. BERSCHEID, and E. WALSTER (1972) "What is beautiful is good." Journal of Personality and Social Psychology 24: 285-290.

DOKE, L. A. and T. R. RISLEY (1972) "Some discriminative properties of race and sex for children from an all-Negro neighborhood." Child Development 43: 677-681.

DOLLARD, J. and N. MILLER (1950) Personality and Psychotherapy. New York: McGraw-Hill.

ERICKSON, E. H. (1968) Identity, Youth, and Crisis. New York: Norton.

GITTER, A. G., D. J. MASTOFSKY, and Y. SATOW (1972) "The effect of skin color and physiognomy on racial misidentification." Journal of Social Psychology 88 (October): 139-143.

HARE, B. R. (1977) "Racial and socioeconomic variations in preadolescent area-specific and general self-esteem." International Journal of Intercultural Relations 1, 3: 31-59.

HARRISON, A., F. SERAFICA, and H. McADOO (1984) "Ethnic families of color," in R. Parke et al. (eds.) Review of Child Development Research. Chicago: Univ. of Chicago Press.

HARRISON-ROSS, P. and B. WYDEN (1973) The Black Child—A Parents Guide. New York: Peter H. Wyden.

HESS, R. D. (1970) "Social class and ethnic influences on socialization," in P. Mussen (ed.) Carmichael's Manuel of Child Psychology. New York: John Wiley.

HILL, R. (1971) Strengths of Black Families. New York: Emerson-Hall.

HORIWITZ, E. L. (1936) "The development of attitudes toward the Negro." Archives of Psychology 28, 194.

HRABA, J. and G. GRANT (1970) "Black is beautiful: a reexamination of racial preference and identification." Journal of Personality and Social Psychology 16: 398-402.

JACKSON, J. S., W. R. McCULLOUGH, and G. GURIN (1981) "Group identity development within black families," in H. McAdoo (ed.) Black Families. Beverly Hills, CA: Sage.

KARDINER, A. and L. OVERSEY (1951) The Mark of Oppression: Explorations in the Personality of the American Negro. New York: Harcourt Brace Jovanovich.

KATZ, P. A. (1973) "Perception of racial cues in preschool children: a new look." Developmental Psychology 8, 2: 295-299.

———and S. R. ZALK (1978) "Modification of children's racial attitudes." Developmental Psychology 14, 5: 447-461.

KATZ, P. A., M. SOHN, and S. R. ZALK (1973) "Perceptual concomitants of racial attitudes in urban grade-school children." Developmental Psychology 11: 135-144.

LANGLOIS, J. H. and C. STEPHAN (1977) " The effects of physical attractiveness and ethnicity on children's behavioral attributions." Child Development 48: 1694-1698.

LEWIS, M. and J. BROOKS-GUNN (1979) Social Cognition and the Acquisition of Self. New York: Plenum Press.

MBITI, J. S. (1970) African Religions and Philosophy. Garden City, NY: Anchor.

McADOO, H. P. (1978) "Factors related to stability in upwardly mobile Black families." Journal of Marriage and the Family 40 (November): 761-776.

———(1977) "The development of self concept and race attitudes of young Black children over time," in W. E. Cross, Jr. (ed.) Third Conference on Empirical Research in Black Psychology. Washington, DC: National Institute of Education.

McADOO, J. (1981) "Involvement of fathers in the socialization of Black children," in H. McAdoo (ed.) Black Families. Beverly Hills, CA: Sage.

MEAD, G. (1934) Mind, Self, and Society: From the Standpoint of a Behaviorist. Chicago: Univ. of Chicago Press.

MORLAND, K. J. (1958) "Racial recognition by nursery school children in Lynchburg, Virginia." Social Forces 37: 132-137.

MUSSEN, P. H., J. J. CONGER, J. KAGAN, and A. C. HUSTON (1984) Child Development and Personality. New York: Harper & Row.

NOBLES, W. W. (1981) "African-American family life: an instrument of culture," in H. McAdoo (ed.) Black Families. Beverly Hills, CA: Sage.

———(1973) "Psychological research and the Black self-concept: a critical review." Journal of Social Issues 29: 11-31.

———(1972) "African philosophy: foundations for Black psychology," in R. L. Jones (ed.) Black Psychology. New York: Harper & Row.

PETERS, M. (1981) "Parenting in Black families with young children: a historical perspective," in H. McAdoo (ed.) Black Families. Beverly Hills, CA: Sage.

PETTIGREW, T. F. (1964) A Profile of the Negro American. Princeton, NJ: Van Nostrand.

PORTER, J. (1971) Black Child, White Child: The Development of Racial Attitude. Cambridge, MA: Harvard Univ. Press.

PROSHANSKY, H. (1966) "The development of intergroup attitudes," in L. W. Hoffman and M. L. Hoffman (eds.) Review of Child Development Research. New York: Russell Sage.

———and P. NEWTON (1968) "The nature and meaning of Negro self-identity," in M. Deutsch et al. (eds.) Social Class, Race and Psychological Development. New York: Holt, Rinehart & Winston.

RADKE, M., J. SUTHERLAND, and P. ROSENBERG (1950) "Racial attitudes of children." Sociometry 13: 154-171.

RAINWATER, L. (1968) "Crucible of identity: the Negro lower-class family." Daedalus 95: 258-264.

SATTLER, J. M. (1970) "Racial experimenter effects in experimentation, testing, interviewing, and psychotheraphy." Psychological Bulletin 73: 137-160.

SCHACTER, F. F. (1979) Everyday Mothers Talk to Toddlers: Early Intervention. New York: Academic.

SLAUGHTER, D. (1983) "Early intervention and its effects on maternal and child development." Monographs of the Society for Research in Child Development 48, 4: 202.

SOLKOFF, N. (1972) "Race of experimenter as a variable in research with children." Developmental Psychology 7, 1: 70-75.

SPENCER, M. B. (1982) "Personal and group identity of Black children: an alternative synthesis." Genetic Psychology Monograph 106: 59-84.

STACK, C. (1975) All Our Kin: Strategies for Survival in a Black Community. New York: Harper & Row.

STAPLES, R. (1971) "Toward a sociology of the Black family: a decade of theory and research." Journal of Marriage and the Family 33 (February): 19-38.

STEPHEN, W. G. and D. ROSENFIELD (1979) "The Black self-rejection: another look." Journal of Educational Psychology 71, 5: 708-716.

STEVENSON, H. and E. STEWART (1958) "A developmental study of race awareness in young children." Child Development 29: 399-410.

WARD, S. H. and J. BRAUN (1972) "Self-esteem and racial preference in Black children." American Journal of Orthopsychiatry 42: 644-647.

WILLIAMS, H. B. (1979) "Some aspects of childrearing practices in three minority subcultures in the United States." Journal of Negro Education 48, 3: 408-418.

WILLIAMS, J. E. and J. K. MORLAND (1979) "Comments on Banks's white preference in Blacks: a paradigm in search of a phenomenon." Psychological Bulletin 86, 1: 28-32.

WILLIAMS, J. E., D. BOSWELL, and D. L. BEST (1975) "Evaluative responses of preschool children to the colors white and black." Child Development 46: 501-508.

WYNE, M. D., K. P. WHITE, and R. H. COOP (1974) The Black Self. Englewood Cliffs, NJ: Prentice-Hall.

YOUNG, V. H. (1970) "Family and childhood in a southern Negro community." American Anthropologist 72: 269-288.

ZIAJKA, A. (1972) "The Black youth's self-concept," in W. R. Looft (ed.) Developmental Psychology: A Book of Readings. Hinsdale, IL: Dryden Press.

ZIGLER, E. F., M. E. LAMB, and I. L. CHILD (1982) Socialization and Personality Development. New York: Oxford Univ. Press.

11

A PSYCHOEDUCATIONAL PERSPECTIVE ON BLACK PARENTING

ANDERSON J. FRANKLIN
NANCY BOYD-FRANKLIN

Well son, I'll tell you:
Life for me ain't been no crystal stair.
It's had tacks in it,
And splinters,
And boards torn up,
And places with no carpets on the floor—
Bare.
But all the time
I'se been a-climbin's on,
And reachin' landin's
And turnin' corners,
And sometimes goin' in the dark
Where there ain't been no light.
So boy, don't you turn back.
Don't you set down on the steps
'Cause you find it's kinder hard.
Don't you fall now—
For I'se still climbin',
And life for me ain't been no crystal stair.

—Langston Hughes,
"Mother to Son" (1959)

The message of Langston Hughes's poem is still relevant for Black parents to communicate to their children today. This chapter will present a discussion of issues confronting Black parents in the psycho-

AUTHORS' NOTE: "Mother to Son," copyright 1926 by Alfred A. Knopf, Inc. and renewed 1954 by Langston Hughes. Reprinted from *Selected Poems of Langston Hughes*, by permission of Alfred A. Knopf, Inc.

logical and educational development of their children. Much of the discussion is based on our clinical work and supervision of psychological and psychiatric services provided to Black families. In the first part of this chapter we will discuss a definition of psychoeducation and the role of parenting as distinct from being the parent. We next present the social and historical context of parenting and examine alternative family structures involved in the child rearing process. An extensive area covered in this chapter is a discussion of the demands faced by Black parents in contemporary times. This includes delineating some of the tasks in parenting, reviewing strategies for coping with single parenthood, emphasizing teaching Black children about racism, and stressing the importance of parental vigilance about social trends. In the end we note some pitfalls in parenting that may result in clinical problems and offer suggestions for their prevention.

INTRODUCTION

A psychoeducational perspective of Black parenting is the view that a child's experiences contain both socioemotional (i.e., affective) and learning (i.e., cognitive) components. These two elements are always interactive in the daily transactions of the child and are not mutually exclusive. This may only vary in terms of degree. Parenting refers to the person(s) responsible for the nurturance and guidance of the child through its developmental periods into adulthood. In no way is this restricted to any particular family model or biological linkage. The focus is on that person(s) or significant others in the life of the child who, by the nature of the relationship, fulfills primary parenting tasks. This person(s), who is defined as a parent by responsibilities, must recognize that parenting is a job requiring skills: If performed within the context of parental "love," the process of child development is enhanced. However, if performed in an atmosphere of contempt and rejection, the process can be detrimental to development.

Nevertheless, the person(s) in the role of "parent" should realize that knowledge and feelings are processed by the child in response to daily learning experiences. Inherent in the job of parenting are the roles of nurturer and teacher. Parenting is the task of guiding the child to mastery over the intrapsychic experiences accompanying the achievement of developmental and life goals. Yet this process is more than teaching survival skills, which in our view is a subsistence goal, but, rather, a larger strategy toward self-actualization. Hence, parental awareness of the psychoeducational features of the child's transactions in daily life gives purpose to the role. Fulfilling the tasks of parenting may take many forms, but the objective is clear. Just how clear parenting objectives are to young Black parents is the question.

For Black people, parenting has too often been consigned to teaching kids to survive and to not submit to the inequities of racism. There is no choice in this regard. However, even this fundamental task in Black parenting is changing. Perhaps as a result of preoccupation with the oppressive socioeconomic depression in the Black community, the new generation of Black parents seems to be overwhelmed by the full responsibilities of parenting the Black child. Caretaking must be accomplished in addition to the nurturance of Black identity and teaching the nuances of racism. Our clinical work with young Black parents has exposed a crucial difference between the teaching of racial consciousness in children from that of previous generations. Young Black parents have not experienced the blatant restrictions of overt public segregation and "Jim Crow" laws. Many do not know what Jim Crow laws were, much less the history. This generation is more the victim of the covert forms of institutional racism. Different from their grandparents, the new generation must be more vigilant about how subtle social policies and practices eclipse opportunities for Black children. They must battle the seduction of pseudo access and participation in society and confront the real status of equal opportunity. Success at this is directly related to preparing Black children to develop a positive self-esteem and skills in negotiating a racist society. Exactly how young parents approach these tasks for their children needs to be researched as well as all other aspects of parenting in the Black community.

As Harrison-Ross and Wyden (1973: xx-xxi) have written, Black parents want "to bring their children up to be comfortable with their blackness, to be secure, to be proud, to be able to love, to grow up being and feeling equal, comfortable, responsible, effective, and at home in the world they live in."

This task is extremely difficult given the hurdles of racism and oppression that any given Black child must navigate in a lifetime. In addition, Black parents must help prepare their children for a bicultural existence in a Black world represented by their home, family, and community, and a white world represented by school, work, and the broader reaches of American society (Comer and Poussaint, 1975).

THE SOCIAL AND HISTORICAL CONTEXT
OF BLACK PARENTING.

In order to understand Black parenting today, the historical factors that influenced current child rearing practices must be acknowledged. One must consider the influence of the African orientation on parenting and children (Sudarkasa, 1981). Most societies in Africa were primarily tribal in organization. Child rearing was a communal task with the entire tribe sharing responsibility for raising a child. The philosophy was based on a collective or "we" focus rather than the Western individualistic or "I" focus (Nobles, 1980; Mbiti, 1970). Children were raised to believe that their primary allegiance was to the tribe. Therefore, if a child did not carry out responsib ::ties, an adult member would provide appropriate discipline. Although one needs to be cautious in drawing direct parallels between African traditions and current Afro-American practices, there are a number of similarities. It is not at all uncommon for Black children in America today to be raised in large extended families in which a number of blood and "nonblood" relatives may provide role models and accept some parenting or child rearing responsibilities (Boyd, 1982; Hines and Boyd-Franklin, 1982). A given family might include mothers, fathers, brothers, sisters, grandmothers, grandfathers, aunts, uncles, cousins, stepparents, boarders, and friends who may live in the same household or in close proximity (Billingsley, 1968; Stack, 1975; White, 1980). The key issue is that parenting may be a shared task that goes beyond the traditional "nuclear family" structure.

The era of slavery within this country introduced changes in family structure and caretaking that have influenced current parenting practices. When slaves were brought to this country from Africa, families were abruptly torn apart. Mothers, fathers, and children often were separated and sent to different plantations. Once separated new "families" often were formed within the slave community. Children were informally adopted by unrelated "parents" when their parents were sold. This pattern of "taking in new family" members in times of adversity has persisted in a variety of ways through the years. Informal adoption practices today are variations on this traditional custom, which was a necessity for survival during slavery (Hill, 1977; Boyd, 1982; Hines and Boyd-Franklin, 1982; Stack, 1975).

Informal adoption today has clear implications for family structure and for parenting roles. Formal adoption of children through social service or adoption agencies is a relatively recent phenomenon in Black communities in this country. Before World War II Black children were not included in this process. Therefore, Black families developed an informal social service network in which children were taken care of in times of crisis. These family crises might include the death of the parents, hospitalization or illness of a parent, separation or divorce, child abuse or neglect, a move by a parent to another location to find work, economic crisis, unemployment or an inability of parents to provide for a child financially, or redistribution of children from a family with many to a family with none. Sending a child to relatives also could occur in order to provide a child with educational opportunities not available at home. A child also could be sent off when a parent was unable to provide adequate supervision or discipline and the child was beginning to get in trouble at school or in the community.

Whatever the parenting unit in the family, whether it is a more traditional nuclear family with mother and father, a single-parent family, adoptive family, or any of the combinations discussed previously, the task of parenting is the same. That task involves the transmission of social and cultural values. These include folkways, religious practices, mores, and socialization in terms of the appropriate behavior for different social situations. These tasks are implicit to psychoeducational development. On the affective level, the task of parenting is to help a child relate to family members. These relationships become the prototype for relationships outside the family: peers, classmates, teachers, and community authority figures. Education also can include encouraging and facilitating the cognitive development and formal training of a child.

CONTEMPORARY BLACK PARENTING

Parenting is an ongoing process with many sociocultural traditions. Knowledge of the process is acquired primarily through imitating parental models. There is little formal training in this central role of the socialization process. Like many tasks in adult development, there is insufficient preparation for the responsibility of raising children. For the most part, many of us are left to the images of our parents raising us and our fantasies of what a parent should be. Our success at being a parent, therefore, is left to our synthesizing experiences from parental models, fantasies, multimedia, and consultation with a myriad of other resources. It is only recently with the rise in divorce in the United States and the restructuring of the traditional family that professionals have focused their interests again on the family and the roles of its members (Bartz and Levine, 1978; Lamb, 1977). Being a responsible parent is a complex task. It encompasses both a psychological and educational domain of knowledge. To have our children approximate our aspirations for them or to achieve the goal of becoming responsible adults necessitates parents acting in a responsible manner. The task of the dutiful parent is to define the parameters of responsible parenthood. Society through its system of values provides one set of parental guidelines augmented by the ethnocentricity of community and family heritage. A parent's interpretation of those values and his or her philosophy of life provides the foundation for his or her own personal parental strategies.

With the increasing technocratic orientation of the contemporary world, new demands for skills and survival are emerging. Computers are redefining the way we communicate and transact business. Concomitantly, the skills required to participate in the job market are changing. Increasing pressure is being placed on parents to evaluate their strategy for raising children as well as the parental goal in the preparation of the child for adulthood. Whatever may come with the twenty-first century, child rearing will require the parent to manage both the psychological and educational welfare of the child.

To approach the task of Black parenting, the status of the Black family must be considered. As noted in the National Urban League's *State of Black America* (1984), there is a rapid growth of Black families headed by women (47%). The income of these families approximates only 62% of white families' in the same circumstances (Noble, 1984). Black families in general have an income that is 56% that of white families. The number of Black families at poverty level is increasing. In 1979, 25% of Black children were born to teenage mothers. Completion of secondary school for Black children is dropping, and the preparation in basic much less marketable skills has fallen to crisis proportions, particularly in our urban areas. Unemployment for Blacks is more than double that for whites, and the rate for Black youth is even higher. The dilemma for the Black family is the loss of momentum toward upward mobility and the increasing noncompetitive status of the next generation of young Black adults.

Perhaps an equal if not greater concern from these statistics is the demands placed on rearing children under these social circumstances. There are obviously less material resources to work with in a state of impoverishment. Moreover, the inability of Black men to find and maintain secure jobs has created instability in family roles and structure.

In spite of the socioeconomic direction of Black families, inferences about the consequences to Black child development can be overly pessimistic. Black families have a resiliency and strength that has withstood social circumstances (Hill, 1972; McAdoo, 1981). These should not be overlooked any less than weakness should go unacknowledged. The task for behavioral scientists as well as Black parents is to be realistic in the appraisal of the social context in which Black child development occurs.

There clearly are many ways to interpret current statistics on Black families. The classic stance taken by sociologists in the 1960s was to "blame the victim" (Moynihan, 1965; Ryan, 1971). On the other hand, we can work toward the development of strategies designed to meet the needs of Black families, particularly single-parent families. First, we must be aware that statistics, particularly those gleaned from Census data, often mask the support systems and coping skills developed by families specifically to manage their life circumstances. Second, researchers and service providers often lose sight of the reality that growing up in a single-parent family does not necessarily predestine children to pathology.

There are some issues unique to single parents, particularly mothers struggling to raise children alone. Some key issues are the financial pressure and the scarcity of resources. Helping to improve the socioeconomic condition of these families is a major political debate, but it must become a national priority. With the dwindling of fiscal support from federal, state, and local authorities, many of these single parents face a constant battle to provide the bare necessities of life for their children. This often preempts concerns about psychoeducational and socioemotional development.

It is not surprising that many a single parent feels overwhelmed by these demands. This feeling is magnified for Black single parents, as over 50% of them are significantly below the national poverty line in contrast to approximately 30% of white single parents (Cummings, 1983). In addition to financial support and necessities such as housing and food, there is the question of emotional support for single parents. In order for a parent to adequately nurture the psychoeducational development of his or her child, he or she must receive some attention to his or her own needs. It is clear that in order to "feed" children emotionally, a parent must be "fed" or nurtured from other sources in his or her own life. Part of this process requires encouraging Black single parents to utilize available resources. First and foremost, they can look to their own extended families for individuals who can help with the psycho-educational task of parenting and provide additional role models for their children. The statistics often mask a reality, which is that although a biological "father" may not be present in the home, a mother's boyfriend or a stepparent may fulfill some of the aspects of the parental role. Where this does not occur, an uncle, grandfather, male relative, or next door neighbor often can be utilized. The fundamental task of the single parent is to create the environment that will enhance the psychoeducational development of the child. *There is nothing sacred about traditional or extended family structures if they do not work.* Single parents some distance from relatives must use such available resources and networks as friends, churches, or community agencies to create the environment for psychoeducational development.

For many generations, Black families also have relied on Black churches to contribute to the psychoeducational development of their children and to provide additional role models. Often a mother struggling alone can enlist the aid of a minister and church members, as well as Sunday school and church activities, to instill values that clearly shape a Black child's development. Churches in the Black community also have provided emotional support to parents overburdened with the task of parenting. Often these churches contribute directly to the formal education of Black children and their cognitive development by providing low-cost day care and/or elementary school programs.

The needs of single parents can be addressed in other areas as well. The task of providing an enriched, supportive educational and social environment for a child is complicated in the case of the working single parent. A key issue here is finding appropriate day care facilities that support the parental values from a very early age. In addition, the single parent faces alone a dilemma that confronts even two working parents; that is, careful attention to monitoring of children after school and attention to important areas such as physical care as well as homework assistance. Many children are alone for hours after school and receive relatively little monitoring. The problem of "latch key children" has reached epidemic proportions throughout this country.

Black parents in many communities have had to band together and demand afterschool services from their school programs, their churches, and, in some cases, to pool their limited resources to provide afterschool babysitting services.

The needs of single parents can be served by support groups that address both survival and parenting issues. These can and should be offered in schools and through other community agencies.

A final aspect of parenting that can affect children raised in single-parent Black families is the tremendous fear that many of these parents express about their perceived inability to protect their children from the "dangerous" elements in their communities. These might include peer influences, drugs, and delinquent activities. This can sometimes result in a parent being overprotective and taking an overcontrolling stance, such as restricting a child from going out into the street to play with peers. It is important that such parents make education about these influences an important part of their child's psychoeducational development and also that emphasis be placed on learning to cope with the realities of urban life. An extreme amount of overprotectiveness can be as detrimental as a total lack of monitoring, because it can stifle the socioemotional development of the child by limiting his or her development of independence, good reality testing, and appropriate social judgment.

Finally, in contrast to single parenthood, there is the issue of multiple caretakers. While providing a very rich socialization experience for Black children, it often creates a question of parental authority; specifically, just who is in charge? For example, it is not an uncommon experience in families in which an adolescent has a child for the child's grandmother to play a significant role in raising both the mother and the child. As the child grows older, he or she, in fact, has two "mothers." This can work well as long as the mother and grandmother are in agreement in terms of important decisions in the child's life. If there is disagreement, however, conflict can develop and ultimately the child can find him- or herself triangulated between these two adults. If this situation continues, everyone loses, especially the child, who may develop serious behavioral and/or emotional problems as a result.

If this situation is to be avoided, Black parents must be particularly conscious of the need for "unified parenting." This involves the coordination and management of parenting so that the key caretakers are all giving a single message to the child. This is essential whether the parenting or executive unit is mother, father, grandmother, parental child, aunt, uncle, babysitter, or any combination. It is important for those involved in parenting to discuss carefully and reach agreement on child rearing practices, especially on disciplinary and socialization issues.

Parents and other key family members have the chief responsibility for creating the social/environmental context for a child. This might include decisions about exposing a child to his or her history, cultural heritage, and the impact of racism. It would include expectations about his or her education and school performance. As a child grows older, questions will arise concerning the amount of responsibility he or she should have for household chores. These all are issues that can lead to disagreements and the communication of mixed messages to the child.

However, with the growing incidence of teenage pregnancy in the Black community, multiple caretaking families will grow and one has to wonder what role parents play or do not play in this statistic. Adolescence is admittedly a complex period in the life span (Franklin, 1982). Social and personal developments are beginning to assume adult form. On the other hand, can we require teenage parents to fulfill the tasks of equipping children with the survival skills that they themselves are still cultivating? It is not so much whether teenage parents can survive, because there is evidence that they do. A more fundamental question is, do we want Black teenagers to be in that position in the first place? If not, then what in the personal and social development of Black teenagers gives rise to these statistics? Equally important, are there social attributes and practices in the Black community that contribute to teenage pregnancy?

In spite of the obvious issues in Black teenager parenthood, a significant aspect of this social phenomenon is its commentary on Black female-male relationships. With the teenager mother and child frequently returning to her family of origin, the teenage father often is on the periphery, if included at all. Although this may be a practical solution, is there a subtle social message being conveyed about the value of family and the structure of male-female responsibilities in parenting? To assume the adult tasks of parenthood fortuitously in adolescence is likewise a comment on parenthood. Black parents must decide if this comment is applicable.

Consequently considering the social context in Black child development is paramount to maximizing psychoeducational development. Children in general negotiate three major environmental settings— home, school, and community. Within each are particular experiences that nurture and direct affective and cognitive development. They are interdependent. Black parents in the past have been sensitive to this interdependency in the teaching of survival skills in a racist society. The poem "Mother to Son" by Langston Hughes (1974), presented at the beginning of this chapter, captures the tenor of Black parenthood and is explored further by Grier and Cobbs (1968).

Much of the critical skills of Black parenthood needed in the past are needed in contemporary Black America. The Black child's response to the conditions at home, in his or her school, and in the neighborhood is a product of his or her ability to understand his or her experiences (i.e., the cognitive domain) integrated with the management of his or her emotional reactions (i.e., the affective domain). That they are not mutually exclusive must be continually stressed. Contained in the approach to managing life experiences is the structure of personality. Achievement or failure, adaptive or maladaptive behavior is simply a manifestation of the child's personal management style. Black parents can play a significant role in shaping that style. Black children must be nurtured in the development of racial identity and self-esteem. They must learn the skills of survival to negotiate the social and racial conditions of society. They must acquire literacy and marketable skills in order to compete in the world of work. But foremost in the tasks of Black parenting is teaching the child about the nuances and impact of racism.

To deny the existence of racism for the Black parent is to misguide the psychoeducational development of the child. No matter if the child is insulated from overt personal confrontations with racism, the vestiges of a racist society are omnipresent. Television is a major culprit in accenting social class differences between the Black child and the screen image. It provides no suitable Black role models based on the reality of life for the average Black child. This technology of the modern world is becoming the "electronic parent" and having considerable influence on shaping the identity of Black children (Pierce, 1974; Berry, 1982). There is no portrayal on television of a competent Black family nurturing their children through the realities of Black life. In fact, a greater insult is perpetrated in television series representing orphaned black children uncharacteristically raised by white families in the absence of Black extended family participation. As Black parents permit this "electronic babysitter" into their homes, they must begin to scrutinize the social messages it conveys about their worth, both as parents and as people.

Too many Black parents are abdicating their child rearing responsibilities to instruments of institutionalized racism. Movies as well as television rarely represent Black life in a positive or supportive manner (Nobel, 1969). Infant and day care centers are reducing parent-child contact at critical periods of development. Moreover, their success at enrichment must be monitored as closely as primary school systems, where the quality of education for Black children remains woefully inadequate and where an alarming number of parents are failing to become involved.

Getting a "good" education remains the Black parent's "hope" for improving the child's access to better life opportunities. Monitoring school achievement is no less important today than in the past. However, the increasing dropout rate of Black students before completion of secondary school requires our scrutiny of what is happening to our youths' future. Schools are social environments, not simply repositories for knowledge. It must be rewarding for both socio-emotional as well as educational reasons. Hence, accountability becomes an important parental task. This include monitoring the child's progress in school in addition to whether the school is fulfilling its commitment to educate. For Black parents cognizant of the ravages of racism, evaluation of the formal educational process becomes upper-most to the task of guiding the psychoeducational development of the child. This obligation is more than signing end of term grade reports. It means the parent fully engages in the configuration of activities that contribute to the affective and cognitive experiences of his or her child.

Hence, parent-school interactions are an equally important domain to child development as to parent-child interactions. Community school boards' decisions can be equally as consequential to the psycho-educational development of the Black child as any parental decisions. Black parents must come to terms with what Ogbu (1978, 1981) poignantly delineates as the cultural-ecological context of Black education. Viewing formal education as an instrument of societal priorities, Black parents must constantly evaluate if those priorities serve the best interests of their children and in what form. One form that has gained in national concern among professionals is standardized testing.

In spite of the admonitions of Black psychologists and educators about the consequences of psychological and educational testing, this pervasive product of the modern world is having increasing parental acceptance notwithstanding its impact on the educational and career opportunities of black children (Miller, 1980; NAACP, 1974, 1983). The National Academy of Science, in a major report, has absolved testing as unduly biased or inherently discriminatory. This endorsement will only increase the use of standardized testing by institutions.

It is the practices and social policies of these institutions that must be carefully monitored by Black parents. In California, the case of Larry P. exemplifies the danger posed by testing (Hilliard, 1983). A dispropor-tionate number of Black and Mexican-American children were placed in special education classes, giving "scientific" support for adherents of stereotypical notions about Black children's abilities. It is these types of social trends that Black parents must be vigilant about. They begin to structure the personal life of the Black child.

A more ominous trend in the future is the development of personal computer software facilitating the administering and *interpretation* of psychological and educational tests. This capability expands the access of these tools to institutions and persons professionally untrained in their use, but in positions to establish social and economic policy on test results. Computers in particular are revolutionizing our way of life, but can shroud their social relevance in technological glitter. However, advancement in technology continues to outstrip the social and moral progress of society. No matter how much things may seem to change, they also seem to remain the same. Black children still experience their parents' facing housing and job discrimination, their siblings with few career options, and upward mobility stymied in the Black community. All Black children at some point in their development must reconcile aspirations for the "American dream" with their odds for attaining it. Psychodynamically, this struggle still is best represented by W.E.B. DuBois (1965: 2) in his *Souls of Black Folks*:

> The Negro is a sort of seventh son, born with a veil, and gifted with second-sight in the American world—a world which yields him no true self-consciousness, but only lets him see himself through the revelation of the other world. It is a peculiar sensation, this double-consciousness, this sense of always looking at one's self through the eye of others, of measuring one's soul by the tape of a world that looks on in amused contempt and pity. One ever feels his twoness—an American, a Negro; two souls, two thoughts, two unreconciled strivings; two warring ideals in one dark body, whose dogged strength alone keeps it from being torn asunder.

Black children must be educated and psychologically prepared for this inevitable feeling of duality in their lives. Guidance through this emotional maze should come foremost from the parents. The Black community, however, always has managed to provide mentors in addition to the parent for this personal experience, and must continue to do so.

EMERGENCE OF CLINICAL PROBLEM:
ISSUES OF PREVENTION

In our role as clinicians, we are too often confronted with the casualties of Black children and families who are unaware of the implications of the issues discussed in this chapter. These casualties can manifest themselves in a variety of symptoms, presenting problems such as learning disabilities, school failure, and behavioral and emotional problems. Although these problems may initially manifest themselves in the family, they are rapidly transmitted to the school and the community context as the child grows older. For our purposes, in this chapter we would like to present preventative strategies for avoiding these pitfalls.

The current literature on learning disabilities, for example, addresses issues such as the role of prenatal factors and early nutrition in providing a sound basis for neurological development. Educating Black parents to the importance of a sound, well-balanced diet in the early years is essential. There is an ongoing debate, for example, on the impact of excessive sugar intake on the development of hyperactive conditions (Davis, 1981; Kolata, 1978). In addition, early recognition of learning problems and clear understanding of "normal" child development would greatly assist Black parents in gaining early diagnosis and remediation of learning problems. Even basic screening programs for the detection of hearing and visual defects often are overlooked in Black communities. This requires an educational program on sex and parenting health and nutrition care in general for future parents that can begin in our junior high and high school courses long before motherhood or fatherhood becomes a reality.

Once the child leaves the home environment and enters the school, his or her social sphere expands considerably. This is occurring at an earlier and earlier age with the tendency toward day care and nursery programs for infants and young children. Black parents need to be educated to the importance of a close working arrangement between parents and teachers. If this does not occur, the child's progress cannot be adequately monitored and problems often will become severe before conferences are sought. As in the case of the diagnosis of learning diabilities, the earlier that school behavioral problems are caught, the more effective intervention strategies can be. Finally, Black parents can benefit greatly from understanding the etiology and prevention of emotional and behavioral disorders. Current child development literature stresses the importance of early bonding and attachment to parenting figures. Parents, who are themselves overwhelmed by serious life and survival realities, often lose sight of these needs. Many hospitals, clinics, and mental health centers now feature infant stimulation and parenting programs. Workshops on these topics are now an important part of many day care programs.

In addition, at times it is possible for the child's parents or caregivers to contribute significantly to the development of emotional and behavioral problems. The key element here is the impact of inconsistent disciplinary practices; for example, a parent who disciplines a child and states that the child will remain in his or her room for a period of time after disobeying a family rule. If this is not followed through and maintained, the child will quickly discover this inconsistency. All children in this position begin to test their parents. If this pattern continues, it can lead to serious emotional and behavior disorders.

It is the perception of many white mental health practitioners that Black parents resort to more "physical" punishment than many white ethnic groups (Boyd, 1977). Many Black parents believe firmly in the philosophy that if you "spare the rod, you spoil the child." Black parents need to be helped to understand that certain forms of spanking may have a place in an overall disciplinary program, but that an exclusive reliance on this form of discipline can be counterproductive. In extreme situations, it can even contribute to child abuse. It is important for Black parents to be exposed to other behavioral paradigms for effective management of disturbing behaviors. Once again, mental health centers, clinics, and schools can provide a much needed service by offering workshops and groups on effective parenting. The key here is that parents have a clear responsibility for guiding, enhancing, and monitoring a child's psychoeducational development in order to avoid the development of problems.

In this chapter we have highlighted another area in which difficulties can occur: lack of unified parenting messages, particularly in situations in which many caretakers may be involved. Here children often become scapegoated (Minuchin, 1974). All parenting figures must be helped to be consistent and clear in their messages to their children.

Finally, it is the task of Black mental health professionals to help change attitudes in the Black community toward seeking professional help when necessary. Many Black families view people who participate in mental health programs as "crazy." These attitudes must be changed by more effective community education and outreach programs. Individual, family, and group therapy are available as well as counseling in the schools and a variety of parent education workshops discussed above.

In conclusion, the struggle to raise children in this world is a difficult task for any parent. This struggle is magnified considerably when a parent and child are Black. Added to all of the other-jobs of the Black parent is the task of preparing a child to feel proud of him- or herself and his or her racial identity in a racist world. If Black children are to have a chance at survival, Black parents must become even more aware of the psychoeducational process and participate in it in a meaningful way. It is only through this process that Black children can have a chance for a viable future and an opportunity to realize their potential as adults.

REFERENCES

BARTZ, K. W. and B. S. LEVINE (1978) "Child rearing by Black parents: a description and comparison to Anglo and Chicano parents." Journal of Marriage and the Family 40, 4: 709-720.

BERRY, G. (1982) "Television, self-esteem, and the Afro-American child," in B. A. Bass et al. (eds.) The Afro-American Family. New York: Grune & Stratton.

BILLINGSLEY, A. (1968) Black Families in White America. Englewood Cliffs, NJ: Prentice-Hall.

BOYD, N. (1982) "Family therapy with Black families," in E. Jones and S. Korchin (eds.) Minority Mental Health. New York: Praeger.

———(1977) "Clinicians' perceptions of Black families in therapy." Ph.D. dissertation, Teachers College, Columbia University.

COMER, J. P. and A. E. POUSSAINT (1975) Black Child Care. New York: Simon & Schuster.

CUMMINGS, J. (1983) "Breakup of Black family imperils gains of decades." New York Times (November 20).

DAVIS, A. (1981) Let's Have Healthy Children. New York: New American Library.

DuBOIS, W.E.B. (1965) The Souls of Black Folk. London: Longmans, Green.

FRANKLIN, A. J. (1982) "Therapeutic intervention with urban Black adolescents," in E. Jones and S. Korchin (eds.) Minority Mental Health. New York: Praeger.

GIROUD, A. (1970) Nutrition of the Embryo. Springfield, IL: Charles C Thomas.

GRIER, W. and P. COBBS (1968) Black Rage. New York: Bantam.

GUTTMACHER, A. (1973) Pregnancy, Birth and Family Planning. New York: New American Library.

HARRISON-ROSS, P. and B. WYDEN (1973) The Black Child: A Parent's Guide. New York: Peter H. Wyden.

HILL, R. (1977) Informal Adoption Among Black Families. Washington, DC: National Urban League Research Department.

———(1972) The Strengths of Black Families. New York: Emerson Hall.

HILLIARD, A. G. (1983) "IQ and the courts: Larry P. vs. Wilson Riles and PASE vs. Hannon." Journal of Black Psychology 10 (August): 1-18.

HINES, P. and N. BOYD-FRANKLIN (1982) "Black families," in M. McGoldrick et al. (eds.) Ethnicity and Family Therapy. New York: Guilford.

HUGHES, L. (1974) Selected Poems of Langston Hughes. New York: Vintage.

KOLATA, D. (1978) "Childhood hyperactivity: a new look at treatment and causes." Science 199:.515.

LAMB, M. E. [ed.] (1981) The Role of the Father in Child Development. New York: John Wiley.

MBITI, J. S. (1970) African Religions and Philosophies. Garden City, NY: Anchor.

McADOO, H. P. [ed.] (1981) Black Families. Beverly Hills, CA: Sage.

MILLER, L. (1980) "Testing Black students: implications for assessing inner-city schools," in R. L. Jones (ed.) Black Psychology. New York: Harper & Row.

MINUCHIN, S. (1974) Families and Family Therapy. Cambridge, MA: Harvard Univ. Press.

MOYNIHAN, D. P. (1965) The Negro Family: The Case for National Action. Washington, DC: U.S. Department of Labor, Office of Policy Planning and Research.

NAACP (1983) Quality of Education, Update. New York: author.

———(1974) Task Force on Minority Testing. New York: author.

National Urban League (1984) The State of Black America. New York: author.

NOBLE, K. B. (1984) "Plight of Black family is studied anew." New York Times (January 29).

NOBLE, P. (1969) The Negro in Films. Port Washington, NY: Kennikat Press.

NOBLES, W. (1980) "African philosophy: foundations for Black psychology," in R. Jones (ed.) Black Psychology. New York: Harper & Row.

OGBU, J. U. (1981) "Black education: a cultural-ecological perspective," in H. P. McAdoo (ed.) Black Families. Beverly Hills, CA: Sage.

———(1978) Minority Education and Caste. New York: Academic.

PIERCE, C. (1974) "Psychiatric problems of the Black minority," in G. Caplan (ed.) American Handbook of Psychiatry, vol. 2. New York: Basic Books.

RYAN, W. (1971) Blaming the Victim. New York: Pantheon.

STACK, C. (1975) All Our Kin: Strategies for Survival in a Black Community. New York: Harper & Row.

SUDARKASA, N. (1981) "Interpreting the African heritage in Afro-American family organization," in H. P. McAdoo (ed.) Black Families. Beverly Hills, CA: Sage.

WHITE, J. (1980) "Toward a Black psychology," in R. Jones (ed.) Black Psychology. New York: Harper & Row.

PART V

INTERNAL ENVIRONMENTS OF CHILDREN'S RACIAL ATTITUDES AND SELF-ESTEEM

12

RACIAL ATTITUDE AND SELF-CONCEPT OF YOUNG BLACK CHILDREN OVER TIME

HARRIETTE PIPES McADOO

The development of the racial and self-attitudes of young Black children over time has been a concern of many. The child's awareness of his or her individual existence and the perceptions of who and what he or she is result from the interaction with his or her environment and how significant others in this domain view him or her and the groups of which he or she is a member.

The importance of parental attitudes as intervening variables in the development has been stressed by many authors (Horowitz, 1939; Goodman, 1952; Cole, 1967; and Lipscomb, 1975). The impacts of external institutions and the mass media also have been singled out as important socializers upon how the child views his or her racial group (Graves, 1975). All of these forces combine to form the child's view of how he or she and his or her ethnic group fit into his or her view of the world.

From the earliest studies in the late 1930s until presently, authors repeatedly have reported that the young Black child has low self-esteem and negative racial attitudes (Clark and Clark, 1939; Clark, 1952, 1963; Goodman, 1952; Asher and Allen, 1969). Self-concept and racial attitudes were assumed to have a linear relationship. The self-hatred hypothesis has been widely accepted in lay and professional literature. Only limited questioning of this view has occurred, although varied

AUTHOR'S NOTE: Gratitude is given to Lorraine Nadelman for her support. The Mississippi and Michigan data were collected with the assistance of a University of Michigan Rachkam Research Grant, 1969. The DC I data collection was supported by a 1972 Howard University Faculty Grant. The DC II data were collected under an Office of Child Development Grant, OCD-CB-282, 1973. Follow-up funds were made through a 1974 faculty Research Grant.

results have been obtained (Porter, 1966, 1971; Greenwald and Oppenheim, 1968).

More recent findings have indicated a more positive view of the Black
child's ethnic identity (J. McAdoo, 1970; Hraba and Grant, 1970; Fox
and Barnes, 1971; Ward and Braum, 1972; Lipscomb, 1975). These
desirable results have been attributed to two factors: improved research
methodology and the increase in Black consciousness and self-pride
within the Black community.

We have collected such data over a period of five years on Black
children that should provide insights in the development of and the
relationship between these variables. I began to look at these variables
as I viewed my own four children experiencing the painful contradictions
of growing up Black in our society. They reached an awareness of race,
made their self-race identities, and then coped with the complicated
process of forming racial preferences.

Proceeding through the socialization process is a complicated one for
all children, filled with hazards and high points. It is even more difficult
for Black children. They have a double developmental task, at first they
must incorporate the dominant values of our society. These values
insidiously include a devaluation of those who are nonwhite. At the
same time, they must incorporate the values of the Black community
and culture, which often are in conflict with the dominant society
(McAdoo, 1974). The conflict of values, which is experienced universally
by American Blacks, must be resolved in some manner so that the
individual may become a functioning adult.

In examining how Black children resolve this apparent conflict, it is
necessary to ask ourselves three questions: (1) How does the average
Black child feel about him- or herself? Is he or she usually happy or sad;
does he or she really feel he or she is a person of worth? (2) What does he
or she feel about being Black? Is he or she really seething with anger,
hatred, or wishful thinking? Or is he or she proud or indifferent to his or
her racial group? (3) How are his or her feelings of self-worth affected by
what he or she feels about his or her racial group?

The traditional view of the resolution of this conflict has earlier been
seen in the literature as resulting in self-hatred. The child, from this
point of view, was seen as developing an acceptance of the societal
preference for white, inferring a hatred for blackness. This preference
for white was seen as a rejection of that which is black: be it skin color,
hair texture, facial and body features, and even speech patterns. If one
blames the Black child and his or her alleged "self-hatred" for his or her
inability to score high on standardized tests, then the purest form of
blaming the victim rather than the system is at play.

In light of the many happy Black youngsters I have seen and my personal dissatisfaction with the view that Black children hate themselves, I was led to reexamine the literature and my old data and to collect follow-up data in order to look at these issues.

Many studies have been made on either self-concept *or* related racial attitudes. These variables, however, have not been combined in empirical investigations until recently (H. McAdoo, 1970; Ward and Braun, 1972). Often authors have collected hard data on only one variable (i.e., race preference) but have extended the discussion into other areas. This happens when out-group-oriented responses given by children to skin color tests are interpreted by a researcher as being indicative of impaired self-concepts. These interpretations may or may not be supported by data. The self-hatred philosophy, which is the prevalent view taught to most graduate students and professionals, appears to be faulty and ultimately damaging to the Black child. The negative expectations that result from these attitudes could be a direct intervening variable in later school performance that has been shown to be related to eventual self-worth.

The possibility that no such relationship between racial attitude and self-concept exists is one that most of us find difficult to conceptualize. We all have been so imbued with the image of a unitary self-concept that it is almost impossible to envision how a child may feel good about him-or herself on one dimension, poorly on another, or even ambivalent on a third, all at the same time. We still tend to feel that if a child picks up the Caucasian doll as the prettiest doll, then he or she hates the other pretty Black doll, and ultimately must hate him- or herself. Presented in these simple terms, the self-hatred view appears absurd. Yet this is exactly how Black child research has been interpreted in the past.

In contrast to the self-hatred theory, a few researchers have begun to take a different theoretical tack (Cross, 1974; McAdoo, 1974) because supposed direct linear relationship between these variables has not been supported by data. Three views of the relationship now appear possible: (1) A curvilinear relationship exists between the two variables; (2) a compartmentalization is possible between the two variables race attitude and self-concept; or (3) no such relationship exists.

Several researchers have hypothesized that there will be a nonlinear relationship between these variables (Spencer, 1973; Cross, 1974). Spencer has found that both negative and positive race attitudes are found in preschoolers who have positive self-concepts. It is possible that Black children are able to compartmentalize their view of themselves from their view of their racial group. My earlier (1970) data have not supported the linear hypothesis. The results obtained partially support both the nonlinear (or curvilinear) view and the compartmentalized view.

My research on the development of the Black child has concentrated on four aspects: the development of self-esteem and racial attitudes in Black children from preschool age and over a period of time; the relationship between these variables; the impact of demographic factors upon these developments; and the occupational and educational aspirations of the children.

RESEARCH DESIGN

SUBJECTS

Data were obtained from three different groups of children, each at two points in time. The original testing was followed up in one year in the mid-Atlantic area, and in five years with the Mississippi and Michigan samples (see Table 12.1). Data were collected in three different demographic areas: an all-Black Mississippi rural town; a racially mixed Michigan urban setting; and a mid-Atlantic urban, predominantly Black setting.

The subjects in the pretest studies consisted of 4½- to 6½-year-old Black children, who were enrolled in full day, year-long day care programs with an educational component.

The Mississippi preschool sample of 43 had a mean age of 5.5 years and 10.8 years upon retesting. They were from Mound Bayou, a town founded by former slaves that has remained in Black ownership. A great deal of pride exists within this town. It was considered an ideal place to test the hypothesis that children in stable, all-Black communities will be able to develop stronger self-concepts.

The Michigan sample of 35 had a mean age of 5.2 years on the pretest and 10.5 on the follow-up. They lived outside of Detroit in a residentially segregated, metropolitan area with integrated schools. All of the children were born in the North, although many of the parents had come from the South to work in the automobile factories.

The District of Columbia (DC) sample was in a predominantly Black residential and school environment, with limited interracial contacts. Sixty-eight children of working-class and middle-class families, whose mean age was 5.4 years, were in the original DC sample. Fifty-five of the children were retested 12 months later.

TABLE 12.1   Testing Time

	1969	1972	1973	1974
Mississippi	X			X
Michigan	X			X
D.C.		X	X	

RESEARCH PROCEDURE

All of the children in the appropriate age group were tested by trained Black adults. The effect of the sex of the examiner was controlled by having each interviewer test half of the boys and half of the girls. To control for the possible effect of father absence in the home, within each sex group, the same proportion of two-parent to one-parent families was maintained, approximately 75% to 25%. These proportions were used to reflect the census data on Black families nationally.

After the data were collected, t-tests were run on all of the data collected by the two examiners. No significant difference between the testers was found and the data were then combined. To avoid the bias that may be introduced if one test was consistently presented first, two orders of presentation were used, thereby preventing the formation of a presentation set. In all cases, the racial identification procedure was presented last, to avoid contamination from this task to the responses for the other instruments. The basic assumption of this study was that race and self-attitudes are multidimensional; therefore, several approaches should be used to obtain data that would accurately reflect the many dimensions of how a child feels about him- or herself.

There are several methodological problems inherent in any follow-up study. We experienced the usual loss of subjects upon retesting that placed serious limitations on the multivariate analyses that were possible. Increasing the number of assessments made for each child enlarged the breadth of the study and attempted to offset the problem of a smaller number of subjects.

The northern sample proved to be very stable. Of the original 35 children, 24 (69%) were found and retested. But only 8 of the original 43 (19%) on whom there was complete data in the South still resided in the area. The dropout rate probably reflected the agricultural changes occurring in the rural Delta area. Giant agribusinesses were moving in, taking over the smaller farms and replacing human labor with giant machines. Many of the parents were reported as having moved North, usually to the Chicago area, looking for jobs and following the migration patterns of earlier relatives. To augment the small southern posttest sample, a cohort group of 13 children, for whom we had partial pretest data, was given the complete battery. The original 8 and cohort 13 were compared on all variables and no significant differences were found on any of the variables. Pre- and posttest comparisons were run for the original group alone and for the combined group. No differences were found in the results. Therefore, the two groups were combined to form the Mississippi follow-up group.

The data are organized on the basis of the three studies: Study I Mississippi and Michigan preschool; Study II DC one-year preschool follow-up; and Study III Mississippi and Michigan five-year follow-up.

DATA COLLECTION INSTRUMENTS

SELF-CONCEPT

Two main procedures were used to collect self-concept (SC) data: the Thomas Self-Concept Values Test and the Engle Self-Concept Procedures.

The Thomas asks 14 bipolar questions that provide an assessment of how the child views him- or herself, and then how the child perceived how he or she is viewed by important reference persons: mother, teachers, and peers. These questions are asked in relation to the child's own Polaroid picture. The questions ask how the child rates him- or herself on the dimensions of appearance, size, ability, sociability, happiness, and strength.

There was one problem with the Thomas: A sex bias against girls was built into the standardized format. Girls were scored lower if they viewed themselves as strong (versus weak) or big (versus small). Because the girls consistently scored themselves similarly to the boys, and because recent sex-role attitudes and the literature did not support this biased scoring, it was eliminated. All sexes were scored in the same manner. Further support for this position was given in the 1976 APA presidential address in which Hartup (1976) stated in summary SC findings that size is positively related to self-concept until the third grade, but there is no correlation afterward.

The Engle self-concept procedure was the second instrument used to measure self-esteem. The child was shown an illustration of two stick figures standing at both ends of a stepladder with five steps. One figure was identified as having positive characteristics (happy) and the other as being negative (sad). The child's self-evaluation statement was rated by his or her placement of a mark on one of the rungs of the ladder illustration. Seven different selections were made (appearance, strength, likeability, ability, happiness, bravery, and following rules).

The self-portrait and story technique used by Porter (1971) was given only in the follow-up study as a measure of self-image and racial group attitude. Each child was asked to select a piece of paper when shown eight sheets of paper (two each of black, brown, tan, and white) in identical random order. They then were given a new box of crayons and asked to draw themselves. They were then asked in a nondirective manner to tell a story about the drawing. Porter set up self-esteem scoring on the assumption that the most detailed, lively pictures indicated a more positive self-image. Facial expression, size, and position on the page were scored as emotional indicators. The thematic content of stories was coded for personal efficacy, powerlessness, and lively descriptions.

Two trained coders worked independently of each other to determine the presence or absence of each category. On each coding disagreement the two coders had to reach a consensus before the final score was assigned.

RACIAL GROUP ATTITUDES

The racial attitudes (RA) was assessed five ways: PRAM II, Clark's dolls test, a racial identification procedure, racial group awareness, and a separate racial content scoring of the self-portraits. The last two were used only with the follow-up group.

The Williams and Roberson Preschool Racial Attitude Measure (PRAM II) was used, in which children are shown a picture of two figures, identical except for skin and color. A story was read to the children describing a person in either negative or positive terms. The children then are asked to point to the person who appears in the story. There are twelve possible picture pairs from which to select. If the choices are due to random selection and there are no relationships between the content of the picture and the child's choices, the score should fall around 6, as in a binomial distribution (Guilford, 1956). A score between 10 and 12 could be considered white-oriented, while 2 to 0 could be considered Black-oriented, using the standardized scoring of Williams and Roberson.

Race preference and race self-identity were obtained with a modification of the original Clark's dolls test. Seven questions were related to the preference of the dark- or light-skinned doll, when children were asked to evaluatively select a doll (pretty, ugly, nice, etc.). The two identity questions found what race the children believed themselves to be (looks like you now, as a baby).

The racial identification score was the number of times the child correctly pointed to the race content picture of the PRAM (3 Blacks and 3 whites) when asked to identify a person of a particular race.

The racial content from the self-portrait procedure was scored according to a scheme that was based on the color of paper chosen and the presence of five ratings of Negroid characteristics (skin and hair color, hair type and style, facial features, and Black cultural artifacts).

The racial group awareness score was obtained when the children were asked, "What type of person do most people in America think is best?" They are given the choices of different groups: Black, Jewish, white Protestant, and white Catholic. The question was repeated until the child had ranked all of the groups.

ASPIRATIONS

The occupational and educational aspirations were obtained by simply asking the child, parent, and teacher how far the child would go in school and what job they would like him or her to have, or would like to have.

RESULTS

STUDY I:
MISSISSIPPI AND MICHIGAN PRESCHOOL DATA

SELF-CONCEPT RESULTS

Self-concept scores were viewed to see how they were affected by demography, sex of the child, and family type. On the Thomas Self-Concept Test all of the samples had positive self-concept scores, within one standard deviation of the mean of 50. The self-hatred hypothesis was not supported by the data because positive self-concepts were found in all groups.

TABLE 12.2 Summary Table of Three-Way Analysis of Variance of Thomas Self-Concept Scores According to Demography, Sex, and Family Type of Children

| Source | df | Modified Scoring | |
		MS	F
Demography (A)	1	610.77	9.31*
Sex (B)	1	188.80	2.88
Family (C)	1	1.67	0.03
A x B	1	29.46	0.45
A x C	1	243.11	3.71
B x C	1	16.81	0.26
A x B x C	1	567.48	8.65*
Error	70		
Total	77		

*$p < .01$

The demographic location of the sample was an important factor; the children in the urban centers had lower self-concept scores than those in the rural areas. On the first testing the preschool children in the southern all-Black town (M = 51.42) had significantly higher self-concept scores than those in the integrated northern urban center (M = 46.63).

A three-way analysis of variance was run on the Thomas Self-Concept scores using the demographic, sex, and family type groups as the independent variables (see Table 12.2). The demographic difference was significant at the 0.1 level $F(1,70) = 9.31$, but the sex and family type differences did not reach significance. The three-way interaction was significant at the .01 level, $F(1,70) = 8.65$ (see Table 12.2). Of the 8 demographic x sex x family type groups, the southern one-parent boys had the highest self-concept (56.56) and the northern two-parent girls had the lowest (41.82) (see Table 12.3).

An analysis of variance with five replications was run on the total and four referent SC scores by demography, using a program of Winer's (1971). The demographic group difference was significant—$F(1,76) = 6.95$, $p < .009$. The reference group's (trials) difference was significant—$F(4,304) = 7.08$, $p < .0001$. The low score of the teacher referent scale score contributed heavily to the lower total northern score. The children felt better about themselves than they felt they were perceived by their teachers or peers, especially in the North. The southern children scored positively on all four referent groups. The interaction between demography and reference groups was not significant (see Table 12.4). The southern children with only Black teachers scored significantly higher on teacher's perceptions of them, $F(1,77) = 7.37$, $p < .01$, and peer rating,

TABLE 12.3 Means and Standard Deviations of Thomas Self-Concept Test for Total Sample and Subgroups

Group	n	M	SD
Total	78	47.84	9.37
Northern	35	46.63	10.16
Southern	43	51.42	7.43
Boys	36	51.66	8.19
Girls	42	47.49	9.42
Two-parent	48	48.94	9.20
One-parent	30	49.83	8.85
Northern			
boys	16	50.69	8.65
girls	19	43.21	10.28
Southern			
boys	23	51.17	7.80
girls	23	50.91	7.31
Two-parent			
boys	23	51.17	7.57
girls	25	46.33	10.18
One-parent			
boys	13	32.46	9.22
girls	17	47.94	8.34
Northern	23	47.78	10.72
Two-parent	12	53.25	7.03
boys	12	53.25	7.03
girls	11	41.82	11.12
Northern			
One-parent	12	44.23	6.64
boys	4	43.00	9.38
girls	8	45.18	9.37
Southern			
Two-parent	25	50.28	7.66
boys	11	49.08	7.80
girls	14	50.71	7.79
Southern			
One-parent	18	53.65	6.63
boys	9	56.56	5.73
girls	8	51.25	6.88

$F(1,77) = 6.73$, $p < .05$. The self-referent rating and mother perception were positive for both groups. A sex difference on reference groups was not found (see Table 12.5).

TABLE 12.4   Repeated Analysis of Variance of Thomas Self-Concept
Score for Demographic Effects with Five Replications
(total, self, mother, teacher, and peers)

Source	df	MS	F
Between	77	294.81	
groups (N & S)	1	1,901.97	6.95**
errors	76	273.66	
Within	312	35.99	
replications	4	233.37	7.08***
G x R	4	68.72	2.08*
error (R)	304	32.96	
Total	389	87.22	

*p < .08; **p < .009; ***p < .0001

TABLE 12.5   Means and F Test of Differences Between Means of North,
South and Boys, Girls on Four Reference Groups (self,
mother, teacher, peers) on Thomas Self-Concept Test

Reference Group	Total	Northern	Sourthern	F Ratio	Boys	Girls	F Ratio
Self	51.27	50.23	52.12	1.83	52.40	50.47	1.64
Mother	50.09	48.23	51.60	2.50	51.51	48.79	1.82
Teacher	46.94	43.17	50.00	7.37**	48.71	45.37	1.79
Peers	47.85	44.91	50.23	6.73*	49.51	46.79	1.23
n	78	35	43		36	42	

*p < .05 1,77 df; **p < .01 1,77 df

An analysis of variance was run on the self-concept scores for each of
the 14 bipolar scores by demography. Differences were found on only
two scales: size and sharing. The southern children scored themselves as
bigger, $F(1,76) = 7.63$, $p < .01$, and also were more willing to share their
toys, $F(1,76) = 4.38$, $p < .05$.

As each child had been weighed and measured, it was possible to
determine if an actual physical difference existed. In fact, the southern
children at 44.65 pounds and 45.53 inches (20.25 kg, 115.65 cm) were
significantly taller, $F(1,76) = 7.66$, $p < .01$, but not heavier than the
northern children at 44.64 pounds and 44 inches (20.25 kg, 111.76 cm).

TABLE 12.6   Means and Standard Deviations of PRAM Race Attitude
Scores for Total and Subgroups

Group	N	M	SD
Total	78	8.79	2.85
boys	36	8.89	2.62
girls	42	8.71	3.06
Northern	35	8.71	3.22
Southern	43	8.86	2.53
Northern			
boys	16	8.94	3.13
girls	19	8.53	3.37
Southern			
boys	20	8.85	2.21
girls	23	8.87	2.83

No sex differences or family type differences were found in the actual size of the child.

The bipolar SC items also were run by family type and sex. The only family type difference was that the one-parent children were more willing to share, $F(1,76) = 5.25$, $p < .05$. The only sex difference was that the boys scored higher on liking "to be with men" than the girls, $F(1,76) = 8.32$, $p < .05$.

RACE ATTITUDE

The mean RA for this sample was higher than chance selection. A moderate out-group-oriented mean score of 8.79 was obtained for the total sample, with no significant demography, sex, or family type differences found (see Table 12.6). This moderate out-group orientation is less than found in earlier data with Black children. These scores were significantly more favorable toward Blacks than the contemporary data of white preschool children using the same procedures with Roberson. Williams and Roberson's (1967) white preschool sample was $t(50) = 3.90$, $p < .01$.

RACIAL IDENTIFICATION

The scores indicate that the children were well aware of proper racial titles, for the average score was 5.65 out of a possible 6. A three-way

ANOVA was run on these scores, with no sex or family differences found. The children in the southern one-parent families all gave perfectly correct identifications (M = 6, SD = 0). The children in the South were able to identify correctly significantly more pictures than those in the North (F [1,70] = 7.58, p < .01).

For these groups the more accurate the race identification score, the more positively oriented was their attitude toward whites. Correctness of race identification correlated significantly with out-group racial orientation for the boys, r = .330, p < .05, and for children from two-parent families, r = .367, p < .05. No intercorrelations were found in the other groups (see Table 12.7).

The accuracy of responses to the picture of the two races was separately correlated with the other variables. No relationship was found with race attitude. A demographic difference was found, with no relationship in the North. In the South positive self-concept was related to the response accuracy of the Black pictures, r = .613, p < .01, but no relationship at all was found in responses to the white pictures. In the North self-concept was not related to either type of picture.

RELATIONSHIP BETWEEN RACE ATTITUDE AND SELF-CONCEPT

The crucial tenet of the self-hate thesis is that race attitude and self-concept are directly related, but the results were found to be mixed. No such relationship was found with northern, one-parent, or either sex group when combined across demography. These groups felt positive about their own self-worth independent of what racial group orientation they held.

A relationship was found with the southern boys, r = .534, p < .01, and the combined two-parent family groups, r = .404, p < .01. In these groups, those with positive self-concepts had more out-group orientation. The southern relationship was attributed to the divergent scores obtained by the southern boys, the group with the highest SC scores.

Self-concept was positively correlated with the accuracy of racial identification for the southern boys, r = .712, p < .01, and southern girls, r = .712, p < .05. The children in the South who were more accurate in designating the race of the picture also scored higher in self-esteem. Different relationships were found in the northern sample. The northern girls, with the lowest self-concept scores, had a significantly negative relationship; those who had positive self-esteem tended to make

TABLE 12.7 Intercorrelation of Self-Concept, Race Attitudes, and Race Identification Scores

Variables	T	N	S	B	G	I	NI	NB	NG	SB	SG
Race Attitudes:											
Thomas self-concept	.196	.080	.355*	.310	.109	.404**	-.041	.043	.534*	.534*	.203
race identification	.090	-.021	.280	.330*	-.088	.367**	-.307	.381	-.343	.364	.233
Thomas self-concept::											
race identification	.087	-.236	.555**	.276	-.043	.100	.036	.103	-.524*	.712**	.461*

NOTE: T = total; N = North; S = South; B = boys; G = girls; I = two-parent; NI = one-parent; NB = northern boys; NG = northern girls; SB = southern boys; SG = southern girls.
*p < .05; **p < .01

inaccurate identifications. No relationships were found among these boys.

To sum up the first study, the children had positive self-esteems, were moderately out-group oriented, and were easily able to identify pictures by their racial labels. The majority tended to compartmentalize their feelings about themselves and their status attitude toward their racial group.

STUDY II:
DC ONE-YEAR FOLLOW-UP—FIRST TESTING

SELF-CONCEPT

On the first testing the 55 urban children had low average Thomas Self-Concepts, M = 44.18; SD = 9.87. There were no significant SC differences between sex, family types, or SES class groups. The analysis of variances run on sex by family type obtained no significant difference, $F(3,48) = 2.75$, nor were differences found between sex by working class groups, $F(3,47) = 2.65$.

The pattern of SC scores for significant others found in this group was similar to that found in Mississippi and Michigan. These children felt that the teachers viewed them negatively, M = 40.05, while they still felt good about themselves, M = 49.07. Scores for peers also were low, M = 41.36. The total lower score can be attributed to their low teacher and peer perception scores.

Similar self-concept results were obtained using the Engle procedure. The children had a very positive mean SC score of 28.69 out of a possible 35, SD = 4.56. No sex, family type, or SES differences were found.

RACE ATTITUDE

These urban children had a moderate out-group orientation, with a mean RA score, M = 8.45, that was almost identical to that of the earlier Mississippi and Michigan sample. No sex differences were found, but significant SES family RA differences were found.

The highest out-group orientation obtained in all studies was found in the DC I two-parent families, M = 10, much higher than those in one-parent families, $t(53) = 3.82$, $p < .01$. Those in middle-class families, M = 9.73, had more white-oriented scores than children from working-

TABLE 12.8   Significant Intercorrelations of Thomas Self-Concept Tests with Racial Attitude Measures

Thomas Self-Concept Intercorrelations	DC I			DC II		
	Group*	R	p	Group*	r	p
PRAM II Race Attitude		no significant relationship		boys	.501	.01
				one-parent	.391	.008
				WC SES	.343	.05
Clark						
Dolls Race Attitude	girls	−.591	.01	boys	−.358	.03
	two-parent	−.593	.04	girls	−.414	.04
				WC SES	−.319	.05
				one-parent	−.336	.03
Dolls Self-ID.	all groups	no significant relationship			no significant relationship	
Dolls Race Pref.	girls	−.556	.02	boys	−.337	.04
	two-parent	−.596	.04			
	MC SES	−.558	.05			

*All other sex, family, or SES groups not listed had nonsignificant relationships.

class families, M = 7.94, t(53) = 3.35, p < .01. When grouped by sex, both groups had moderate out-group orientation, while those from one-parent and working-class families had mean scores in the chance range, M = 7.92, 7.94, respectively.

On the Clark race preference and identity dolls test, all of the groups displayed a positive evaluation of the white doll, regardless of sex, SES, or family type group. There were two dolls subscores obtained: race attitude and self-identity. All group mean scores were out-group oriented, M = 2.62, more than in the Mississippi and Michigan samples. In addition, they were able to exhibit correct self-identification only half of the time, M = 0.93, with no group differences. By contrast, all children in the Mississippi sample gave correct self-identification. Certain factors in Washington may have caused these differences: status, values, and power relations within the capital.

RELATIONSHIP OF RA AND SC

No support for the self-hatred hypothesis was found. No relationship was found between Thomas self-concept and racial attitude, or between self-concept and dolls self-identity. Relationships were found on doll race preference questions for three subgroups: the girls (r = −.556), two-parent (r = −.596), and middle-class (r = −.588) groups. When they were high on self-concept, they also were out-group oriented. No relationships were evident in the other groups. Again, the children's

TABLE 12.9   Means, Standard Deviations, and t-Tests for
             Total Group on Major Variables, DC I and DC II

Variables	DC I		DC II		df	t
	M	SD	M	SD		
Thomas Self-Concept (total)	44.18	9.87	49.38	10.77	54	3.05**
Thomas Self-Concept Reference Groups						
self	49.07	6.99	50.82	7.09	54	1.33
mother	47.64	10.36	51.58	10.07	54	2.23*
teacher	40.05	10.59	47.16	12.97	54	3.43**
peer	41.36	10.06	48.02	10.06	54	3.80**
Engle Self-Concept	28.69	4.56	27.85	6.16	54	0.90
PRAM-Race Attitudes	8.45	2.08	8.56	2.90	54	0.22
Dolls Race Preference	2.53	2.32	2.47	2.66	54	0.12
n = 55						

$*p < .05; **p < .01$

self-concept was intact, regardless of how they felt about the status
differential of racial groups (see Table 12.8).

SECOND TESTING

One year later the 55 children were retested, using identical procedures. Self-concepts had improved, while race attitudes remained the
same.

SELF-CONCEPT

The average Thomas self-concepts had increased significantly from
44.18 to 49.38 by the second year, $t(54) = 3.05$, $p < .01$ (see Table 12.9).
The greatest improvement had occurred in the girls who were in two-
parent families and who were middle class (see Figure 12.1).

The self-concept increase also is accounted for by the marked
increase in three reference scores. The children continued to view
themselves positively, but they indicated a significant increase in
important persons in their lives who now viewed them more positively:
the scores for mother, $t(54) = 2.23$, $p < .05$; teachers, $t(54) = 3.43$, $p < .01$;
and peers, $t(54) = 3.80$, $p < .01$; all had significant increases (see Figure
12.2).

The children felt much more positive about their own self-worth by
the second year. The Engle scores did not change, remaining high for

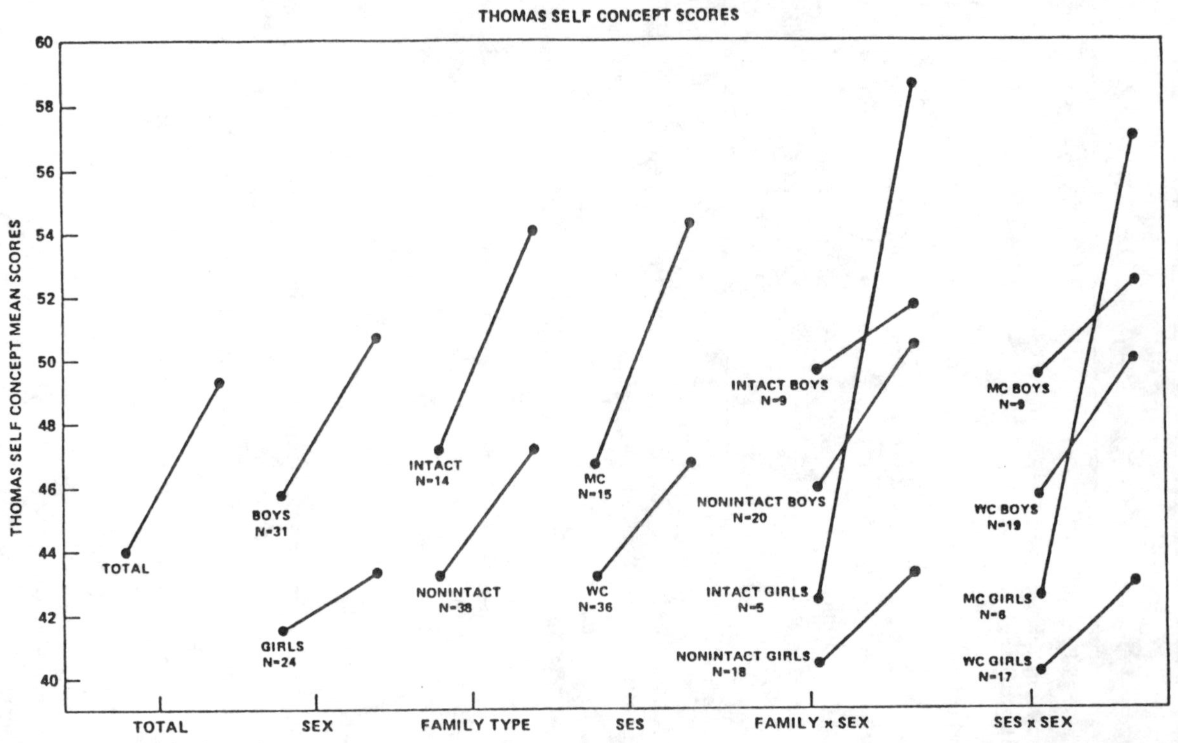

Figure 12.1 Mean Thomas Self-Concept Values Scores of the Follow-Up Sample in D.C. for Total Group and Subgroups

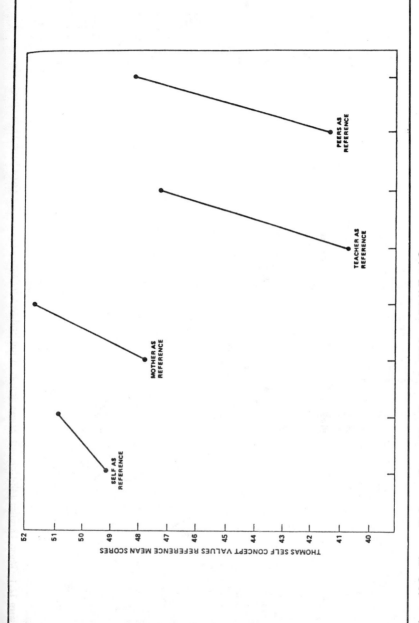

Figure 12.2 Thomas Reference Groups Mean Scores for DC I and DC II Total Groups

TABLE 12.10 Means, Standard Deviations and t-Tests of Self-Concept Measures by Socioeconomic Status, Sex, and Family Type

Sample Group		N	Mean	*Thomas* SD	t	N	Mean	*Engle* SD	t
DC I	Boys	31	45.87	10.23	1.67	31	28.48	4.91	1.06
	girls	24	41.58	8.77		24	29.79	4.22	
	two-parent	14	47.14	6.64	1.58	14	29.29	4.29	0.23
	one-parent	38	43.37	9.77		38	28.97	4.37	
	middle SES	15	46.87	6.50	1.57	15	29.33	4.37	0.33
	working SES	36	43.17	9.96		36	28.89	4.38	
DC II	boys	31	50.81	9.23	1.12	31	28.87	5.94	1.39
	girls	24	47.42	12.47		24	26.54	6.31	
	two-parent	14	54.07	8.70	2.28*	14	31.86	5.71	3.02*
	one-parent	38	47.11	10.93		38	26.45	5.76	
	middle SES	15	54.40	8.31	2.69**	15	30.40	6.31	1.84
	working SES	36	46.78	11.10		35	26.89	6.00	

*p < .05; **p < .01

both years. The one-dimension design of the Engle procedure did not appear to be as sensitive as the multidimensional design of the Thomas. When compared by groups on the Thomas, the children from two-parent homes had significantly better self-concepts, t(54) = 2.28, p < .05. The middle-class children were also significantly more positive about their self-worth than those who were working class, t(54) = 2.69, p < .05. The boys tended to be nonsignificantly higher than the girls in both years (see Table 12.10).

Significant sex by class group differences were found, F(3,47) = 3.72, p < .05. The middle-class girls felt positive, M = 57.00, about themselves, while the lowest scores were obtained from the working-class girls, M = 43.00.

RACE ATTITUDE

No changes were noted in RA or on the race attitude or self-identity. The children remained out-group oriented in all groups.

RELATIONSHIP BETWEEN RA AND SC

For three groups of children the self-hatred hypothesis was not rejected. Those with high SC scores were out-group oriented. Significant relationships on Thomas SC were found the second year in the boys, one-parent and working-class homes, r = .501, p < .01, r = .391, p < .008

and r = .343, p < .05, respectively. These two groups could be considered the most vulnerable within the sample. For the children from the three most "secure" groups—girls, two-parent and middle-income families— no such relationship was found (see Table 12.8), rejecting the view of Black self-hatred. Self-concept and self-race identity were not related for any of the groups. A relationship between high self-concept and out-group orientation was found with four of the groups.

In summary, over one year the children had shown remarkable self-concept increases in the preferred direction, but their racial attitudes had remained out-group oriented. The increase came mainly from improvement in their perception of teacher, peer, and mother ratings. Even though the day care center staff was stable, the children felt their teachers now valued them more highly. Those in what could be considered the more vulnerable groups—boys and those from one-parent and poorer families—tended to be more out-group oriented when their self-value was high. The most secure Black groups in our society—girls and those from two-parent and middle-class families— showed no relationship between self-attitudes and racial group acceptance. The self-hatred theories were not given support when Black children are in environments of security.

STUDY III:
FIVE-YEAR FOLLOW-UP

In the final study the original Mississippi and Michigan children were retested five years later.

CHANGES

Changes over the years in both SC and RA were significant for the combined samples. Self-concepts mean scores increased significantly, t(29) = 2.26, p < .05, and race attitude dramatically changed in the pro-Black-oriented direction, t(31) = 6.03, p < .001 (see Table 12.11).

Children in the North had developed significantly more positive self-esteems, t(22) = 2.46, p < .05. This increase accorded in all four reference groups, with a significant change in the peer reference score, t(22) = 2.09, p < .05. The southern sample maintained their high self-esteem scores. The southern group also moved significantly from a moderate out-group orientation to a score that fell in the chance or no preference range, t(62) = 4.34, p < .001.

TABLE 12.11   Means, Standard Deviations, and t-Tests for Thomas Self-Concept Scores and Reference Groups

Variables	n	Pre M	Pre SD	Post M	Post SD	dt	t
		Combined Mississippi and Michigan Groups					
Thomas SC Total	00	46.69	9.65	51.10	9.56	29	2.26*
Reference Scores							
self	30	50.09	6.90	52.90	5.48	29	1.80
mother	31	48.39	10.65	53.16	7.07	30	2.54
teacher	30	43.50	12.87	47.93	13.73	29	1.42
peer	30	44.80	11.85	49.23	11.02	29	1.87
PRAM-Race Attitudes							
		Total Mississippi Test Group					
Thomas SC Total	43	51.42	7.43	19	51.74	10.09	60	0.14
Reference Scores							
self	43	51.70	6.38	19	53.37	4.27	60	1.04
mother	43	51.60	7.89	19	54.26	5.53	60	1.33
teacher	43	50.00	8.55	19	49.58	13.28	60	0.15
peer	43	50.23	6.46	19	48.89	12.38	60	0.56
PRAM-Race Attitudes	43	8.91	2.56	21	5.95	5.54	62	4.34***

NOTE: Total Mississippi group combines the 8 original and 13 cohort groups.
*p < .05; **p < .01; ***p < .001

The northern racial attitudes moved from a modified white orientation to become markedly more Black-oriented, moving from a mean of 8.50 to one of 4.13, t(23) = 5.21, p < .001.

SELF-CONCEPT STATUS

The demographic differences on self-concept no longer existed in retesting on the Thomas SC, Engle SC, or Porter self-awareness score. The children had positive self-concepts on all measures (see Table 12.12), both in the North and in the South.

A two-way analysis of variance was run on the four reference scores of Thomas. The self-referent score analysis resulted in no main effect significance of sex or demography. A significant difference on the interaction between sex and demography was present, F(1,37) = 18.78, p < .002 (see Table 12.13). In the South the girls had higher self-concept scores (girls, M = 55.50; boys, M = 51.82), but the boys were higher in the North (boys, M = 59.40; girls, M = 49.23).

The analysis of the mother as a reference score found a similar demography × sex interaction difference, F(1,37) = 5.88, p < .04. Again,

TABLE 12.12 Means, Standard Deviations, and t-Tests of Major
Variables on Post Michigan and Mississippi Sample

| | Michigan | | | Mississippi | | | | |
Variables	N	M	SD	N	M	SD	df	t
Thomas Self-Concept	23	51.78	7.99	19	51.74	10.09	40	0.02
Reference Scores								
self	23	52.78	6.04	19	53.37	4.27	40	0.37
mother	24	52.42	7.30	19	54.26	5.54	41	0.94
teacher	23	49.22	11.31	19	49.58	13.28	40	0.09
peer	23	50.48	8.88	19	48.89	12.38	40	0.47
Engle Self-Concept	24	31.29	3.71	20	30.70	4.04	42	0.50
Pierce Harris SC	24	63.13	9.57	21	65.43	8.77	43	0.84
PRAM-Race Attitudes	24	4.13	2.42	21	5.95	2.54	43	2.46*
Porter Self-Awareness	23	9.83	1.83	21	9.55	1.60	42	0.24
Circle Test	24	8.29	1.85	21	7.33	1.98	43	1.68

*p < .02

the girls had higher SC in the South and the boys were higher in the North. It should be remembered that no such sex differences were found in the original tests. No sex × demography interaction differences were found in the teacher or peer scores for this sample.

Because of the similarity between the two sites on major variables, they were pooled to look for sex differences. None was found on any of the self-concept scores. All children tended to feel positive about themselves.

RACE ATTITUDE STATUS

While both groups improved from an out-group to more of an own-group orientation, the northern children by 10 years of age were more Black-oriented, RA score $t(43) = 2.56$, $p < .02$. The analysis of the RA scores on demography by sex was significant only for the demography main effect, $F(1,36) = 6.48$, $p < .03$. No sex or interaction effects were found (see Table 12.14). The northern children were moderately white-oriented while the southern scores were in the chance range.

The self-portraits were scored using a procedure developed for race content, because the original Porter scoring had no means of picking up racial attitude content, despite its title. A score of 0 would indicate no

TABLE 12.13 Summary Table of Mean Scores by Sex and Two-Way Analysis of Variance of Thomas Self-Concept According to Demography and Sex

Source	Sum of Square	df	Mean Square	F
Self Reference SC				
Main Effect	77.43	2		
Sex	71.27	1	71.27	3.82
Demography	1.03	1	1.03	0.06
Sex x Demography	350.30	1	350.30	18.78*
Residual	690.16	17	27.95	
Total	1117.90	40		
Mother Reference SC				
Main Effect	112.23	2		
Sex	78.88	1	78.88	2.00
Demography	17.53	1	17.53	0.45
Sex x Demography	231.42	1	231.42	5.88**
Residual	1456.84	37	39.37	
Total	1800.48	40	45.01	

Mean Scores			Boys	Girls
Self as Reference SC		Michigan	59.40	49.23
		Mississippi	51.82	55.50
Mother as Reference SC		Michigan	56.50	49.50
		Mississippi	53.27	55.63

*p < .002; **p < .04

identifiable racial content. These children tended to have several recognizable race-related characteristics in their pictures, unlike Porter's sample, in which few racial features were drawn, causing her to drop that feature of her scoring. The northern and southern children had similarly high race content, $t(42) = 1.24$, n.s., indicating a strong identification as Blacks in their self-identity drawings. They identified themselves as being Black by the frequent use of identifiable Black motifs in their drawings of themselves. Their self-concepts remained positive, while there was a greater increase in the North to allow them to become on par with the earlier high southern self-concept scores.

Demographic differences again were found on the rankings of the groups "most Americans prefer." Consistent with the more pro-Black race attitude responses, the northern children ranked Black as more

TABLE 12.14 Intercorrelation of Education Expectation for Children with Parental Education Level and Expectations for Him or Her of Significant Others

Group	Education Expected	
	Parents	Teacher
Michigan		
parents		
teachers	.151	
children	.508	.365
Mississippi		
parents		
teachers	.580**	
children	.402	.486
	Parental Education Achieved and Expected	
Michigan	.6	
n = 15		
Mississippi	.531*	
n = 19		

*p < .02; **p < .01

preferred over the other racial groups, significantly higher (.01) than did the Mississippi children. Blacks were ranked highest in Michigan by 60% of the children, while only a slight preference existed between mean ranks of preferences in the southern sample.

RELATIONSHIP OF SELF-CONCEPT AND RACIAL ATTITUDE

No relationships were found on any measures of SC and RA scores, again supporting the compartmentalization of how the children were able to feel good about themselves, independent of their feelings about their racial group. The only significant relationships found were between the various self-concept tests that were essentially measuring the same concepts (see Table 12.15).

EDUCATIONAL AND OCCUPATIONAL ASPIRATIONS

Another dimension of self-evaluation could be the occupational and educational aspirations held by the child for him- or herself and for the child by significant others (teachers and parents). The northern data

TABLE 12.15   Summary of Two-Way Analysis of Variance of Race
Attitude According to Demography and Sex

Source	Sum of Square	Df	Mean Square	F
Main Effect	36.43	2		
sex	0.08	1	0.08	0.02
demography	36.03	1	36.03	6.48*
sex x demography	1.34	1	1.34	0.24
residual	200.13	36	5.56	
total	237.90	39		

RA Means

	Boys	Girls
Michigan	3.90	4.28
Mississippi	6.09	5.80

*p < .03

showed no correlation between these educational expectations in terms of the years of schooling that the child is expected to complete. In the South the educational expectations of parents and teachers were significantly correlated, $r = .580$, $p < .01$. This would indicate a desired match between home and school expectations (see Table 12.16). In neither site were the child's own expectations related with those held for him or her by parents or teachers.

The correlation was made between the obtained education of the parent and how far he or she expects the child to go. Significant correlation existed in both sites (Michigan, $r = .605$; Mississippi, $r = .531$, $p < .02$.). The parents with higher educational levels had greater expectations for their children.

And, finally, the occupational aspirations of the child, teacher, and parent were intercorrelated, using a phi coefficient. High agreement was found on occupation goals between the Mississippi parents and children (phi coefficient = .870, $p < .01$). No such relationships were found in Michigan. It would appear that the southern children were in an environment in which there was a greater agreement between the home, school, and child than those in the North.

DISCUSSION

These children felt that they were competent and valued individuals and believed that they were perceived positively by their mothers. They

TABLE 12.16   Intercorrelations of Self-Concept and Race Attitude Scores on Retesting of Five-Year Sample

| | Mississippi | | | Michigan | |
	r	No. Pairs	P	r	No. Pairs
	Self-Concept and Race Attitude				
TSC	102	19	—	-.086	23
Reference Group:					
self–RA	-.046	19	—	-.269	23
mother–RA	-.042	19	—	-.183	24
teacher–RA	.172	19	—	-.116	23
peer–RA	.109	19	—	.088	23
Porter and RA	.161	21	—	.256	23
	Self-Concept Scores				
Porter SC and TSC	-.412	19	.04	-.364	22*
Porter SC and Thomas SC					
self	-.414	19	.04	-.252	22
mother	.116	19	—	-.477	23***
teacher	-.424	19	.035	-.423	19**
peer	-.358	19	—	-.201	22

*p < .05; **p < .04; ***p < .01

felt that they were as highly regarded by their teachers. These findings of positive feelings of self-worth would provide data that would cause one to question the commonly held view of a lower value that minority children place upon themselves because of the negative messages communicated to them in the environment. The self-hatred hypothesis would have to be rejected for these groups based on these findings. Their feelings of self-worth were not related to their evaluation of their own ethnic group. In the preschool testing the southern children felt better about themselves. Because of their all-Black environment, they were not placed in the position of being reminded of the ethnic group's lowered status position by contact with non-Blacks. Therefore, there may have been a greater sense of security. The southern children may not have been placed in a defensive posture of protecting themselves from subtle and overt antagonism that is predicted by the general attitudinal preferences for non-Black. The northern preschool children had not been provided this shelter, but were forced to face the lowered school expectations and other negative experiences that all too often occur in Black/white settings. All groups felt that their teachers had a better evaluation of them upon retesting.

One interesting differential sex change occurred. Originally, the boys tended to be higher in all three sites. The boys kept their advantage in the North, while in the South and in D.C. the girls' self-concept improved markedly. The northern and urban girls seem to be receiving and internalizing positive feedback from their environments and are feeling better about themselves, while in the North boys were being reinforced. Could it be that girls are more secure in the all-Black or southern environment, whereas boys are more secure in the integrated urban community? The groups in the urban all-Black preschool that would probably be receiving the most supportive instruction, those of middle income, girls, and those from two-parent homes exhibited the greatest increase in self-concept. There is a need to examine the environmental reinforcers that appear to be provided differentially to the different groups.

All had a strong sense of their Black membership, as shown by the frequent use of Black motifs in their delightful self-portraits at the later age. This is consistent with the findings of Bolling and Hassibi (1976) that race identification items in drawings increases with age. All three groups were moderately white-oriented on the preschool level. They were able to accept the dominant preferences while compartmentalizing their feelings of their individual self-worth to feel good about themselves.

The preschool findings supported those of other researchers who found Black children giving fewer white-oriented responses than those found from 1930 through the early 1950s. In contrast, white children, earlier and still, have been found to consistently prefer their own racial group in preschool and middle childhood. The children became more pro-Black by middle childhood.

Only the northern children ranked Blacks higher than other ethnic groups. Although the question asked for society's preference, it can be assumed that they were expressing their own views. The mixed results are consistent with the evaluative responses to the racial picture stories. The southern children remained more ambivalent on racial responses, while those in the North gave clearly pro-Black responses. The children had clear assessments of correct racial identification even at the preschool level. The southern children with positive self-esteems also were able to correctly identify the pictures by race, especially the Black pictures, while remaining moderately out-group-oriented. These relationships were not found in the northern urban setting, where the race identity accuracy was much lower. The preschool children in the all-Black setting appeared to have become more keenly aware of racial differences as they developed positive feelings of self-worth. The southern children may have been developmentally advanced in their racial self-identification; however, by the end of the five years the northern children moved to become more like the southern children on all measures.

These findings indicate that Black children develop more positive attitudes toward their own group over a period of time. The more supportive environmental changes that had occurred over the five years have increased the developmental changes and have resulted in these children being able to place a positive evaluation on their own ethnic group.

REFERENCES

ASHER, S. and A. ALLEN (1969) "Racial preference and social comparison processes." Journal of Social Issues 25, 1: 157-166.

BARATZ, S. and J. BARATA (1970) "Early childhood intervention: a social science based institutional racism." Harvard Educational Review 4, 1: 29.

BILLINGSLEY, A. (1968) Black Families in White America. Englewood Cliffs, NJ: Prentice-Hall.

BOLLING, J. and M. HASSIBI (1976) "Sex differences versus sex identification: cultural considerations." Presented at the Empirical Conference on Black Psychology III, Cornell University, October.

CLARK, K. (1963) Prejudice and Your Child. Boston: Beacon Press.

——— (1952) "Racial identity and preference in young children," in Maccoby et al. (eds.) Readings in Social Psychology. New York: Holt, Rinehart & Winston.

——— and M. CLARK (1939) "The development of consciousness of self and the emergence of racial identification in Negro preschool children." Journal of Social Psychology 10: 591-599.

COLE, R. (1967) The Antecedents of Self-Esteem. San Francisco: Freeman.

CROSS, W. (1974) Personal communication.

DEUTSCH, M. (1960) "Minority group and class status as related to social and personality factors in school achievement." Society of Applied Anthropology, Monograph 2.

DIGGORY, J. (1966) Self-Evaluation: Concepts and Studies. New York: Crowell-Collier.

ENGEL, M. and W. RAINE (1963) "A method of the measurement of the self-concept of children in third grade." Journal of Genetic Psychology 102: 125-137.

FOX, D. and U. BARNES (1971) "Racial preference and identification of Blacks, Chinese, and white children." Presented at the American Educational Research Association Meeting, New York.

GOODMAN, M. (1964) Race Awareness in Young Children. New York: Crowell-Collier.

——— (1952) Race Attitudes in Young Children. Boston: Addison-Wesley.

GORDON, T. (1970) "Self-concept and sex identity in Black pre-adolescent boys." University of Michigan. (unpublished)

GRAVES, S. (1975) "How to create positive racial attitudes." Presented at the biennial meeting of the Society for Research in Child Development, Denver.

GREENWALD, H. and D. OPPENHIEM (1968) "Reported magnitude of self-misidentification among Negro children—artifact?" Journal of Personality and Social Psychology 8, 1: 49-52.

GUILFORD, J. (1956) Fundamental Statistics in Psychology and Education. New York: McGraw-Hill.

HARTUP, W. (1966) "Presidential address." Annual meeting of the American Psychological Association, Washington, DC.

HRABA, J. and J. GRANT (1970) "Black is beautiful: a reexamination of racial preference and identification." Journal of Personality and Social Psychology 16, 3: 398-402.

HOROWITZ, R. (1939) "Racial aspects of self-identity in nursery school children." Journal of Psychology 1: 91-99.

JOHNSON, R. and G. MEDINUSS (1965) Child Psychology: Behavior and Development. New York: John Wiley.

LIPSCOMB, I. (1975) "Parental influences in the development of Black children's racial self-esteem." Presented at the meeting of the American Sociological Association, San Francisco.

McADOO, H. P. (1976) "A reexamination of the relationship between self-concept and race attitudes of young Black children." National Association for Education of Young Children Monograph.

——— (1974) "The socialization of Black children: priorities for research," in L. Gary (ed.) Social Research and the Black Community. Washington, DC: Howard University.

——— (1970) "Racial attitudes and self-concepts of Black preschool children." Ph.D. dissertation, University of Michigan. (University Microfilms 71-4677)

——— (1969) "An exploratory study of racial aggressiveness in Black preschool children." University of Michigan. (unpublished)

McADOO, J. (1973) "Modification of race attitudes in Black children." Presented at the annual meeting of the Association of Black Psychologists, Detroit.

——— (1970) "An exploratory study of racial attitude change in Black preschool children, using differential treatment." Ph.D. dissertation, University of Michigan. (University Microfilms 71-468).

MORELAND, J. (1958) "Racial recognition by nursery school children in Lynchburg, Virginia." Social Forces 37: 132-137.

Mound Bayou Diamond Jubilee (1962) Handbook for the 75th Mound Bayou Celebration.

PALMER, R. and J. MASLING (1969) "Vocabulary for skin color in Negro and white children." Developmental Psychology 1, 4: 394-401.

PORTER, J. (1971) Black Child, White Child. Cambridge, MA: Harvard Univ. Press.

——— (1966) "Racial attitude formation in preschool age children." Ph.D. dissertation, Harvard University.

SPENCER, M. (1973) Personal communication.

SPRINGER, D. (1950) "Awareness of racial differences by preschool children in Hawaii." Genetic Psychology Monograph 41: 215-270.

STEVENSON, H. and E. STEWART (1958) "A developmental study of race awareness in young children." Child Development 29: 399-410.

THOMAS, W. (1967) The Thomas Self-Concept Values Test: Project on Student Values. Grand Rapids, MI.

TROWBRIDGE, J. (1947) "The south," in V. Wharton (ed.) The Negro in Mississippi, 1865-1890. New York: Harper & Row.

VALENTINE, (1971) "Deficiency, difference, and bicultural modes of Afro-American behavior." Harvard Educational Review 41: 135-157.

WARD, S. and J. BRAUN (1972) "Self-esteem and racial preference in Black children." American Journal of Orthopsychiatry 42, 4: 64-74.

WHARTON, V. [ed.] (1947) The Negro in Mississippi, 1865-1890. New York: Harper & Row.

WILLIAMS, J. and K. A. ROBERTSON (1967) "A method for assessing racial attitudes in preschool children." Educational and Psychological Measurement 27: 671-689.

WINER, B. (1971) Statistical Principles in Experimental Design. New York: McGraw-Hill.

13

MODIFICATION OF
RACIAL ATTITUDES AND PREFERENCES
IN YOUNG BLACK CHILDREN

JOHN LEWIS McADOO

Black children's ethnic identity has been extensively studied over the last half-century with mixed and confusing results. The early social scientists (Clark and Clark, 1939, 1950; Goodman, 1952; Morland, 1963; Stevenson and Stewart, 1958) found that Black children rejected their ethnic identity and chose to identify with the predominate culture. The Black child was found to have a negative self-image and a preference for things white (Proshansky and Newton, 1968).

McAdoo (1974) reviewed the white preference in Black children and noted that all of the earlier studies assumed that the Black child is unable to adjust to sometimes competing and conflicting developmental tasks. This lack of adjustment was assumed to have serious negative consequences to the child's self-esteem. The child was seen as being placed in a developmental bind of adjusting and incorporating the values of his or her Black community and that of the dominant society. The inability to complete these tasks successfully lead the child to reject his or her own identity, to self-hatred, white preference.

A growing number of researchers (Hraba and Grant, 1970; Harris and Braun, 1971; Gregor and McPherson, 1968; Moore, 1976; Winnick and Taylor, 1977) have begun to test those assumptions. They suggest that one cannot assume that all Black children will develop negative identity because of the racial prejudice that surrounds their community.

The findings from these series of studies using essentially the same methodology as earlier studies suggest that Black children exhibit a positive ethnic identity. The proponents of this view would point to the 33% to 77% of the subjects in the Clark (1939) studies, the 87% of the subjects in the Greenwald and Oppenheim study (1968), and the 46% to 68% of the subjects in Morland's (1962), who did not select the white doll as being like themselves as support for the position that Black children are as positive toward their own identity as children of other ethnic groups.

Banks (1976) reanalyzed the data on Black children from the major racial preference studies from 1939 to 1974 and reported that in a majority of those studies (69%) the children did not accept or reject their ethnic identity. In 24% of the studies, the Black children were found to be more positive in the attitudes toward their own ethnic group. Black children in 6% of the studies were found to exhibit a positive white preference.

The racial attitude/preference studies reviewed here provide some support for Proshansky and Newton's (1968) notion that the inescapable reality of being Black in America shadows the Black child's emerging sense of self, making the development of racial identification an integral part of his or her total self-esteem. Racial identification or racial preference—the child's development of who he or she is in relation to other ethnic groups—begins around the age of 3 and is completed around the age of 6 (Clark and Clark, 1939, 1950; Morland, 1962). As noted earlier, most Black children are able to satisfactorily develop their ethnic identity and self-esteem (Hraba and Grant, 1970; Winnick and Taylor, 1977; Spenser and Horowitz, 1973). However, our focus will be on the efforts to modify the negative ethnic preference of children who exhibit such an identity.

For those young Black children who are not able to develop positive racial identification and reject their own ethnic group, the literature provides little information on how to modify these negative attitudes. Katz (1973) notes that there are three possible reasons for this. The first is that few social scientists have focused on racial attitude modification techniques. The second reason is the relative lack of theories that suggest change techniques. Finally, most of the early instruments used to assess racial attitude suffer from reliability and validity problems (Banks, 1979). However, newer studies have been found to be more technologically sophisticated in terms of types of measures used. Thus, there is a need for more studies that evaluate the effectiveness of measures used to modify racial attitudes and preferences in young children.

This chapter will report on two studies of racial attitude and racial preference change in Black preschool children that were carried out in two different locations. One goal of the study was to determine the degree to which these children reflected the negative racial attitudes and preferences found in earlier studies. The other goal was to determine the degree to which operant learning procedures can be utilized to modify preschool children's racial attitudes and preferences.

Williams and Morland (1976) and their students (Renninger and Williams, 1966; Williams and Edwards, 1969; Williams et al., 1975) have done the most extensive work using positive and negative reinforcement to change preschool and kindergarten children's color concept attitudes. They consistently have found that white children associate positive evaluations to the color white and negative evaluations to the color black.

In all of the North Carolina studies, positive reinforcement was found to modify the white children's responses to a more positive association to the color black. White children who had a more positive association to the color black also were found to have a more positive attitude toward dark-skinned people (Williams, 1967; Williams and Edwards, 1969; Renninger and Williams, 1966).

Traynham (1976) replicated Wiliams's study in Arkansas, controlling for possible geographical bias. He found that the white kindergarten children in his sample were even more positive in their color concept attitude change than the Williams subjects. Spencer and Horowitz (1973), in the only modification study found utilizing both Black and white preschool children, noted that both Black and white children exhibit a negative evaluation of the color black. While operant learning procedures did reduce white color bias in Blacks, the change was not found to be significant.

In summary, operant learning procedures have been found to differentially affect Black and white children's racial concept attitudes. White children's negative evaluations of dark-skinned people have been consistently modified using operant learning procedures. Black children's racial concept attitudes have been modified using the same procedures, but not significantly. The question this study asks is whether we can modify black preschool children's racial attitudes using operant learning procedures. Furthermore, I wish to learn the degree to which these procedures change the children's racial preferences. Finally, I wish to determine the degree to which there are regional variations in racial attitudes and preference changes in children.

TABLE 13.1   Frequency and Percentages of the Michigan
             and Washington, D.C. Treatment Groups

Treatment Groups	Michigan		Washington, D.C.	
	F	%	f	%
Positive reinforcement	22	34	32	33
Negative reinforcement	20	31	32	33
Black consciousness	23	35		
Control			33	34
Total	65		97	

METHODOLOGY

Two different geographical sites were chosen: the Washington, D.C., metropolitan area and the Detroit, Michigan, metropolitan area. In the Michigan sample 65 working-class preschool children ages 3½ to 5½ were selected to take part in the study. Twenty-two children were placed in the positive reinforcement group, 20 were placed in the negative reinforcement group, and 23 were placed in a Black consciousness curriculum (see Table 13.1).

Ninety-seven Black working-class preschool children living in Washington, D. C., ages 3½ to 6 years, were randomly placed in three treatment groups. Thirty-three children were placed in the positive reinforcement group and 33 were placed in the negative reinforcement group. One child dropped out halfway through the process because of illness. Thirty-two children were placed in a control group.

MATERIALS

Children in both geographical locations received the Clark dolls test (1939) and the Williams Preschool Racial Attitude Measure (PRAM, 1967) as pretests and posttests.

In the Clark dolls test two dolls were used. The dolls were identical in dress and age and all physical features except for skin color. The black doll had a medium brown skin coloring whereas the caucasian doll had a pinkish tan coloring.

The Clark dolls procedures required that the dolls be randomly placed in a prone position before the child and then the child was requested to select the doll that represented his or her response to the positive or negative questions. An example of the questions was, "Which doll is the nice color?" The children's racial preference was determined by the number of times they selected the black doll in response to a positive question. There were nine questions; however, the Michigan sample responded to a shortened four-question version of the Clark dolls test.

The PRAM is described by Williams (1967) as a series of 18 Black and white human figures. These figures were similar in age, sex, and all physical features except for skin and hair color. The Black figure had medium brown skin and black hair. The white figure had pinkish tan skin and yellow hair. The children were shown a picture containing two figures and they were told a story about each picture. They were asked to select the person in the picture that the story was about. A typical story was "Here are two girls. Everyone says that one of them is pretty. Which is the pretty girl?"

The children received a point each time they identified a Black person in response to a negative question and a white person in response to a positive question. The children could accumulate up to 12 points with 0 to 3 points indicating a pro-Black racial orientation and a 9 to 12 score indicating a pro-white orientation. Children scoring in the 4 to 8 range exhibited no racial preference orientation or chance response (Banks, 1976).

COLOR MEANING PICTURE SERIES

The color modification picture series developed by Williams (1967) was used in both geographical areas for the positive (PR) and negative reinforcement (NR) groups. There was a total of 12 pictures, 6 were of animals and 6 exhibited toys. The pictures contained either two animals or two toys that were identical except for color. The children in the PR and NR groups were shown a picture and told a two- to three-sentence evaluative story about each picture. A typical story was, "One of these rabbits is good. He helps his mother care for his brothers and sisters. Which is the good rabbit?"

All of the pictures were shown with four stories. For each of the pictures, the children were given 24 opportunities to respond to the black and white animal stories. They were positively or negatively reinforced for their response according to their treatment groups.

TREATMENT GROUPS

POSITIVE REINFORCEMENT

In the positive reinforcement group the children were rewarded each time they selected a black animal for a positive story or a white animal for a negative story. The Michigan group received three M&Ms and the Washington D.C. group received two pennies. The children were rewarded for any selection they made of toys.

Two weeks later, the procedure was repeated; however, the first 12 responses were not rewarded. At the end of the game both groups were given a handful of pennies.

NEGATIVE REINFORCEMENT

The negative reinforcement groups in both geographical locations were given 30 pennies to hold. They were told that they would have to forfeit 2 pennies each time they gave a wrong response. The children were requested to give up 2 pennies each time they selected a white animal for a positive response or a black animal for a negative response. At the end of the game they were given a handful of M&Ms.

CONTROL GROUPS

The control group was shown the color meaning series on two occasions. The stories were not read at the end of each session. They were given a handful of pennies.

BLACK CONSCIOUS GROUP

The Black consciousness group was taught a series of classes related to some positive aspects of Black culture. Games, poems, arts and crafts, and songs related to Black history were used in 18 one-hour sessions with the Michigan sample. This curriculum was administered by six trained Black teacher aides.

RESULTS

THE MICHIGAN SAMPLE

Negative reinforcement was found to be the most significant modifier of racial concept attitudes. Black preschool children responded more

TABLE 13.2 Means, Standard Deviations, and t Test of Differences of Race Attitude and Race Preference for the Three Treatment Methods and Control Group for the Michigan and D.C. Samples

Variable	Sample	Group	Pre			Post		
			N	M	SD	M	SD	P
Race attitude	Michigan	positive reinforcement	22	7.45	2.77	7.77	2.74	ns
		negative reinforcement	20	8.50	2.95	6.30	3.03	.01
		black consciousness curriculum	23	7.48	2.78	8.48	2.15	ns
Race attitude	D.C.	positive reinforcement	33	6.94	1.85	5.88	1.52	ns
		negative reinforcement	32	6.56	1.64	5.28	1.46	ns
		control	32	6.97	1.92	6.46	1.78	ns
Race preference	Michigan	positive reinforcement	22	6.68	1.25	7.77	1.45	ns
		negative reinforcement	20	6.25	1.33	6.40	1.77	ns
		black consciousness curriculum	23	6.52	1.34	6.39	1.44	ns
Race preference	D.C.	positive reinforcement	33	2.48	2.15	3.79	2.47	ns
		negative reinforcement	32	3.74	2.99	2.63	0.14	ns
		control	32	3.44	2.70	2.57	1.61	ns

positively to the loss of pennies in this group and were able to move from a slightly negative evaluation of the Black figure to a more even selection of both Black and white figures in response to positive and negative stories.

No significant color concept change was observed in either the positive reinforcement group or the Black consciousness group. Neither approach was effective in changing the choices of the children (see Table 13.2).

Although negative reinforcement was seen as a significant modifier of racial concept attitudes in the Michigan sample, withdrawal of pennies did not lead to a modification of the preschool child's racial preference. Children who selected the white doll for positive evaluative stimuli before entering the three treatment groups selected the white doll in the same pattern after the treatment. No significant difference in social preferences was found in the three treatment groups.

In summary, we found that Black preschool children in the Michigan study were not extremely positive or extremely negative in their color concept attitudes. Negative reinforcement did significantly change the children's patterns of responses in the desired direction, partially because the procedure closely approximated the child rearing patterns in the children's homes. Pennies were felt to be a more powerful stimulus than candy for working-class children. None of the operant learning procedures was able to change the child's racial preference. Although change in the color consciousness curriculum appeared in the opposite direction than predicted, it was felt that we were observing changes as they were beginning to occur and probably would need to continue using the curriculum over a longer period of time in order to gain a true evaluation of its effectiveness.

WASHINGTON, D.C. SAMPLE

The results from the Michigan study indicated several design changes. First, as pennies were felt to be a more powerful influence in working-class families, they were used for both the positive and negative reinforcement conditions. Second, the Black consciousness group was dropped in favor of a control group because of the apparent length of time needed to change attitudes with this approach. And, third, children were randomly selected to participate from five nurseries located in different areas, and they were randomly placed in one of three treatment conditions.

The children in the three treatment groups were found to be equally neutral in their racial concept attitudes on the pretest. No significant differences were observed on the racial color concept attitudes on the posttest for the three treatment groups. The children were found to be equally positive toward the white and Black figures (see Table 13.2).

The total Washington, D.C. sample was found to be moderately out-group-oriented on the racial preference test. Positive and negative reinforcement produced no significant changes in the children's racial preferences. The children in this study were similar to the ones in Michigan in their patterns of responses to the racial preference study; they chose the white doll more often regardless of operant learning conditions.

DISCUSSION

The Black preschool children in both the Michigan and Washington, D.C. sample equally chose the Black and white figures in response to positive and negative evaluative meaning stories. This democratic attitude and lack of apparent personal bias has led us to believe that these children have a clear sense of their own ethnic identification. It is felt that only children who have a clear sense of their own personal identity will be free enough to evaluate others without racial bias (Lewin, 1948). The equivalence of the children's selection of both dark- and light-skinned figures suggests lack of racial prejudice at this point in their lives.

The findings in these two studies were similar to Spencer and Horowitz's (1973) study. We were able to nonsignificantly modify racial attitudes, but not racial preference. These findings suggest that Black children who are secure in their racial identity will not be greatly influenced by efforts to change their racial attitudes. A reappraisal of Spencer's data supports this point of view. Her data went even further to suggest that Black children who were democratic in their racial attitudes also were found to have positive self-esteems. McAdoo (1974) also found that Black preschool children in Michigan and Mississippi, while selecting the white doll over the black doll for positive stimuli, had high self-esteem.

We were not able to modify the children's racial preferences in both groups. They randomly chose the white doll or the black doll. The racial preference results provide partial support for Bank's (1976) random choice theory. The data do not provide support that they rejected their blackness.

There are several reasons that our study failed to confirm other findings, and we will explore them here. The first explanation may be found in a lack of a theoretical framework to explain and predict racial identity formation and change in young Black children. For a theory to be helpful, it must differentiate between racial self-rejection or self-hatred or rejection of one's own racial group, racial prejudice, and racial preference in young children.

The majority of the studies assumed that racial self-rejection and white preference are dominant themes in Black children and that these constructs, which underlie negative racial identity in Blacks, are similar to the constructs that underlie racial prejudice in white children. The above assumptions appear to be the foundation in the development of operant learning force choice procedures by Williams (1967) in diagnosing and treating negative racial attitudes in Black children and racial prejudice in white children. Our data do not provide support for the assumptions as they apply to Black preschool children.

A second reason may be found in the limitations of force choice methodologies in helping us to identify negative ethnic identity. The racial preference studies all assumed that Black children who selected one doll automatically rejected the nonselected doll and this rejection may be said to have serious implications for his or her attitudes toward family and own ethnic group, particularly if he or she consistently chose the white doll for positive attitudes and the black doll for negative stories. Lerner and Schroeder (1975), in a methodological test of these assumptions with white children, found that their responses were similar to that of other white children in other studies; they preferred the white doll. However, they also found in their choice of the white doll there was a complete lack of perjorative rejection of the black doll.

The white children apparently attached little significance to their selection process, and this may be why Williams (1967) and his group have been able to see such dramatic changes in the children's choices after treatment. Black children who expressed negative racial preference also should evaluate negatively their own worth. Spencer and Horowitz's (1973) study provided a test of the above, and found that their Black children had high self-esteem, providing further support for our findings that Black children do not apply the same meaning to their doll choice processes as developmental psychologists.

A third reason may be found in the geographical difference of this and Williams's series of studies. The Michigan and Washington, D.C. studies were done in highly urbanized areas. Most of Williams's studies of racial attitude change were done in southern and southeastern areas, where the populations were less dense. The children living in urban areas may be more sophisticated in their understanding of the expectations in forced choice games. They merely were expressing an opinion about a doll or a story in much the same manner that we might choose an automobile. When we select a Ford as our preferred automobile, it does not mean we rejected, hated, or experienced personal identity problems because we did not choose a Dodge.

Closely related to urban-rural differences are the racial differences in the different geographical areas. Almost all of the studies utilizing Williams's (1967) racial modification strategy used only white subjects. They were able to demonstrate significant modification in the white children's selection process. The children in these series of studies appeared more positive in their selection of the Black figure. Black children in both of the studies reported here and in the Spencer study did not make the change in their choices to the same dramatic degree, suggesting that problems related to color concept formation and its meaning may be different for the Black and white child.

In summary, when you control for race of the examiner and geographical region, Black preschool children's racial attitude and racial identity are found to be as positive as any other ethnic group, using both the Williams and Clark procedures. The findings are that Black children in the Michigan and Washington, D.C. sample have a positive racial identity, and this may be the principal reason why operant learning procedures were found to be ineffective in modifying their racial attitudes and preferences.

Operant learning procedures have been found to be effective in the reduction of racial color concept in white children. However, because the Black children did not display the same degree of biased choice selections, the procedures were ineffective in influencing Black children's choices. Future modification research may need to focus on identifying Black children who exhibit the same degree of extreme selection bias in the opposite direction as whites.

Differences in the racial modification studies may be explained in terms of the interaction of racial and geographical differences and lack of a theoretical framework. We seem to be asking Black and white children different questions using the same methodology and expecting that these will lead to a change in personal identity in Black children and to a decrease in racial prejudice in white children. A theoretical framework may be helpful in controlling our conceptualizations and the assumptions we make, while at the same time allowing us to more reliably predict racial attitudes and racial prejudice change.

In future research in this area, we may need to develop better techniques of evaluating the formation and process of identity development, racial attitudes, and preferences in Black children. Banks (1976) has observed correctly that, given the stimulus materials developed by Clark (1939) and Williams, we have no way of knowing if Black children may have problems in this area. Our data suggest that Black preschool children's racial identity is developing as well as that of any other child.

We need at least to determine whether the child's selection processes lead to negative consequences for his or her personal identity.

Once we have identified the problems of ethnic identity formation faced by Black children within a given theoretical framework, we can develop more appropriate modification techniques. Given the data of our studies and the Spencer study, the modification procedures may need to be changed in order to positively deal with the consequences of negative identity formation and low self-esteem. One questions whether we might be more effective in modifying the child's attitudes, behavior, and beliefs about his or her personal and racial identity by including his or her family in the modification process.

The evaluation process and changes of the interaction processes within families of children experiencing identity problems may lead to significant departures in the way we understand the process of identity formation and change in all families. Negative identity formation from this point of view would be seen as a reflection of something wrong in the socialization practices in the home, rather than a sign that the preschool child's uncontested personal acceptance of some of society's negative attitudes of his or her racial group membership.

Developmental theory would have us believe that the family serves as the major mediator between the preschool child and society. I believe that many Black families may be over protective and thus delay the indirect impact of racial prejudice on their children. Future research may need to evaluate the consequences of this child rearing approach on identity formation and development in Black children. By turning our focus away from problematic Black families, we may identify effective modification strategies that could be used successfully in remedying identity problems in all families.

I began by asking the question, to what degree can operant learning procedures, used so effectively in modifying negative color concept attitudes in white preschool children, have the same effect on Black preschool children. The responses in both studies were surprising and forced a reexamination of the conceptual foundations of the Williams and Morland (1967) color modification procedures. I am led to believe from the evidence presented above that the theoretical framework underlying racial attitudes and racial attitudes change may be overly simplistic and may not have a firm foundation in the breadth of human experiences—at least in the way that Black children experience it. The most important point is this: Whereas white children do need to modify their ethnocentric attitudes, Black children are increasingly indicating their nonbiased choices. Therefore, the racial preferences of young Black children may no longer even need to be modified.

REFERENCES

ASHER, R. and V. ALLEN (1964) "Racial preference and social comparison process." Social Issues 25, 1: 157-166.

BANKS, W. C. (1976) "White preference in Blacks: a paradigm in search of a phenomenon." Psychological Bulletin 83, 6: 1179-1186.

———and W. J. ROMPF (1973) "Evaluative bias and preference behavior in Black and white children." Child Development 4: 776-783.

BANKS, W. E. (1979) "On the importance of white preference and comparative difference of Blacks and others: reply to Williams and Morland." Psychological Bulletin 86, 1: 33-36.

BRAND, E. S., R. A. RUIZ, and E. PARILLA (1974) "Ethnic identification and preference: a review." Psychological Bulletin 81: 860-890.

BRODY, E. B. (1963) "Color and identity conflict in young boys." Psychiatry 26: 188-201.

CLARK, K. and M. CLARK (1950) "Emotional factors in racial identification and preference of Negro children." Journal of Negro Education 14: 341.

———(1947) "Racial identification and preference in Negro children," in T. M. Newcomb and E. C. Harley (eds.) Readings in Social Psychology. New York: Holt, Rinehart & Winston.

———(1939) "The development of consciousness of self in the emergence of racial identification in Negro preschool children." Journal of Social Psychology 10: 591-599.

GOODMAN, M. E. (1952) Race Awareness in Young Children. New York: Collier-Macmillan.

GREENWALD, H. J. and D. B. OPPENHEIM (1968) "Reported magnitude of self-misidentification among Negro children." Journal of Personality and Social Psychology 5: 149-152.

GREGOR, A. J. and D. A. McPHERSON (1968) "Racial preference among white and Negro children in a deep south standard metropolitan area." Journal of Social Psychology 68: 95.

HARRIS, S. and J. BRAUN (1971) "Self-esteem and racial preference in Black children." Proceedings of the 79th Annual Convention of the American Psychological Association 6: 259.

HRABA, J. E. and G. GRANT (1970) "Black is beautiful: a reexamination of racial preference and identity." Journal of Personality and Social Psychology 16: 398.

KATZ, P. A. (1973) "Stimulus predifferentiation and modification of children's racial attitudes." Child Development 44: 232-237.

———and S. R. ZALK (1974) "Doll preference: an index of racial attitudes?" Journal of Educational Psychology 66, 5: 663-668.

LERNER, R. M. and C. SCHROEDER (1975) "Racial attitudes in young white children: a methodological analysis." Journal of Genetic Psychology 27: 3-12.

LEWIN, K. (1948) Resolving Social Conflicts. New York: Harper & Row.

McADOO, H. (1974) "The socialization of Black children: priorities for research," pp. 66-76 in L. E. Gary (ed.) Social Research and the Black Community. Washington, DC: Institute for Urban Affairs.

MOORE, R. L. (1976) "The racial preference and attitudes of preschool Black children." Journal of Genetic Psychology 129: 37-44.

MORLAND, J. K. (1963) "Racial self-identification: a study of nursing school." American Catholic Sociological Review 24: 231-238.

———(1962) "Racial acceptance and preference of nursery school children in a southern city." Merrill Palmer Quarterly of Behavior and Development 8: 271-280.

PROSHANSKY, H. and P. NEWTON (1968) "The nature and meaning of Negro self-identity," pp. 178-218 in M. Deutsch et al. (eds.) Social Class, Race and Psychological Development. New York: Holt, Rinehart & Winston.

RADKE, M. and H. TRAEGER (1950) "Children's perceptions of the social roles of Negroes and whites." Journal of Psychology 29: 3-33.

RENNINGER, C. A. and J. E. WILLIAMS (1966) "Black-white color connotations and racial awareness in preschool children." Journal of Perceptual Motor Skills 22: 77-78.

ROTH, R. (1969) "The effects of integral curriculum on Negro and white students." Ph.D. dissertation, University of Michigan.

SEWARD, G. (1956) Psychotherapy and Culture Conflict. New York: Ronald Press.

SPENCER, M. B. (1982a) "Personal and group identity of Black children: an alternative synthesis." Genetic Psychology Monographs 106-59-84.

———(1982b) "Preschool children's social cognition: a cognitive developmental interpretation of race dissonance findings." Journal of Psychology 112: 275-286.

———and F. D. HOROWITZ (1973) "Effects of systematic social and token reinforcement on the modification of racial and color concept attitudes in Black and white preschool children." Developmental Psychology 9, 2: 246-254.

STEVENSON, H. W. (1967) "Racial awareness in young children," pp. 206-213 in W. W. Hartup and N. L. Smotherhill (eds.) The Young Child: Review of Research. Washington, DC: National Association for the Education of Young Children.

———and E. C. STEWART (1958) "A developmental study of racial awareness in young children." Child Development 29: 390-409.

TRAYNHAM, R. N. and K. L. WITTE (1976) "The effects of modifying color meaning concepts on racial concept attitudes in five and eight year old children." Journal of Experimental Child Psychology 26: 165-174.

WEINER, B. J. (1962) Statistical Principles in Experimental Design. New York: McGraw-Hill.

WILLIAMS, J. E. (1967) "Connotations of racial concepts and color names." Journal of Personality and Social Psychology.

———(1964) "Connotations of color names among Negroes and caucasians." Journal of Perpetual Motor Skills 18: 721-731.

———and C. D. EDWARDS (1969) "An experimental modification of color concepts and racial attitudes in preschool children." Child Development 40, 3: 737-750.

WILLIAMS, J. E. and J. K. MORLAND (1979) "Comments on Banks' white preference in blacks: paradigm in search of a phenomenon." Psychological Bulletin 86, 1: 28-32.

———(1976) Race, Color, and the Young Child. Chapel Hill: Univ. of North Carolina Press.

WILLIAMS, J. E. and J. K. ROBERTSON (1967) "A method for assessing racial attitudes in preschool children." Educational and Psychological Measurement 27: 671-689.

WILLIAMS, J. E. and C. A. ROUSSEAU (1971) "Evaluation and identification responses of Negro preschoolers to the colors black and white." Perceptual and Motor Skills 33: 50-54.

WILLIAMS, J. E., D. L. BEST, and D. A. BOSWELL (1975) "Children's racial attitudes in the early school years." Child Development 46: 494-500.

WILLIAMS, J. E., D. A. BOSWELL, and D. L. BEST (1976) "Evaluative responses of preschool children to the colors white and black." Child Development 46: 501-508.

WILLIAMS, J. E., J. K. MORLAND, and W. L. UNDERWOOD (1970) "Connotations of color names in the United States, Europe, and Asia." Journal of Social Psychology 82: 3-14.

WILLIAMS, K. H., J. E. WILLIAMS, and R. C. BECK (1973) "Assessing children's racial attitudes via a signal detection model." Perceptual and Motor Skills 36: 387-398.

WINNICK, R. H. and J. A. TAYLOR (1977) "Racial preference—36 years later." Journal of Social Psychology 102: 157-158.

14

INTERRACIAL CONTACT IN SCHOOLS AND BLACK CHILDREN'S SELF-ESTEEM

NEAL KRAUSE

The influence of social scientific thought on government policy is perhaps nowhere more evident than in the area of school desegregation. The testimony of social scientists and educators in the *Brown v. Board of Education* trial, as well as in a series of decisions at the state level, helped to establish the official government policy that segregation in public schools is harmful to the self-esteem of minority school children (see Stephan, 1978). This testimony, and the policy established from it, was based on the assumption that segregation of Black school children "from others of similar age and qualifications solely because of their race generates feelings of inferiority as to their status in the community that may affect their hearts and minds in a way unlikely ever to be undone" (*Brown v. Board of Education*, as quoted in Stephan, 1978: 217). The theoretical basis for this "contact hypothesis" can be found in Alport's (1954) important work on prejudice and is supported by a number of studies on the integration of military units during World War II (see Amir, 1969 for a review of this research).

Following the development of the contact hypothesis, a second competing view emerged about the effects of increased interracial contact on Black self-esteem. Advocates of this alternative view, which will be referred to here as the "insulation hypothesis," maintain that

AUTHOR'S NOTE: A more detailed presentation of the research discussed in this chapter may be found in Krause (1983).

instead of bolstering the self-esteem of Black students, increased contact with majority members may actually lower Black self-esteem. Proponents of the insulation hypothesis argue that as Black school children experience increased contact with white students they will internalize the negative image of Blacks held by whites and eventually will come to view themselves in the same disparaging terms. The basis for the proposition that minority self-esteem is negatively influenced by contact with whites may be traced to the work of early social theorists, such as Cooley (1902), who argued that self-concepts are formed as reflections of the responses and evaluations of others in the environment.

Increasingly, the weight of the empirical evidence tends to favor the insulation hypothesis. These studies suggest that Blacks in segregated school settings enjoy much higher levels of self-esteem than Blacks in integrated settings (see Epps, 1978; St. John, 1975; Stephan, 1978; and Wylie, 1979, for reviews of this literature).

In attempting to explain why Black students in predominantly white schools have lower self-esteem than Blacks in segregated institutions, Rosenberg (1977) identified three factors that mediate the impact of racial contact on feelings of self-worth. He referred to these factors as the dissonant communications environment, the dissonant cultural environment, and the dissonant comparison reference group.

Rosenberg (1977) maintains that, compared to Blacks in segregated settings, a minority child in a majority setting will be more likely to be exposed to negative communications about him- or herself as a group member (i.e., racial teasing) and about his or her group in general (i.e., his or her group's status in the majority world). Blacks in integrated settings will therefore experience lower levels of self-esteem because of this "dissonant communications environment."

Minority students in integrated settings also may suffer a loss of self-esteem when they realize that their norms and values are different from those of the white majority, and that whites consider Black culture to be inferior. Rosenberg (1977) mentions racial differences in family structure as one example of this "dissonant cultural environment." He argues that Blacks from single-parent families will be stigmatized by whites from intact (two-parent) families and will suffer a loss of self-esteem as a result.

According to Rosenberg (1977), Blacks in integrated settings may also be confronted by a "dissonant comparison reference group." Here he argues that people tend to compare their social characteristics with the characteristics of those people in immediate social settings. This poses no problems for Blacks in segregated schools because they are comparing themselves with other Black students. Blacks in predominantly white schools, however, will compare themselves with whites, and they will experience a decline in self-esteem because of their relatively unfavorable position.

Academic performance represents one of the most important areas in which students make status comparisons. As Rosenberg (1977) observes, the academic performance of Blacks generally is below that of whites. This does not create a problem for Blacks in segregated schools because it is impossible for wide racial discrepancies in academic performance to exist in these institutions. However, when Blacks in white-dominated schools compare their academic performance with that of their white classmates, their relatively low academic standing will result in a loss of self-esteem.

The purpose of this chapter is to evaluate the insulation hypothesis by assessing whether levels of self-esteem among Black school children decrease as the amount of contact with whites increases. If this hypothesis is true, the mechanisms by which this effect operates also must be examined. In the analysis that follows, the three aspects of the dissonant school environment will be used to explain why Blacks experience lower levels of self-esteem as they come into contact with whites.

DATA AND MEASURES

The data used in this study were collected in 1968 by Rosenberg and Simmons (1972) in Baltimore, Maryland. A random sample of students in grades 3-12 were selected from a stratified cluster sample of 23 schools (see Rosenberg and Simmons, 1972: 146-150). The analyses in the present study were based on the responses of Black students only.[1] The sample was partitioned into the following three groups for separate analyses: elementary school students, grades 3-6 (N = 761); junior high school students, grades 7-9 (N = 302); and senior high school students, grades 10-12 (N = 202).[2]

The impact of racial contact cannot be fully understood unless a precise conceptual model is developed that specifies the processes that transmit its effects. The theoretical bases for the relationship between racial contact and self-esteem have been discussed above. These processes are illustrated in Figure 14.1, which portrays the mechanisms that transmit the effects of racial contact.

As shown in Figure 14.1, self-esteem is divided into two distinct dimensions: positive and negative self-esteem. These two dimensions, which are formed from positively and negatively worded items, were derived from a factor analysis of the self-esteem scale. These two

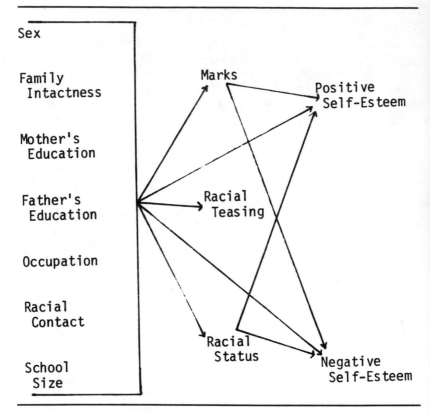

Figure 14.1   A Conceptual Model of Self-Esteem

dimensions reflect the fact that a person's self-concept contains a range of self-evaluations that include both positive and negative feelings.

The variables that were used in the analyses reported below, along with their codes, are described in Table 14.1. A high score on either self-esteem factor reflects high self-esteem.

The variable CONTACT stands for the amount of racial contact that a Black student has with white students. When information about the actual amount of contact between Blacks and whites is unavailable, estimates must be made of the opportunities for (or the probability of) racial contact within schools. When using cross-sectional data, the only information that is usually available is the relative numbers of Black and white students in each school or school class. Typically researchers who are interested in examining the effects of racial contact on Black self-esteem have used the proportion of white students as a measure of racial contact (Crain and Mahard, 1978a; 1978b; Wilson, 1979). The percentage of white students has been thought to represent the probability

TABLE 14.1   Description and Coding of Variables in the Analysis

Variable	Concept	Measurement
SEX	male-female differences	0 = female 1 = male
INTACT	family intactness	0 = living with one parent 1 = living with both parents
MED	maternal education	coded in years of schooling completed from 6 ordinal categories
FED	paternal education	
OCC	occupation of house- hold head	7 ordinal categories reflecting occupational prestige
CONTACT	contact with whites	logarithm of the product of the proportion white students and the number of Black students
SIZE	school size	logarithm of school size
MARKS	discrepancy between white and Black grades	average of all white grades in each school minus indivi- dual Black grades
TBLACK	racial teasing	How often have you been teased because you are (Black)? often = 4 sometimes = 3 not very often = 2 never = 1
STATUS	perceived racial status	Who do Americans consider best Jewish, white catholic, Negro, white pretestant)? 4 = Blacks best 3 = Blacks 2nd best 2 = Blacks 3rd best 1 = Blacks 4th best
POSSE	positive self-esteem	I am able to do things as well as most other kids. I am satisfied with myself. I am as good as most other kids I know. How happy are you with the kind of person you are? I like the kind of person I am.
NEGSE	negative self-esteem	I am no good at all. I do not like myself. I think I am no good at all. I'm not much good at anything. There's a lot wrong with me.

of exposure to white students. Although interracial contact is partially a function of the percentage of white students, under the simplest set of assumptions it can be shown that the expected volume of racial contact is equal to the product of the proportion of white students and the number of Black students: N_c (volume of contact) = N_b (number of Black students) X P_w (proportion of white students). This is a common measure of exposure among groups (see Coleman, 1964; Reed, 1972; Becker, 1980). The measure of contact used here differs slightly from the measure of contact used by other researchers. Most of these measures include a component that reflects the total number of persons, both Black and white, in the unit under consideration.

The measure of racial contact used in this study is expressed in person-units, and ranges from zero to the number of Black students. As a reflection of the volume of contact with whites for Black students in a school, this indicator expresses the risk of exposure to racial prejudice and institutional definitions of racial status.

The measure N_c can be disaggregated into its constituent parts by taking its logarithm as follows:

$$Ln (N_c) = Ln (N_b) + Ln (P_w).$$

According to the proponents of the insulation hypothesis, increased racial contact leads to more negative self-evaluations by Black students. We further expect this effect to be mediated in part by the influence of racial contact on the dissonant communications environment, the dissonant cultural environment, and the dissonant comparison reference group (Rosenberg, 1977).

The relationship between the dissonant communications environment and self-esteem is examined below by using measures of the reported amount of racial teasing (TBLACK) students experience and their beliefs about the standing of their racial group in the larger community (STATUS).

The effects of the dissonant cultural environment were assessed in this study with a measure of the student's family (INTACT).

As noted earlier, academic performance is one of the key dimensions that Black students use for making status comparisons with whites. In testing this aspect of the dissonant comparison reference group, most researchers have merely examined the effects of Black grades on Black self-esteem (Rosenberg and Simmons, 1972). Although this may be of some interest, it fails to capture the essence of the comparative process. What is needed is a measure of Black grades relative to those of whites. A more precise indicator of this construct was constructed in the following manner: First, the average grades of white students in each school were computed. Then the grades of each Black student were subtracted from the average grades of whites in their school. We predict that the greater the discrepancy between Black and white grades, the greater the likelihood of Black students making negative status comparisons. The measure is scored so that the higher the score on the grade discrepancy measure (MARKS), the more unfavorably Black grades compare to white grade averages in each school.

Following the recommendations of Wylie (1979) and others, controls were established for the influence of several demographic variables. These variables are mother and father's education (MED and FED), the occupation of the household head (OCC), and gender (SEX).[3]

The more rigorous operationalization of racial contact, self-esteem, and black/white grade discrepancies highlights many of the problems in the existing literature. Furthermore, by controlling for the effects of the background variables in a multivariate framework, we can obtain more accurate estimates of the effects of racial contact on Black self-esteem.

RESULTS

Estimates of the relationships among the variables depicted in Figure 14.1 were obtained with Joreskog and Sorbom's (1978) program, LISREL IV. These coefficients are presented in Tables 14.2-14.4 for elementary, junior high school, and senior high school students respectively.[4]

Does racial contact influence the self-esteem of Black school children? The data in Tables 14.2-14.4 reveal that although racial contact does exert a slight effect on self-esteem, in no instance are any of the effects statistically significant.

As Figure 14.1 indicates, racial contact may influence self-esteem indirectly by increasing the amount of racial teasing that Black students are exposed to and by lowering their perception of the status of Blacks in American society.[5] The data in the tables indicate that increased racial contact was associated with increased racial teasing for elementary school students only. Racial teasing, however, was not associated with self-esteem at any grade level. Similarly, increased contact with whites was not associated with self-esteem at any grade level. Similarly, increased contact with whites was not associated with Black students' perception of their racial status. The results do suggest, however, that perceived racial status exerts a significant impact on negative self-esteem for senior high students only ($b = .086$; $p < .05$).[6] These results suggest that among senior high school students, the belief that Blacks

TABLE 14.2 Sample Estimates of a Linear Structural Equation Model of Black Self-Esteem: Elementary School Children (n = 761)

Predetermined variables	DEPENDENT VARIABLE				
	MARKS	TBLACK	STATUS	POSSE	NEGSE
SEX	.074**	−.119	−.076	.034	.008
	.066***	−.059	−.035	.079	.011
INTACT	.011	−.057	.045	.008	.037
	.009	−.027	.020	.018	.049
MED	.018	.008	−.021	.004	.010
	.065	.016	−.039	.036	.052
FED	−.029*	−.007	.006	.002	−.007
	−.112	−.015	.012	.017	−.043
OCC	.021	−.057	−.004	−.004	.018
	.049	−.075	−.005	−.022	.067
CONTACT	.014	.252*	.039	−.008	−.031
	.012	.117	.017	−017	−.040
SIZE	−.137	−393	.196	−.044	.096
	−.038	−.061	.028	−.032	.041
MARKS				−.017	.036
				−.046	.055
TBLACK				−.015	−.024
				−.070	−.067
STATUS				−.008	.022
				−.043	.065
1-R^2	.985	.981	.996	.981	.976

NOTE: X^2 (114 df) = 380.858; X^2/df = 3.34.
*p < .05.
**metric coefficient
***standardized coefficient

occupy a low status in society is associated with more negative feelings of self-worth. Taken as a whole, these findings provide little support for the effects of the dissonant communications environment.

Family intactness, as one indicator of the dissonant culture environment, was hypothesized to lower Black self-regard because Blacks from single-parent families would be stigmatized by whites from two-parent (INTACT) families. This hypothesis predicts an interaction effect between family intactness and racial contact. Separate analyses (not shown here) were conducted to test for this interaction effect. These

TABLE 14.3   Sample Estimates of a Linear Structural Equation
Model of Black Self-Esteem: Junior High School
Students (n = 302)

	DEPENDENT VARIABLE				
Predetermined Variables	MARKS	TBLACK	STATUS	POSSE	NEGSE
SEX	.100**	.204*	−.196	.057	.084*
	.060***	.121	−.086	.191	.132
INTACT	−.183	−.119	−.170	.068*	.100*
	−.106	−.068	−.072	.223	.152
MED	−.031	.003	−.009	.007	.003
	−.075	.007	−.015	.099	.017
FED	.053*	.067*	.077*	−.001	−.026*
	.152	.190	.163	².011	−.197
OCC	.070	−.039	−.244	−.012	.004
	.111	−.062	−.262	−.107	.018
CONTACT	.202	−.175	−.033	−.024	.001
	.161	−.139	−.019	−.110	.001
SIZE	.046	.270	−.402	−.032	−.114
	.009	.050	−.056	−.034	−.057
MARKS				.021	.024
				.121	.065
TBLACKS				.003	−.029
				.016	−.077
STATUS				.015	−.029
				.114	−.105
$1-R^2$	.906	.938	.910	.873	.909

NOTE: X^2 (114df) = 271.673; X^2/df = 2.38.
*$p < .05$
**metric coefficient
***standardized coefficient

analyses failed to reveal any significant interaction between family intactness and racial contact in any of the grade levels.[7]

The additive effects of family intactness also were examined (see Tables 14.2-14.4). Essentially, these analyses test whether family intactness influences self-esteem independently of the effects of racial contact. The data in Table 14.3 indicate that for junior high school students, Blacks coming from single-parent families are more likely to have lower scores on both self-esteem factors than Blacks from two-parent families.

TABLE 14.4   Sample Estimates of a Linear Structural Equation
             Model of Black Self-Esteem: Senior High School
             Students (n = 202)

Predetermined Variables	DEPENDENT VARIABLE				
	MARKS	TBLACK	STATUS	POSSE	NEGSE
SEX	.259**	.247*	.009	.024	−.042
	.193***	.144	.004	.045	−.042
INTACT	−.013	−.249*	−.082	.010	.040
	−.009	−.141	−.038	.018	.039
MED	.020	.015	−.053	−.001	.029
	.063	.038	−.104	−.009	.121
FED	−.025	−.006	−.008	−.021	−.016
	−.082	−.015	−.017	.171	−.069
OCC	−.012	.011	.088	−.022	−.020
	−.023	.018	.109	².106	−.053
CONTACT	.524*	.025	−.247	−.029	−.029
	.424	.016	−.127	−.059	−.032
SIZE	−1.531	4.518	−1.992	.888	3.436
	− .048	.110	− .039	.069	.144
MARKS				−.016	−.102
				−.040	−.137
TBLACK				−.028	−.019
				−.089	−.033
STATUS				−.014	−.086*
				−.053	.183
1-R	.782	.944	.960	.954	.916

NOTE: X^2 (114df) = 233.707; X^2/df = 2.05.
*$p < .05$
**metric coefficient
***standardized coefficient

The discrepancy between Black grades and white grade averages
within each school represents one way of assessing the effects of the
dissonant comparison reference group hypothesis: The greater the
discrepancy between Black and white grade averages, the lower the
self-esteem of Black students will be. The data presented in Tables
14.2-14.4 fail to support this hypothesis. No statistically significant
associations between the grade discrepancy measure and self-esteem
were found at any grade level.

CONCLUSIONS

The purpose of this study was to assess the insulation hypothesis by examining the effects of racial contact on Black self-esteem and by evaluating several specific causal mechanisms that might transmit these effects. Essentially, little support was found for the hypothesis that increased contact with whites lowers the self-esteem of Black school children.

The findings from this study must, however, be viewed within the limitations imposed by the data that were used. This study focused on the opportunity for racial contact instead of actual amount of interracial contact. In addition, the data used were cross-sectional. It is imperative that longitudinal studies be conducted that include measures of self-esteem both before and after Black students come into contact with white students. Finally, many of the hypotheses discussed earlier may operate at the classroom level rather than at the school level as examined here. For example, it is possible that the grade comparisons made by Black students are based on the performance of whites in their classrooms, and not on the average performance of all the whites in their school.

Apart from the limitations of the existing data, there appear to be some important substantive explanations that might help us to understand why racial contact failed to influence Black self-esteem in this study. The insulation hypothesis rests on the assumption that Black students automatically will internalize all the negative views that whites hold about them. Recently, social psychologists have begun to realize that this represents an oversocialized view of people—one in which human beings are seen as passive and conformist (Gecas and Schwalbe, 1983). Instead of merely accepting the appraisals of prejudicial whites, Rosenberg (1979) suggests that Blacks may selectively incorporate the views of others (usually the views of other Blacks), and that they make selective comparisons with those around them (other Blacks are used as a reference group).

What factors might help Blacks to resist the negative self-image presented to them by whites? Perhaps the answer can be found in the work of sociologist Simmel (see Wolff, 1950), who noted that conflict increases the solidarity within groups that are confronted by a threatening situation. Applying this concept to the school integration process, Crain and Mahard (1983) demonstrated that community conflict early in the desegregation process created stronger cohesion within the Black community and increased the academic self-esteem of Black students (see also Drury, 1980).

Clearly, more definitive statements about the validity of the contact hypothesis or the insulation hypothesis await studies that examine the interrelationships among interracial contact, conflict, and group cohesiveness.

NOTES

1. Pairwise deletion of missing data was used in the data analysis.

2. It was necessary to weight the data because the school-specific sampling fractions of Black students did not correspond to the true number of Blacks in these schools. The data were adjusted in such a way as to either underrepresent the cases in which a disproportionately high number of Black students were interviewed or overrepresent the cases in which a disproportionately low number of Blacks were selected. The formula that was used in this weighting procedure was $n_h M / N m_h$, where n_h equals the size of subpopulation h, M stands for the total sample size, N represents the total population size, and m_h is the size of the sample in subpopulation h. See Smith (1976) for a further discussion of this weighting approach. A table of school sizes, percentage of the white students, and the number of Black students for each school is available from the author.

3 A series of ordinary least square regression analyses were conducted to determine if there was an interaction effect between gender and racial contact on self-esteem. Separate analyses were performed for each grade level. No statistically significant interactions were found.

4. The structural disturbance terms between the positive and negative self-esteem construct equations were allowed to be correlated in the computational process. Similarly, the structural disturbance terms were correlated among the equations in which marks, racial teasing, and racial status were the dependent variables. These parameters were allowed to be correlated to reflect the mutual influence that variables outside the model exert on the respective constructs.

5. The model presented in Figure 14.1 was designed to test only for the main effects of racial teasing, perceptions of racial status, and course marks on self-esteem. In additional data analysis, not shown here, I used ordinary least square regression analysis to test for any possible interaction effects between these mediating factors and racial contact on self-esteem. No significant interaction effects were found in these analyses.

6. Unstandardized coefficients will be presented in discussing the results, so that inaccurate comparisons will not be made across grade levels because of differences in item variances.

7. Tests for the interaction effect between family intactness and racial contact were conducted using ordinary least square regression analysis. A multiplicative term was created by multiplying family intactness by the racial contact variable. The multiplicative term then was regressed on positive and negative self-esteem. All of the variables in Table 14.1 were included in these analyses. The unstandardized regression coefficients for the effects of the multiplicative term on positive and negative self-esteem respectively were as follows: elementary school (b = −.31, p < .432) (b = .50, p < .269); junior high school (b = .04, p < .783) (b = .25, p < .236); senior high school (b = .17, p < .751) (b = .34, p < .605).

REFERENCES

ALPORT, G. (1954) The Nature of Prejudice. Reading, MA: Addison-Wesley.

AMIR, Y. (1969) "Contact hypothesis in ethnic relations." Psychological Bulletin 71: 319-342.

BECKER, H. (1980) "Racial segregation among places of employment." Social Forces 58: 761-776.

COLEMAN, J. (1964) Introduction to Mathematical Sociology. New York: Free Press.

COOLEY, C. (1902) Human Nature and the Social Order. New York: Scribner.

CRAIN, R. and E. MAHARD (1983) "Controversy and institutional change." American Sociological Review 47: 697-708.

———(1978a) "School racial composition and Black college attendance and achievement test performance." Sociology of Education 51: 81-101.

———(1978b) "Reply to Eckland." Sociology of Education 51: 125-128.

DRURY, D. (1980) "Black self-esteem and desegregated schools." Sociology of Education 53: 88-103.

EPPS, E. (1978) "The impact of school desegregation on the self-evaluation and achievement orientation of minority children." Law and Contemporary Problems 42: 57-76.

GECAS, V. and M. SCHWALBE (1983) "Beyond the looking-glass self: social structure and efficacy-based self-esteem." Social Psychology Quarterly 46: 77-88.

JORESKOG, K. and D. SORBOM (1978) LISREL IV: Analysis of Linear Structural Relationships by the Method of Maximum Likelihood. Chicago: National Educational Resources.

KRAUSE, N. (1978) "The racial context of Black self-esteem." Social Psychology Quarterly 46: 98-107.

REED, J. (1972) "Percent Black and lynching: a test of Blalock's theory." Social Forces 50: 356-360.

ROSENBERG, M. (1979) Conceiving the Self. New York: Basic Books.

———(1977) "Contextual dissonant effects: nature and causes." Psychiatry 40: 205-217.

———and R. SIMMONS (1972) Black and White Self-Esteem: The Urban School Child. American Sociological Association.

SMITH, K. (1976) "Analyzing disproportionately stratified samples with computerized statistical packages." Sociological Methods and Research 5: 207-230.

ST. JOHN, M. (1975) School Desegregation: Outcomes for Children. New York: John Wiley.

STEPHAN, W. (1978) "School desegregation: an evaluation of predictors made in Brown v. Board of Education." Psychological Bulletin 85: 217-238.

WILSON, K. (1979) "The effects of integration and class on Black educational attainment." Sociology of Education 52: 84-89.

WOLFF, K. (1950) The Sociology of George Simmel. New York: Free Press.

WYLIE, R. (1979) The Self-Concept: Theory and Research on Selected Topics, vol. 2. Lincoln: Univ. of Nebraska Press.

NAME INDEX

SUBJECT INDEX

CONTRIBUTORS

NA'IM AKBAR, Ph.D., is a Clinical Psychologist in Florida State University's Department of Psychology and Black Studies. He is Associate Editor of the *Journal of Black Psychology* and has served as the Southern Regional Representative to the National Association of Black Psychologists' Board of Directors and as the American Muslim Mission's Development Director. Formerly, he was Associate Professor of Psychology at Norfolk State University and at Morehouse College, where he was Chairman of the Psychology Department. His publications include *The Community of Self; Natural Psychology and Human Transformation; From Miseducation to Education;* and *Chains and Images of Psychological Slavery.*

A. WADE BOYKIN is Professor of Psychology at Howard University. He holds a B.A. from Hampton Institute and an M.A. and Ph.D. in Experimental Psychology from the University of Michigan at Ann Arbor. His primary research interests are in culture, motivation, and cognitive performance.

JAMES P. COMER, M.D., is the Maurice Falk Professor of Child Psychiatry and the Director of the School Development Program at the Yale Child Study Center. He also is Associate Dean for Student Affairs at Yale Medical School. He received his A.B. from Indiana University, his M.D. from Howard University College of Medicine, and his M.P.H. from the University of Michigan School of Public Health. He has published several articles and chapters and three books: *Beyond Black and White* (New York Times Books, 1972); *Black Child Care* (Simon & Schuster, 1975); and *School Power: Implications of an Intervention Program* (Free Press, 1980).

MARIAN WRIGHT EDELMAN is President of the Children's Defense Fund, author of *Portrait of Inequality: Black and White Children in America* (1980), and coauthor of *Children Out of School in America* (1974) and *School Suspensions: Are They Helping Black Children* (1975), all published by the Children's Defense Fund. She received her B.A. from Spelman College, her J.D. from Yale Law School, and among her many honorary doctorate degrees are those awarded this year from Columbia University, University of Pennsylvania, Saint Joseph College, Trinity College, Yale University, Amherst College, and Barnard College. Recently, she received a MacArthur Foundation Award for her accomplishments in public affairs. Her research interest focuses on children, families, and poverty.

ANDERSON J. FRANKLIN is Professor and Associate Director in charge of Child, Adolescent, and Family Training for the Clinical Psychology Program at the City College and the Graduate School of the City University of New York. He is a coeditor of *Research Directions of Black Psychologists* (1979), with research interests in the psychosocial factors of mental health for Blacks as well as cross-cultural issues in human development and clinical treatment. Currently, he serves as a member of the New York State Board of Psychology.

NANCY BOYD-FRANKLIN is Clinical Assistant Professor at the University of Medicine and Dentistry of New Jersey in Newark, where she serves as Supervisor in the Child and Adolescent Unit and teaches family therapy. She also is in private practice, in which she sees couples, families, children, and adults. Her work includes teaching and writing about family therapy, particularly the treatment of Black families. She received her training in family therapy at the Philadelphia Child Guidance Center with Dr. Salvador Minuchin.

BRUCE R. HARE is Assistant Professor of Sociology at the State University of New York at Stony Brook. He received his B.A. in Sociology and M.S. in Elementary Education from the City College of the City University of New York, and his M.A. in Sociology of Education and Ph.D. in Social Psychology from the University of Chicago. He taught at the Manhattanville Child Development Center, the University of Massachusetts at Boston, and the University of Illinois and served on the President's Commission on Mental Health. Recently, he was awarded a Rockefeller Foundation, Minority Group Scholars Program Fellowship for a longitudinal study of child self-esteem.

ALGEA O. HARRISON is Associate Professor of Psychology at Oakland University. She received her B.A. from Bluefield State College and her M.A. and Ph.D. from the University of Michigan. She has served as a consultant to various public and private agencies and coordinated conferences for such groups as Empirical Research in Black Psychology and the Society for Research in Child Development. She is on the editorial board of *Child Development* and her work has appeared in *Child Development; Journal of Social and Behavioral Sciences; Journal of Marriage and the Family; Teaching of Psychology;* and *Psychology of Women Quarterly.*

BERTHA GARRETT HOLLIDAY received her B.A. in Psychology from the University of Chicago, her Ed.M. in Counseling and Guidance from Harvard University, and her Ph.D. in Community Psychology from the University of Texas at Austin. She has served as a counselor at the Greater Kansas City Mental Health Foundation, an evaluation specialist and senior project management specialist in manpower and education at the Model Cities Department of Kansas City, MO, and Assistant Professor at Peabody College of Vanderbilt University. She was appointed to a three-year term on the U.S. Office of Education's National Advisory Committee on Black Colleges and Universities and Black Higher Education. Recently, she was awarded an SRCD Congressional Science Fellowship.

NEAL KRAUSE, Ph.D., is Assistant Professor in the Department of Family Medicine and the Department of Preventive Medicine and Community Health at the University of Texas Medical Branch at Galveston. His research focuses on stress and health. He has recently completed an NIA-funded community survey on stress and health among the elderly. In addition, he has published a series of papers on the effects of chronic role strains among Mexican Americans.

HARRIETTE PIPES McADOO is a Professor at the School of Social Work at Howard University. She received her B.A. and M.A. from Michigan State University, her Ph.D. from the University of Michigan, and has done postgraduate work at Harvard. She is the editor of *Black Families*, a Sage Focus Edition, and has published on racial attitudes and self-esteem in Black children, mobility patterns of middle-class Blacks, support networks of single mothers, and adolescent pregnancy. She is a Director of the National Council on Family Relations and the Society for Research in Child Development.

JOHN LEWIS McADOO received his M.S.W. and his Ph.D. from the University of Michigan. He has completed postgraduate training at the University of Michigan Institute of Survey Research, at The Johns Hopkins University in public health, and at the Harvard Graduate School of Education. He has published several articles in the areas of racial attitudes and self-esteem in Black preschool children, father-child interaction patterns in Black families, patterns of parent-child interactions and self-esteem in young children, and fear of crime morale and well-being of Black elderly people.

MARIE FERGUSON PETERS, former member of the faculty of human development and family relations at the University of Connecticut and P.I. Toddler and Infant Experiences Studies, received her Ed.D. from Harvard and her undergraduate degree from Fisk University. She was Secretary of the National Council on Family Relations, Director of the Groves Conference on Marriage and the Family, and edited the Black family issue of *Journal of Marriage and the Family* in 1978. She conducted research on socialization, stress, and development of children in Black families, and was honored by the National Council on Family Relations when they named a major award in her honor, the Marie Peters Award. She was named, posthumously, a member of the Groves Academy of the Groves Conference on Marriage and the Family. Marie died on January 6, 1984, after living a full and active professional and personal life.

JOHN SCANZONI is Professor of Child Development and Family Relations at the University of North Carolina at Greensboro. He is the author of several books, including *Shaping Tomorrow's Family: Theory and Policy for the Twenty-First Century* (Sage, 1983); *Sexual Bargaining: Power Politics in American Marriage* (University of Chicago, revised edition, 1982); *Family Decision-Making: A Developmental Sex Role Model* (with M. Szinovacz; Sage, 1980); and *Sex Roles, Women's Work, and Marital Conflict: A Study of Family Change* (D.C. Heath, 1978). His articles have appeared in several scholarly journals, including *Journal of Marriage and the Family; American Sociological Review;* and *American Journal of Sociology.*

MARGARET BEALE SPENCER is Associate Professor at Emory University. She received her B.S. in Pharmacy from Temple University, her M.A. in Psychology from the University of Kansas, and her Ph.D. from the University of Chicago. She is coeditor (with G. Brookins and